Hunting for Justice

SUNY series in Contemporary Continental Philosophy

Dennis J. Schmidt, editor

Hunting for Justice
The Cosmology of Dikē in Aeschylus's *Oresteia*

KALLIOPI NIKOLOPOULOU

Cover: *The Vision of Orestes* (pen and ink) by Henry Fuseli (Johann Heinrich Füssli). Private collection. Photo © Christie's Images/Bridgeman Images.

Published by State University of New York Press, Albany

© 2025 State University of New York

All rights reserved

Printed in the United States of America

No part of this book may be used or reproduced in any manner whatsoever without written permission. No part of this book may be stored in a retrieval system or transmitted in any form or by any means including electronic, electrostatic, magnetic tape, mechanical, photocopying, recording, or otherwise without the prior permission in writing of the publisher.

Links to third-party websites are provided as a convenience and for informational purposes only. They do not constitute an endorsement or an approval of any of the products, services, or opinions of the organization, companies, or individuals. SUNY Press bears no responsibility for the accuracy, legality, or content of a URL, the external website, or for that of subsequent websites.

"Odysseus Elytis on His Poetry," excerpt translated by Olga Broumas, from *Eros, Eros, Eros: Selected and Last Poems*. Copyright © 1998 by Olga Broumas. Reprinted with the permission of The Permissions Company, LLC on behalf of Copper Canyon Press, coppercanyonpress.org.

EU GPSR Authorised Representative:
Logos Europe, 9 rue Nicolas Poussin, 17000, La Rochelle, France contact@logoseurope.eu

For information, contact State University of New York Press, Albany, NY www.sunypress.edu

Library of Congress Cataloging-in-Publication Data

Name: Nikolopoulou, Kalliopi, author.
Title: Hunting for justice : the cosmology of dikē in Aeschylus's Oresteia / Kalliopi Nikolopoulou.
Description: Albany : State University of New York Press, [2025]. | Series: SUNY series in contemporary continental philosophy | Includes bibliographical references and index.
Identifiers: LCCN 2024027039 | ISBN 9798855801286 (hardcover : alk. paper) | ISBN 9798855801293 (ebook) | ISBN 9798855801279 (pbk. : alk. paper)
Subjects: LCSH: Aeschylus. Oresteia. | Justice in literature. | LCGFT: Literary criticism.
Classification: LCC PA3825.A6 N55 2025 | DDC 882/.01—dc23/eng/20240928
LC record available at https://lccn.loc.gov/2024027039

*For Edward and our sons,
Achilles and Theseus*

μέγα τι θηρεύειν ἀρετάν

(A great thing it is to hunt virtue)

—Euripides, *Iphigenia at Aulis*

Everything passes away—suffering, pain, blood, hunger, pestilence. The sword will pass away too, but the stars will remain when the shadows of our presence and our deeds have vanished from the Earth. There is no man who does not know that. Why, then, will we not turn our eyes toward the stars? Why?

—Mikhail Bulgakov, *The White Guard*

Poetry on a certain level of accomplishment is neither optimistic nor pessimistic. It represents rather a third state of the spirit where opposites cease to exist. There are no more opposites beyond a certain level of elevation. Such poetry is like nature itself. Which is neither good nor bad, beautiful nor ugly; it simply *is*.

—Odysseus Elytis, "Odysseus Elytis on His Poetry"

Contents

Acknowledgments		ix
Chapter 1.	*Cosmos/Phusis*, Dikē, *Pragmata*: An Introduction	1
Chapter 2.	Tragedy and the Seriousness of Culture: Aristotle and Walter Burkert	29
Chapter 3.	Like a Dog, or in Artemis's Night: Dikē in *Agamemnon*	77
Chapter 4.	Hermes of the Axis Mundi: Gē and Dikē in the *Choephoroi*	107
Chapter 5.	Beyond Justice: Apollo's Youth and Athena's Dikē in the *Eumenides*	139
Epilogue	A Lying Shepherd and the Limits of Human Dikē	185
Notes		197
Works Cited		227
Index		239

Acknowledgments

I would like to thank my colleagues at the University of Buffalo's Comparative Literature Department. Particular mention should go to Rodolphe Gasché, David Johnson, and Ewa Ziarek, who have offered intellectual feedback and institutional support in many forms. Conversations with Donald Cross and Krzysztof Ziarek always left me with more ideas. The Humanities Institute at the University at Buffalo and the Office of the Vice President for Research and Economic Development have generously supported indexing and subvention fees for this publication.

I am thankful to Kristi Sweet for her invitation to deliver part of this manuscript as a lecture at the Collegium Phaenomenologicum's course "Cosmology and Cosmopolitanism," in Città di Castello, Italy. Other portions of the manuscript formed a talk at the International Hermeneutics Symposium at Radboud University, the Netherlands, on an invitation by Theodore George. An abridged version of chapter 4 on the *Choephoroi* appears in *The Routledge Handbook on Women and Ancient Greek Philosophy*, edited by Sara Brill and Catherine McKeen. My gratitude to both of them for soliciting the essay and for their remarks.

The SUNY series in Contemporary Continental Philosophy has been the best home that I could wish for this manuscript. I am grateful to the series editor, Dennis Schmidt, whose encouragement has been generous over the years. His own work on tragedy and the Greeks has been a long-standing inspiration for me. I would like to acknowledge the two anonymous reviewers whose summations recast my argument in a crisp and original manner that opens future lines of inquiry for me. (In particular, I should mention Jason Winfree, who has since identified himself, and whose work has been a crucial source for my reflections on the connection between philosophy and anthropology.) Michael Rinella deserves many thanks for his efficient guidance throughout the process.

Most of this manuscript was written during my sabbatical, which coincided with the onset of the COVID lockdowns. This experience would have been much bleaker without the friendship shown to me and my entire family by Bronia Karst. Amid the strangeness of social distancing, she gave me the gift of togetherness in our many conversations about literature, justice, teaching, and much more. Family in Greece and in the United States did their utmost to sustain me. My mother, Eleni Kosmidou, kept track of my writing progress over Skype calls. Yanna Panagiotopoulou and Kjetil Helland in the Greek summers, and Carol and David Barans in the Buffalo winters, have been great listeners, and I am thankful for the time they spent playing with our "little heroes." Edward Batchelder has provided me with continual and unwavering support.

Chapter 1

Cosmos/Phusis, Dikē, Pragmata

An Introduction

"Teach him to study the trees"

To study the trees, one must look upward then downward, from the tops of their trunks and the tips of their foliage shimmering against the sky to their roots in the earth, bulging under and bursting over the soil. Then one must do the same in reverse. To study the trees, the mortal gaze must become a ladder between two realms that collide and complement each other—celestial repose and earthly conflict. Whoever studies the trees must have a passion for the vertical: a willingness to rise but also a readiness in case of fall. The trees want a pupil who is calm and patient, who can count them one by one and memorize their unique markings; but no less do they want someone who loses his bearings amid their shadows, listens attentively to the sound of rustling leaves, yields to their massiveness as they do to strong winds: one who is *alafroiskiotos* (light-shadowed) like Angelos Sikelianos's sprite-like poet whose nearly weightless, translucent existence serves to illumine nature's mysteries.[1] Then one may learn to stand like them: upright, yet able to bend and sway at storm; a trunk, a pillar, a *style*. Style—from *stylus*, the sharp writing instrument—comes in turn from *stylos* for "pillar," or "temple column," and even the urbane ironist Baudelaire wrote of the forest as a temple of living pillars.[2]

Where, then, to learn this exquisite method of attention and vertigo, of logic and prayer? What would be the right proportion of these opposing attitudes, and when is it most urgent to gain this knowledge? Let me turn briefly to a poem for some clues, and for a guidepost to what the larger poem—the drama of the *Oresteia*—will unfold for us:

> Now that you are leaving, now that the day of payment
> dawns, now that no one knows
> whom he will kill and how he will die,
> take with you the boy who saw the light
> under the leaves of that plane tree
> and teach him to study the trees. (Seferis 21)

"Teach him to study the trees" is the ending of "Astyanax," a poem by the modern Greek George Seferis, whose work consistently invokes Aeschylean lineages. (In fact, the poem preceding this one in the collection references the sufferings of Orestes.) What makes this verse especially poignant for my project is that it is written against the background of war—the Trojan War as analog of a modern catastrophe—that begs the question of dikē as the day of payment, the advent of a terrible fulfillment, the pleroma of time: "Now that the day of payment [πληρωμής] dawns." But what this payment of dikē consists in, what or who gets fulfilled and in what timeframe, are all questions that contain an inexorable element. Here, the confluence of necessity and chance outstrips but also unwittingly underlies justice qua human distribution of fairness. Justice is thus only a partial, *exceedingly* anthropocentric, translation of dikē, and risks perhaps too great a hubris when it refuses to acknowledge the structure of cosmic arbitrariness that ironically undergirds its own most secular, rational, immanent institutions. The trees, whose sheer longevity alludes to a longer and deeper view of history than does the modern embrace of acceleration, might have something to say about all this.

Reflecting on the Asia Minor catastrophe of 1922, which uprooted the Greeks of Ionia, including the poet's family, Seferis imagines the aborted future of Hector's son, a little boy whom the Achaeans threw off the city walls to preempt any future threat from Troy—that ancient city on the promontory of Asia Minor from where it was now the Greeks' turn to flee. But in imagining this lost future and thus providing an escape route, which is all the more devastating because there was no actual escape (neither for Astyanax nor for many of the poet's compatriots), Seferis does not speak of the boy as the king that he will have grown to become. This future, which is so movingly invoked because it never came, would have been the time allotted to the child to study the trees. It is not clear to whom exactly the imperative "teach" is addressed: presumably to the boy's mother,

Andromache, whose husband has left for battle, perhaps even to servants or mentors tending to the young prince, or whomever else was tasked to remove him from the ills of war. What remains crucial is the imperative itself. The fulfillment of Astyanax would not have been his kingly destiny but his apprenticeship with the trees. One should not have to die before the chance to receive this precious lesson, and the healing—if any—from the historical disaster of being cut from one's roots could come only in learning (from) the trees.

We might have expected Seferis to exhort us to study history so as not to repeat it, thus falling prey to a cliché that history itself repeatedly falsifies; or to remember the disaster with equal parts condemnation and victimization, turning the poem into a rallying cry for justice against human atrocity; perhaps it would have been more "responsible" had he first drawn up a nuanced list of all the complicities and complexities of the warring parties before offering such controversial advice—except that these nuances become quickly meaningless within the history that alone authorizes them, since this same history relativizes and revises its own previous judgments, now at a vertiginous rate of speed. The poet, however, avoids all such pieties, not least because they are proven so nebulous by the history to which they appeal. Instead, he concludes that time is better spent studying the trees, for a tree, as Homer said, knows how to yield to the wind while firmly rooted (*Il.* 12.132–34). To study history, one must study first natural history.

Though a strange imperative, it makes perfect sense in light of the preceding stanza:

> The olive trees with the wrinkles of our fathers
> the rocks with the wisdom of our fathers
> and our brother's blood alive on the earth
> were a vital joy, a rich pattern
> for the souls who knew their prayer. (Seferis 21)

Inhuman nature, animate and inanimate, is personified. The gnarled olive trees look like the wrinkled faces of the ancestors, and the stones endure quietly with the wisdom of those ancestors. Then comes a scandalous addition, though delivered evenly, with the simple conjunction "and," without a leap and without the expected rupture, which is why it probably registers as a scandal: the brother's blood spilled freshly on the earth—alluding to *human* violence and the chthonic demand for justice—is woven *seamlessly* together with inhuman nature into a "rich pattern" (πλούσια τάξις). Such an orderly arrangement appears to those, like the poet, who understand dikē not as a matter of political convention alone but first and foremost as a prayer addressing itself to the inscrutable nature of reality. Reality here is shorthand for those famous "things that come to pass" even when one least expects them, and that are mentioned in the concluding lines of so many tragedies. These things are notoriously opaque, though they erupt with an exorbitant luminosity; they prove strangely unpredictable, though they may send palpable signals before they occur. Human beings have always been aware of their existence, yet human beings consistently miscalculate their precise arrival. Accidental though these things are/appear, one cannot underestimate their underlying permanence, since they have never ceased affecting human life, though they themselves remain largely unaffected by the ever-changing principles of human reasoning.

Trees and rocks live longer than human beings. They teach us to contemplate scale. They are witness to our history, and their indifference—their offering of shade and rest both to perpetrator and victim—stands as a solemn objectivity against the pettiness that hides beneath human depravity. This indifference—which is not the same as "frivolity," and which could be dismissed as "irresponsible" *only at the risk* of a hubris that totalizes everything into a politics—belongs to the cosmic order of dikē that is exempt from human deliberation. Seferis recites this description (and warning) from the tragic playwrights who all in various ways situated human action, whether individual or collective, against the backdrop of cosmic dikē. If Aeschylus's *Oresteia* commands here pride of place, it is because it lays out most systematically such a cosmology, while concluding that cosmic dikē does not withdraw itself after the inception of the court of jury but continues to underpin the administration of human justice. While it is not surprising that a cosmological view of dikē would underlie the judicial ethos of Aeschylus's time—such fact confirms the modern tendency to either patronize or disparage ancient people for their "naive" link to nature—it is intriguing to see it appear unexpectedly, often in a twisted or stifled guise, among the legal and moral tenets of contemporary conceptions of justice.

Aeschylean Dikē and Cosmological Anthropology: Hunting and the *Oresteia*

This study is not a monograph on Aeschylus. Its ambition is far more limited, its arguments quite local: focusing exclusively on the *Oresteia*, with only some passing references to other tragedies, it tackles the question of justice—or more precisely, of dikē[3]—foregrounding its cosmological rather than political expressions. Such inquiry has been motivated in large part by concerns regarding justice in our time, yet it is vital to stress that, for essential reasons, the contemporary aspect remains peripheral, and of the order of the symptom, throughout the study. Indeed, its conscious displacement thematizes my core premises, which function both as groundwork and goal of this project, and which I hope to make as explicit as possible in this brief list: first, a general methodological reticence toward the fetishization of "relevance" and its frequently reductive presentisms; second, and as a direct result of the first, a preference for letting Aeschylus speak with the fewest possible theoretical ventriloquisms, albeit without losing view of the rich tradition of commentary; finally, an ethical choice to foreground nature in light of its suppression by modernity's increasingly technocratic, though also paradoxically anthropocentric, impetus.[4]

The first two items in this list emerge from my disquiet with interpretive practices that claim to "enliven" the past, whether by means of cultural translation, revision, or even outright invention. To enliven something, one must first presume it dead, and "deadness" stands in these interpretations as a predicate for tradition. This insistence, however, on a living tradition rarely does what it says it does, since it understands "enlivening" chiefly as a one-way epochal translation that consistently reads the present back into the past and scarcely the other way around. The risk of solipsism from such unidirectional translation is then justified as a theoretical necessity: From where else can we read anything than our current position?

The paradox of Theseus and his ship comes to mind. The story is laid out in Plato's *Phaedo* (58a-c), attributing the delay of Socrates's execution to the ship's delayed ritual mission, which must be completed before executions resume. Upon Theseus's defeat of the Minotaur and his deliverance of the Athenian youth, Athens vowed to send a yearly sacred mission—a *theoria*[5]—to Delos in praise of Apollo and as reenactment of Theseus's initial journey to Crete. Thus, theory's meaning here is one of salvific voyage and sacred ambassadorship. According to legends reported in Plutarch's *Life of Theseus* (23.1), the ship to Delos was the original ship of Theseus, and the Athenians tried to maintain it by replacing its decaying parts with new ones. Still according to Plutarch, having undergone so many material alterations, the vessel became a philosophical paradox about identity and difference, with some arguing that it was the same ship while others that it was not. Gregory Nagy reads the *Phaedo* as the most sophisticated rendering of this philosophical debate, since the mythological *theoria* allegorizes Plato's Forms: "The Athenian Ship of State that is sailing to Delos and back while Socrates is having the last dialogue of his life is materially the exact replica of the supposedly original ship. The ship of the *theōriā* or 'sacred journey' in myth is the absolute ship, the ideal ship, comparable to an ideal ship in Plato's Theory of Forms, whereas the ship of the real world is not absolute, not ideal, just as the things of this world are not real in terms of Plato's Theory of Forms" (550). Nagy adds that the salvific journey of Theseus's ship finds its parallel in Socrates's version of philosophical salvation and immortality—namely, the theoretical voyage "that will forever be fueled by the living word of Socratic dialogue" (550). Thus, Socrates translates the mythological *theoria* into its modern meaning, suggesting that great ideas do not die: insofar as they live on *theoretically*—that is, through theory, or *in theory*—the ship too could well be considered the same ship. How we might now read this expression—"in theory"—is key.

Theory's modern meaning emerges from the doubleness implied in Socrates's allegorical performance. To say that this theoretic ship remains theoretically the same after numerous material changes—and in the philosophical parallel, after numerous conceptual modifications—can be read in two ways. At face value, it means that great ideas persist by appearing in different guises but remain *essentially* the same: they are immortal, in some sense. However, Socrates is an ironist, and if, as Nagy suggests, his very gesture performs the translation of theory from its sacred to its modern meaning, then "theoretically" also anticipates some later connotations: abstractly, though not ideally, hypothetically, possibly, *not really*. In other words, *in principle*, or *in theory*, this may be viewed as Theseus's ship, but *in reality*—which is to say, *in essence*—it is far from it. In reality, this is a new ship (new idea/theory) that instead enlivens itself by appealing to tradition while also wounding it. Socrates, who dies in the *Phaedo* defending the immortality of the soul, may in fact be equivocating on the immortality of ideas as they cross from ideality to history: ideas can be given their fixed, immortal name, but their actual contents could well be inversions of the very name they claim. From the vantage point of intellectual history, both Thrasymachus and Socrates speak about the same, immortal justice, though the former identifies it with power and the latter with righteousness; it is hardly likely that Socrates would have been content with such equivalence, though he may have capitulated to its *theoretical* possibility, a capitulation that perhaps even begs to be thought of as "tragic." From such perspective, it is no more the idea that necessitates and delimits interpretation but the interpretation that authorizes itself in the name of the idea; and rather than the idea being infinite, its malleability is infinitized instead, until eventually the idea ceases to exist except as a nominal vestige that designates something bearing little to no kinship with its source.

What I meant to exemplify with this Thesean interlude is my reserve vis-à-vis theoretical approaches that use the tradition nominally, only to render it unrecognizable, while sidestepping any hermeneutical counter-pressure ancient texts may apply to modern assumptions. To enliven the tradition, one must perhaps find recourse to another paradox: enlivening it by letting it speak in its "deadness," its illegibility, oddity, and anachronism—that is, by letting it speak even when it sounds alarmingly contrary to our categories and sensibilities. Tending toward this direction, my approach to Aeschylus favors what *he* has to say rather than aiming at a critique, or "translation," since I happen to think that the latter term, too, now chiefly operates—or, *itself translates*—as a euphemism for (ideological) critique that naturally remains uncritical of its own ideologisms. To put all this in terms more familiar to continental-philosophical readers of the Greeks, I eschew the postmetaphysical (but tacitly utilitarian) twists that intend to make the ancient text audible *for us*; or the German Idealist gesture of "completing" the Greeks by pinpointing what Aeschylus could not hear *in himself* because he was foreign to himself; or the claims of the Heideggerian hermeneutics of *Destruktion*; and so on. All such readings implicitly or explicitly assume the posture of the hermeneutic superiority of modernity in its radical novelty, exalting its violent translation of the past as a historical and interpretative necessity. Instead, positioned rather humbly vis-à-vis Aeschylus, and rather polemically vis-à-vis our own moral and hermeneutic certainties, the book attempts to preserve, and even foreground, that which *we do not want to hear* from Aeschylus.

Now I return to the third point in my initial list, which concerns nature, a word used often interchangeably with "cosmos" throughout the study, though a difference between them must also be noted: the cosmos and the cosmological refer typically to an ordered, patterned universe that is divinized rather than to mere, chaotic nature. However, to speak of ordered nature does not imply that it is a human fantasy projecting its patterns onto outward randomness, or that, conversely, the universe becomes immaterial outside of humanity's meaning production. On the contrary, I submit that if human beings feel drawn at all to even produce such fantasies or constructs, it is because the cosmos compels them to signify it. That it is in our nature to signify is itself a condition granted to us by the cosmos. Furthermore, as I show through Aristotle's theory of tragic mimesis, the worthier significations are those that honor the phenomenon as their very motivation, and thus yield it faithfully, rather than those that exaggerate creativity or self-consciousness in order to displace nature as the originary cause of art. This is, in effect, tragedy's "realism," despite its remaining in many other ways an antirealist genre, as Nietzsche noted.[6]

The priority of nature/cosmos forms the crux of my reading. By foregrounding this priority from Aristotle's mimesis to Aeschylus's cosmology, the study steers clear of the modern dismissal of nature and the concomitant pursuit of an exclusively immanent politics grounded on human voluntarism; it also distances itself from hermeneutical and phenomenological readings that overstate *the symmetry* in this otherwise reciprocal relation between nature and human beings. In various ways, the chapters argue that while the ancient polis is patterned on the cosmos, the reverse is neither necessary nor true: the polis needs the cosmos, but the cosmos exceeds the polis. A famous example of this from another playwright, cited in chapter 4, is the distinction Sophocles's Antigone makes between the laws of the city and those of the underworld: rebuking Creon's argument that Eteocles deserves burial as the city's defender, but traitor Polyneices does not, she denies his correspondence between upper and nether earth, saying that the gods below are not bound by this logic. In effect, she spells out that while Thebes is grounded on the earth, the earth in its chthonic and cosmic determinations extends beyond the political entity of Thebes. Overall, the preponderance of nature throughout my argument serves to illumine another crucial idea as well—namely, that the very notions of priority and hierarchy are themselves indispensable to (tragic) seriousness. To conclude my earlier point about patterned nature qua cosmology, I reiterate that the *-logy* does not refer to human invention or projection but rather to the *discovery* of the *logos* already embedded in nature's workings. Without delving into the intricacies of Heraclitus, it is helpful to recall that, for him, the logos was nature's mode of disclosure before it became a privileged means of human knowledge. This extends to Aeschylean theodicy: randomness somehow gathers itself into a pattern, as divine dikē arrives suddenly yet with a statistically consistent probability of recurrence; during this arrival, *things* converge in a manner that steers the world aright after disorder and disharmony.

Admitting to such hierarchy invites the objection that my argument falls prey to long-standing but simplistic binaries of nature/culture, nature/artifice, or nature/technology, which have been nuanced by contemporary thought; yet, I would argue that current theoretical tendencies of renouncing nature as "oppressive" because it limits human choices, or diminishing its facts by reducing them to "cultural constructs," is hardly nuancing. Behind the critique of natural determinism often hides the strange anthropocentrism of an age that otherwise describes itself as posthumanist and ecological.[7] That at present, and all the more increasingly, nature is as selectively invoked as it is dismissed in accordance to various programmatic ends,[8] is quite evident to anyone who *desires* to see—namely, to anyone who attests to the referentiality and factualness of *things*. This referentiality involves the thing's patency before various interpretive apparatuses curate it into multiple, often self-contradictory meanings.

I should take this opportunity to underline that the most capacious definition I could give for my use of "nature/cosmos" involves precisely this referentiality, or thingliness, which from the Latin *res* for "thing," yields the concept of reality.[9] Nature/cosmos in this project serves as the placeholder for the ineluctability of reality, and thus, for the inescapability from *external reference*. Human beings are contained within this reality, but despite their contestation of this containment, they prove unable to control its ordering. This is what Aeschylus's Prometheus means when he declares that "craft is far weaker than necessity"—a line this project revisits twice, particularly since it is uttered by the patron deity of crafts, indeed the patron deity of modernity in the latter's march toward technological progress. The human being may attest to and give meanings to this thing, or things (*pragma/pragmata*), but those things wield a sovereignty beyond the human being and its meaning production. Thus, in this element of enduring referentiality converge the categories of necessity and inexorability, which are central to the tragic genre. Nature shows necessity as delimitation and restriction, but it also shows something even more rigorous: recognizing necessity as such is itself a *necessary* precondition for becoming human; this is the necessity of necessity as that which can never be dispensed with.

Additionally, here, in the world of necessary things, one can contemplate the notion of scale in an experience of time that appears macroscopically: time in longer swathes like those of geological erosion and the lifespan of trees rather than the fast and transient changes that register within human culture. The language of objective reference, which modernity at least since Kant has destabilized by delimiting the thing-in-itself as beyond the capacities of *theoretical* reason, had found in the past a salient medium of presentation in tragedy, for tragedy was not a theory but a *theoria*.[10]

With the mention of Heraclitus, I have already hinted at Aeschylus's pre-Socratic affinities. From a historical standpoint, this makes good sense: Socrates was born in 470 BC, shortly before Aeschylus died in 456 BC; Aeschylus's so-called archaism owes most likely to this naturalist view of the world, which remains predominant even when he is negotiating political and juridical questions at the dawn of Athens's rise as a democratic polity. Here I should mention another pre-Socratic figure, Anaximander, whose sole surviving fragment addresses precisely the notion of dikē, this word that now gets insufficiently translated as "justice": "ἐξ ὧν δὲ ἡ γένεσίς ἐστι τοῖς οὖσι, καὶ τὴν φθορὰν εἰς ταῦτα γίνεσθαι κατὰ τὸ χρεών· διδόναι γὰρ αὐτὰ δίκην καὶ τίσιν ἀλλήλοις τῆς ἀδικίας κατὰ τὴν τοῦ χρόνου τάξιν" (From what things existing objects come to be, into them too does their destruction take place, according to what must be: for they give recompense and pay restitution to each other for their injustice according to the ordering of time).[11] Dikē is the *apeiron*'s mode of dispensing necessity's dues: the coming-to-be and the passing away of things. This cycle of birth and decay is needed for the perpetual balancing of finite entities, which must perish (or decline and return to the infinite) in time to make place for others to go forth—namely, it describes a repeatable process of changing states.

Discussing Anaximander's formation of the world order as a process of separation of opposites, John Mansley Robinson clarifies that this "crime" (ἀδικία) does not occur at the level of the finite existing things but is the injustice inherent in the very structure of oppositions from which the world emerges. He thus calls it "the injustice of opposites" (34), which must alternate in payment to one another, in an economy of compensation that keeps the cosmos in balance. Such law of compensation is "the root of tragedy," adds Robinson (36, 37), and this remark is most pertinent to the present study. The example he gives from our ordinary experience of this tragic law of compensation sums up the main argument I will be advancing about the *Oresteia*: "The roots of our confidence in the law of compensation lie deep in human nature. We feel 'instinctively' that an unusually mild autumn will have to be 'paid for' by an unusually severe winter" (36). Likewise, the excess of destruction from the *Oresteia*'s blood feud will be in time duly compensated and followed by an age of prosperity because this is in accordance with the order of things. Of course, in Aeschylus the purveyor of this balance of opposites takes on the name of Zeus, but the apportionment the god brings about is of the kind described in Anaximander's cosmology.

Heraclitus will revisit Anaximander in establishing his own philosophy of becoming that, nonetheless, also relies on the regularity and repeatability of a pattern (*taxis*). Change, in other words, is by necessity supported by a substructure of permanence, which—even if "indefinite"—remains secured in its place as the origin of what goes forth and as the eventual receptacle of what returns. When Karl Reinhardt remarked that, even in their worst trials, Aeschylus's heroes are never abandoned but are always granted a "sense of belonging" (3), he attributed this security historically to the as-yet-unfixed boundary between mortal and divine spheres to which Aeschylus's overall "archaism" testifies. It may equally be said that this sense of belonging corresponds to this secure cosmology from which dikē proceeds, and of which the gods are brilliant poetic instantiations.

Heidegger, who devoted a seminar to these sparse lines of Anaximander, read them for their originary, cosmological, and ontological significance, which for him preceded the legislative and moral character that dikē later acquired. Regarding tragedy, and more specifically dikē's relation to techne, Heidegger elaborated on it in his reading of *Antigone* in the *Introduction to Metaphysics* (171–78).[12] Thus, since my understanding of Aeschylean dikē is embedded in a cosmo-ontological framework, I would be perhaps expected to offer a Heideggerian reading as well. However, this too is not my purpose, for two reasons. First, insofar as my source is Aeschylus, I prefer not turning the tragedian into an illustration of Heidegger, nor, for that matter, of Anaximander or Heraclitus. In fact, it may be more interesting to reassess the current philosophical overemphasis on becoming after encountering the registers of constancy Aeschylus describes, and does so, significantly, in a monumental language and authoritative tone. Second, even if I were to subordinate Aeschylus to Heidegger, I would stop short of Heidegger's eventual—albeit oblique—involvement with historicity and politics, which projects the ontological and physical categories into "new beginnings," thus attempting ever so subtly the prescriptive step of translating cosmology into history/politics.[13] As I have tried to stress, despite my acknowledgment of the political potentials granted by this cosmology, I withdraw as much as possible from epochal declarations of "newness," in part because I think that it is the temptation for epochality, novelty, and the resultant absorption of nature into history that account for much of human and political hubris. Moreover, I find that such a historicist ontology falls inevitably prey to the utilitarian, cultural motto of "updating the classics"; thus, despite whatever its merits, or even necessities, this ontology remains unconcerned with its own deficiencies while being overly confident of the virtues of its "radicality." For instance, it cannot respond efficaciously to charges of relativism regardless of how intensely it may protest its alignment with cultural or moral relativism; often, it also risks treating the tradition as a "cultural product" in need of perpetual tweaking to fit new demands—again, despite Heidegger's express reticence to treating things as available resources.

In contrast, my fascination with Aeschylus involves moments where *phusis* escapes from a symmetrical relation with human history, and shows itself as a primordial necessity that precedes and exceeds this history. The truth of this necessity is thus not subject to differential historical expressions, since, *by nature* of its definition, it designates a force that does not need human beings for its manifestation (for it is its own self-manifestation), though it sets in motion human history, among other things. Accordingly, the sea in Clytemnestra's red-carpet speech reproduced itself before human beings arrived on this earth, and continues to do so regardless of the human usage of its resources. *Phusis* in this project names the realm of the referent that needs no transcendental subject or hermeneutical agent for its appearance, though such a subject is bound to interact with, interpret, and appropriate nature for its own ends. Furthermore, nature's *indifference* to our history might be of ethical significance, and not only in the typically negative way in which we have come to view any link between nature and ethics. For instance, I suggest—with no intent to provoke, though aware that I might inadvertently do so—that nature's indifference can be contemplated in a rich correlation with the historical notions of judicial neutrality, objectivity, and "blindness" that all aimed at *isonomia* (equality before the law) but that are now under attack in the name of justice and equality before the law.[14]

Were I to put all this schematically, I would say that while much scholarship invests in translating Aeschylus from the cosmological to the political—with the *Oresteia*, for obvious reasons, being the main text—I traverse the journey backward to highlight the cosmological platform that undergirds human history.[15] A notable example of this gradual trajectory from nature to citizenry and morality is Richard Kuhns's study of the trilogy, which I otherwise found quite useful at several instances of my own analysis. This gesture of extricating morality from nature is predominant in commentary at least since Hegel, and is present in the historian Christian Meier, whose remarks on the *Eumenides* inform my discussion of divine genealogy in chapter 5. Jan Kott, who schematizes Aeschylus's axis mundi in *Prometheus Bound* as a relation between the chthonic Furies and the Uranian Fates (Moirai), also understands this antithesis as a dialectical contestation between nature qua myth and history. The Furies in their fixation with the past and with memory refer to the repetitive, cyclical temporality of myth, whereas the Fates' openness toward the future signals a linear, unidirectional time associated with history. This passage from Kott encapsulates his position, which for the most part is implied in my argument as well, albeit with a significant difference regarding the dialectics of history and myth:

> In the Aeschylean cosmos, split into the above and the below, a cosmos in constant flux, even destiny is antithetic. Moiras weave the thread of time; Furies are memory, relentless and inflexible. In the Greek topocosm, Moiras were placed at the very pinnacle of the heavenly structure; the Furies were the deities of the underground. Moiras and Furies seem to be images of two different "necessities." The Furies were deities of revenge, of paying for blood with blood, for death with death, and so they saw to it that the cycle was repeated. The white Moiras are measures of time—*moira* means a share or a phase. Moiras are bound neither by memory nor by the duty of revenge. They are of necessity free from repeating the past. . . . But it seems that Moiras and Furies depict, as it were, two different notions of time: historic time, which is unidirectional, and mythic time, which is cyclic. (12–13)

In interpreting the *Eumenides*, I similarly lay out the contrast between two necessities—that of life's continuity, thematized by the erotic argument of Apollo at Delphi and by the legal deliverance of the son as last murderer, and that of the death-principle, thematized by the Furies' demand for endless revenge. However, I refrain from articulating this antithesis dialectically *between* mythic and historical time, highlighting instead that the antithesis between Fate and Fury is already present *within* the natural world. The projective momentum of Moira is not necessarily an escape from nature into linear history but itself belongs to the great cosmic cycle of moving forward and being thrown back. I do not mean to suggest that

Kott's correspondences are wrong; in fact, his notion of the axis mundi proves helpful in visualizing the vertical, indeed vertiginous, arrival of tragic dikē. However, as already mentioned, I choose to step back from historical translations because I find that the injection of history shifts the perspective in ways that now obscure rather than illuminate reality—this being in part an effect of our long-standing removal from nature's logos.

Consequently, the text that has provided me with the most fecund guidelines for interpretation is rather unexpected: not a work on Aeschylus, and not even scholarship on literature or moral and judicial philosophy, at least not by conventional disciplinary boundaries. Walter Burkert's *Homo Necans* helped me elucidate various terms and structures in Aeschylus's conception of dikē, though it is, disciplinarily speaking, a study on the anthropology of ritual: specifically, the anthropology of hunting.[16] Since a ritual involving such a naturalist activity—one that concerns the life and death of animals, the season of preparation, and the time spent in nature to catch prey—was understood as reenactment and mirroring of cosmic time, I tend to think of this book as a cosmological anthropology. That the *Oresteia* shows justice to be an actual pursuit by bloodhounds—in effect, a hunting scene—makes *Homo Necans* all the more fitting as a companion text.

Hunting, according to Burkert, initiated the history of ritual sacrifice as atonement for killing, and thus inculcated through religious feeling the sense of seriousness that became indispensable for the development of culture as a complex system of moral ideas, values, and institutions. In elaborating this theory of sacrifice out of the hunt, *Homo Necans* further proves relevant to the sacrificial themes of the *Oresteia*. For instance, as my chapter on *Agamemnon* shows, the original cause of the trilogy does not consist in Helen's abduction, which the chorus cites as the casus belli of the Trojan War (*Ag*. ln. 40–45), but in the wrath of the huntress, Artemis, against her father, Zeus, whose eagle killed her sacred hare, in an omen described by the same chorus (ln. 134–38). In this, I am in agreement with John Peradotto, who reads this sacrificial scene as the structuring incident of the whole trilogy (237), and who also notes the significance of the hunt in the omen (246–48).[17] It was the transport of this divine power struggle into mortal conflict that obliged Agamemnon to sacrifice his daughter at Artemis's altar. In turn, it is for this sacrifice that Clytemnestra, the maiden's mother, holds Agamemnon responsible, initiating a cycle of revenge. At the origin of the *Oresteia*, we are thus confronted with the interrelated scenes of hunting and sacrifice, while the claim of justice replaces the need for atonement still through the logic of sacrificial ritual and reenactment.

What are the implications of justice stemming from the hunt? I would argue that the trilogy shows the institution of human justice to be expiating for this original and originary hunt. By the end of the *Oresteia*, we have nothing else but the stopping of the hunt that the Furies have perpetuated on Orestes. Vicious canines, chasing after the smell of blood, the Furies would be later symbolically translated as personifications of the guilt that hunts down the murderer (the hunter). However, Orestes's atonement through this hunt is simultaneously *their* atonement: having undergone enormous sufferings, he is delivered of their chase, and his deliverance allows them to rest from their exhaustion. One way to phrase Burkert's argument is that sacrifice offers the crucial link between nature and theodicy. Sacrifice also provides *the* scene that, in disclosing the interdependence of life and death, epitomizes the feeling of seriousness, which is important not only to the tragic genre, according to Aristotle, but to the building of culture, according to Burkert.

Nevertheless, the broad scholarly consensus that hunting serves as the main metaphor for the Furies' justice has resulted in commentators treating it as merely that: a metaphor. This implies a hesitancy to admit that justice, now an intensely idealized concept, may have more than a passing, figurative kinship to hunting—a practice now deemed barbaric and outdated. By stressing the metaphorical rather than structural relationship between hunting and justice, one is able to exaggerate the difference between revenge and justice so as to align the former with predation while allowing the latter to be infinitely idealized. Historically, this supports the claim that we are now well beyond the archaic equation of justice with revenge, having reached an enlightened form of this concept. In other words, Theseus's ship has changed, and in this case, it is deemed preferable to emphasize the radical newness rather than the continuity that otherwise secures the concept's legitimacy in a long tradition. The present study problematizes this assumption of linear historical progress, but I will return to this issue briefly toward the conclusion of this chapter.

Apart from reading *Homo Necans* as a cosmological anthropology, I detect in it a nascent phenomenology of seriousness, particularly in the connections it draws between the necessary violence of the hunt, the ensuing need for atonement, and the ways in which culture and morality proceed from the amplification of the physiological traits once required of the hunter—namely, overall discipline, visual focus, and bodily patience.

Summarily, Burkert argues that the most important evolutionary step for the creation and maintenance of culture was the human being's transformation into a predator. Homo sapiens as a thinking being would have been impossible without *homo necans* because it was the reality of predation that first compelled humans to develop and exercise the traits that later proved necessary for the building of organized, long-term projects. To survive, predators required a heightened sense of vigilance, attention, and discipline over their hunger and fear as they waited for food indefinitely while exposed to an inhospitable landscape. Thus, the anthropology of the hunt dramatizes humanity's physical and ethical confrontation with the danger and inscrutability of the natural world. In such a primal scene, the human being is first presented with the serious question of life and death—a seriousness Burkert then locates symbolically in the middle moment of a sacrificial ritual, the moment coinciding with the killing of the animal, which he calls, after Rudolf Otto, the mysterium tremendum. Although Burkert does not explicitly elaborate on seriousness as a conceptual topos unto itself, the few citations of this term are sufficient clues for reading his anthropology as emergent out of this concept. Read this way, hunting provides a narrative scaffold from which to contemplate life-and-death questions, for these are the only type of questions that deserve the designation "serious," according to Burkert. Seriousness is born of necessity, and seriousness is *serious* when it arrives at the threshold of life and death. This means that his anthropology turns out to describe an ontological state of exposure, which, however, is inextricably tied to the concrete ontic contents of this primal scene: the danger of the unknown, the physical threat of wild nature, the darkness of night, and the eventual survival and death allotted to each of the participants in this deadly encounter.[18]

Indeed, as I insist variously throughout the book, it is important to understand that, in tragic cosmology, the being-at-stake of life and death must be taken quite literally. There is a reason why in common parlance "seriously" and "literally" are often used as synonyms. In other words, the materiality of the danger is not to be dismissed as mere ontic content that can vanish into some higher ontological dimension of finitude or rhetorical death. Here, in the plane of the referent and of Ananke, the ontic-ontological difference collapses: in fact, it may be said that the ontic shows itself as that which stands firmly affixed, hovering over the changing history of its subjective and cultural interpretations that we call "ontological." Tragedy's seriousness—its mimesis of a serious act, according to Aristotle—probes this terrifyingly real space, which is now philosophically diminished precisely because of its intense reality. Yet, to begin with, it is this space of objective terror, which cannot be diluted into a historical hermeneutic, that makes the human being capable of ontological contemplation. Burkert's observation that the very definition of "act" refers us to this ancient act of killing should give us pause (3n4), particularly at a time when activism is idealized as the highest form of contemporary justice: ironically, though it is very much connected with justice, it is not so through some enlightened renewal, but again through this inaugural act of (necessary) murder. This is where Theseus's ship remains uncannily the same. In Burkert's description of animal sacrifice as a symbolic reenactment of the hunt, I thus glean an articulation of tragic seriousness in its unfolding from Dikē's hunt of human beings to the human hunt for justice—justice being, of course, considered one of the most serious moral ideas in human culture.

Having offered a rough sketch for my adoption of *Homo Necans* as a companion text to Aeschylus, I will now address some criticisms and potential objections to its methods. Though Burkert is recognized as a leading scholar of Greek and Near Eastern religions, and this book in particular enjoyed many scholarly accolades for its original and provocative insights, he is also critiqued, often for what is provocative in his contributions. The two main critical fronts against *Homo Necans* object to: (a) its functionalism—namely, its subordination of cultural forms to rigid material functions (for instance, the reduction of religious expression to the survival instinct, which is possibly a kind of vulgar materialism of "you are what you eat"); and (b) its naturalism, especially in its indebtedness to Darwin's evolutionary theory, which, once transported into the sociocultural plane, can easily derail into all sorts of unpalatable -isms.

Concerning the critique against functionalism, I think that appearances deceive: although Burkert starts with an evolutionary-biological paradigm, he is led to conclusions that hardly qualify as crude materialism. For instance, arguing that only cultures with a strong religious feeling survive the onslaught of time, and that it is religion rather than economy that supports culture, turns the tables. While it is not surprising that the indebtedness to biology and zoology is construed as reductionist, I stress that *Homo Necans*'s enlisting of these sciences in its theorization of hunting affords us a cosmological view of morality: the human encounter with nature signals the passage into moral being precisely because nature's so-called determinism is another name for its self-presentation as law; in fact, for its presentation of law *as* necessity. In confronting this realm of necessity with its demands and consequences, the human being also apprehends the need for a corresponding orderly pattern in its own existence—namely, the need for the moral law as obligation and prohibition. This important ethical dimension, one most vividly shown in Burkert's discussion of the gravity of the mysterium tremendum, makes this book much more than a document of "cultural anthropology." Were it merely cultural anthropology, it would espouse a cultural constructivism—namely, a moral relativism, according to which humans invent their moral codes with no reference outside of themselves, and then attach some symbols to them, investing them with different meanings in different times. Such relativism, however, understands little of the weight of *compulsion* that underlies the feeling of obligation, obligation being the par excellence moral feeling for which any serious moral theory would have to account. On the contrary, *Homo Necans*'s reflection on sacrificial ritual offers such a theory of obligation, and one that is not precipitated out of cultural or historical incidentals, but out of an originary exposure to nature as threshold, necessity, urgency, and compulsion.

Homo Necans's structure reflects this fruitful tension between matter and symbolic presentation: in the first part, Burkert lays out his method, influenced by the fields of biology and ethology; the second part is devoted to case studies from ancient Greek ritual. Even though these case studies are there to illustrate the method, they also do something else: the overwhelming myths they tell, and the gruesome reality to which they point, suggest that it was *they* that necessitated the recourse to this particular method. Therefore, we must read the book again, now backward, from the examples to the method. After this second reading, we realize that the method will not unlock the meaning of myths and rituals, but rather the violence of the myths and the rituals *will have led* Burkert to seek in evolutionary biology, animal ethology, and the anthropology of the hunt viable modes of explanation. In this, *Homo Necans* provides me with an exemplary hermeneutic instance where the referent (*pragma*) enjoys its due precedence, leading the interpretation, not vice versa. Rather than relegating Burkert to a vulgar functionalism, I approach his thought from within a rich tradition of physiological readings of culture that includes figures as illustrious as Freud and Nietzsche, despite the latter's absence from *Homo Necans*'s citation index.

On the second, and graver charge of Darwinism, there is much to be considered, but for the sake of brevity, I will touch only on a few issues. Perhaps more than Darwin himself, who, apart from his sociopolitical applications, is hailed as a consummate materialist by progressive, secular modernity,[19] the name that proves problematic is that of Konrad Lorenz, whose ethological studies of animals are crucial for Burkert. For these seminal studies that established the scientific vocabulary and field of modern ethology, Lorenz (along with Karl von Frisch and Nikolaas Tinbergen) was awarded the Nobel for Physiology or Medicine in 1973, but the award was contested in light of his earlier positions regarding racial purity during the Nazi regime. Lorenz had since regretted such a position, and revised his early understanding of National Socialism.[20] Nevertheless, his stance during the thirties continues to cast his name into doubt and controversy at the same time that his ethological findings have been crucial for modern zoology. Burkert's intellectual debt to Lorenz's animal studies can therefore be easily politicized, and Burkert can be charged for complicity. Appreciating the legitimacy of such political objections, but troubled by their limitations as well, I would counter them with two general responses before reasserting more positively the indispensability of Burkert's work for my present project.

The first, easier response is historical in nature, pointing out the fact that the charge of political complicity is not always applied consistently. When considering accusations so strong as to discredit the majority, or even entirety, of an author's work, it is edifying to recall other canonical thinkers who have been accused yet have not suffered irreparable consequences; for instance, the criticism against them did not result in a total eclipse of their name, nor did discussion of their work necessarily lead to guilt by association for the discussant. There is no need to name names and continue the controversy since the polemic itself is not particularly fruitful. Nonetheless, this selectivity, which may not even always reflect the actual degree of complicity on the part of the thinkers charged, is an intriguing symptom within broader intellectual and academic history.

The second response is more oblique, but somehow also more essential, because it involves the concept of seriousness itself—namely, the very concept that Burkert develops out of the human being's encounter with nature. Seriousness assumes a structural importance because such political objections are delivered in the form of highly serious charges against the commission of equally serious intellectual (and perhaps not only) infractions. In the case of Burkert's anthropology, its reliance on the concept of aggression[21] may invite criticisms of espousing violence and other such disagreeable sociopolitical ideas. What a political critic, however, might find objectionable—namely, Burkert's thesis that the human entrance into culture presupposes the increasingly conscious exercise of power over life and death—does not invalidate by fiat the descriptive resonance of this concept and its literary, ritual, ethnological, and archaeological examples. On the contrary, the logic presupposed by this objection confirms rather than undermines Burkert's argument about the violence that inaugurates and maintains culture. In other words, to problematize theories that contemplate the undesirable—hence, tragic—necessities delimiting human existence and culture, one must fall back on the notion of seriousness as death-inducing: the critic, then, may attempt to build a consensus that such theoretical descriptions pose serious—because actual and life-threatening—sociopolitical risks, and must thus be delegitimized.

It is worth noting here that such critiques of naturalism when it comes *solely* to the human life sciences are symptoms of the intricate tension between, on the one hand, the glorification of science as an indisputable pillar of post-Enlightenment modernity with its debunking of gods, myths, and superstitions, and, on the other, the postmodern critique, relativization, and regular revision of what counts as science so as to forge an increasingly seamless alignment between science and official ideology. Conversely, when misalignment is suspected, charges of determinism abound, and the idea that science discloses the indifferent and neutral logos of nature is displaced and disqualified; instead, both nature and science are subordinated under the rubric of culture, being spoken of as "cultural constructs." This is, however, an enormous topic at the heart of the so-called dialectic of the Enlightenment, and can hardly be negotiated, even preliminarily, in this study. I have mentioned it only insofar as it generally pertains to the possible critiques of Burkert's biologism and to the limits of such critiques.

In closing this discussion on the politics of Burkert's anthropology, and grateful for the critical pressures this problematic exercised on my manner of responding to it, I wish to highlight once again the positive reason for which *Homo Necans* remains indispensable for my analysis. Insofar as its method and its literary and ritual examples foreground the phenomenon as a manifestation of inexorable necessity—that is, insofar as they disclose nature as an ineradicable referent, as *the thing* that sends and receives human destiny but remains independent of it—*Homo Necans* marks another way of telling the Aeschylean Ananke. I would go as far as to say that *Homo Necans* repeats Aeschylus in another discipline. Furthermore, preempting philosophical objections to anthropology's epistemic limitations in probing philosophical and literary questions, I would underscore that tragedy without anthropology is an oxymoron. Conversely, to think that there can be an *anthropos*, and by extension an anthropology, without tragedy is hubristic, for it misunderstands humanity as invincible, and in control of all nature and necessity. Burkert's anthropology meets and honors both these conditions.

Having laid out the main conceptual threads and textual sources that appear in this study, I now provide a summary of the ensuing chapters as a rough roadmap for the reader, after which I will conclude by returning to the secondary issue of the contemporary impetus behind the book. Following this introduction, chapter 2 delves more deeply into the concept of the prioritization of nature during (tragic) mimesis in Aristotle and in the ritual anthropology of Burkert. In effect, I propose a ritual reading of Aristotle after the recent secularization of his *Poetics*, as for instance by Stephen Halliwell. The chapter also offers a detailed discussion of the notion of seriousness in relation to the mysterium tremendum. It recognizes in Burkert's tripartite temporality of the sacrificial ceremony an analog for tragic temporality, and more specifically, for the trilogic sequence of the *Oresteia*. It concludes with the recovery of the original semantics of authenticity, which refers to the act of killing, thus reinforcing further the concept of seriousness in a life-and-death context. Finally, with the help of this cluster of concepts of priority, hierarchy, seriousness, and authenticity, it establishes the dilemmatic structure of "either/or" as the syntax par excellence of tragedy.

Chapters 3, 4, and 5 are close readings of each of the tragedies in the trilogy—*Agamemnon, Choephoroi (Libation-Bearers), Eumenides*—with respect to the notion of dikē each imparts. In each chapter, one or more deities preside over the sending of dikē, thus revealing it in slightly different facets. With Artemis as the main deity in *Agamemnon*, dikē shows its origins in the scene of the hunt, but also as the appropriation of one's own destiny—dikē in its syntactical usage as the word "as"—seen exemplarily in the guard's self-understanding of his task: to be "as a dog," a vigilant protector of his city. The stargazing of the guard, the portent of the eagles and the hare, and the sea in Clytemnestra's beguiling red-carpet speech are three important images in this analysis of Aeschylean cosmology.

In the *Choephoroi*, Hermes embodies the axis mundi as he travels from his Olympian heights to agitate the underworld and disclose dikē in its chthonic form. Here, the motifs of the buried warrior and erstwhile hunter who keeps vigil over his community and demands revenge for his murder are the anthropological correlates of what Walter Otto describes as a cosmological, objective demand for payment after blood shedding.[22] I pay attention to the chthonicity of the male figure (the dead hero), especially in its relation to the buried but life-giving image of the vegetal seed. This is important because the *Choephoroi* offers the background for this image that reappears to support the winning argument of Apollo against the Furies, an argument thus critiqued for its blatant patriarchy.

The chapter on the *Eumenides*, with Apollo and Athena as key deities, presents most starkly, and perhaps unconventionally, this reading backward from politics to cosmology. While this concluding tragedy has furnished the exemplary instance for scholars to mark the progress from the benighted revenge of the "age of nature" to the enlightened justice of the polis, I highlight the persistence of natural processes and precepts throughout the institution of the court. I argue that the interruption of the cycle of revenge is not simply the result of judicial progress, but rather the reflection in the city's microcosm of a cosmic process by which nature regularly checks its own destructive momentum and lets life resume. We must not forget that the Furies are already asleep in the beginning of the *Eumenides*, having abandoned their pursuit well before the trial starts, and being chastised by the plaintiff they are supposed to defend. Physical exhaustion caught up with them before forensic argument. Finally, the epilogue attempts a short excursion into Sophocles, aiming to sketch the endurance—at least in Attic tragedy—of dramatizing the limits of human justice in front of cosmic Dikē.

Coda: Ananke—Then, Now, and Always

As stated earlier, this project is not unaffected by contemporary questions about the nature and implementation of justice. After all, justice has long claimed one of the top spots in the history of human ideas and cultural institutions, and in its current iteration as "social justice," it has arguably sent many other virtues—goodness, temperance, prudence, equanimity, humility, detachment—to court for moral inadequacy. It would be impossible to think about the *Oresteia*, this seminal text of the *progress* from blood feud to civic justice (or so we have been told), without also noting how its main ethical categories of justice and revenge, vigilance and vigilantism, jury duty and equality before the law, are inflected in our world; how they may have altogether receded from our understanding; or how they may still be repeated wittingly or unwittingly. Thus, a range of questions opens up, involving but not limited to: (a) the concept of equality before the law (*isonomia*) whose universality now suffers from identitarian critiques that posit the agents' social identity rather than the nature of the act as the ultimate criterion for the verdict—in effect, giving precedence to the incidental markers that used to sway justice arbitrarily *before* the notion of *isonomia* came to remedy the incidental's outranking of the essential; (b) the official, albeit not always consistent, shunning of extrajudicial violence that in some cases could qualify as vigilantism even if not designated so; and (c) the legal and cultural demand for redress of historical injustices, which presumes a preponderantly *collectivist* and *intergenerational* conception of justice, therefore inevitably but tacitly relying on the archaic and retaliatory logic of "sins of parents visited upon children." All these conundrums, and others not elaborated here, find mirroring examples and an arsenal of concepts in the *Oresteia*.

Nevertheless, and as I have also pointed out at the beginning, it is equally critical to underscore that these modern concerns remain overall peripheral and epiphenomenal to my inquiry: their sporadic appearance at the end of sustained discussions of Aeschylus as mostly disquieting moments of comparison, and their more frequent placement in brief footnotes, show concretely their auxiliary character for my purposes. In this conscious, and even tactical hierarchy that it sets up, the study remains loyal to its own argument for hierarchical priority that it locates in the very structure of tragedy's "either/or" syntax. With these qualifiers in mind, then, I will append some thoughts on these current topics so as to also highlight by contrast an important conclusion to which I have been led—namely, that justice is not an adequate, nor is it a "just," translation of dikē since it compromises dikē's cosmological and ontological provenance, reducing it to an exclusively immanent politics. Interestingly, in this lopsided translation, the one thing that survives intact is the structure of arbitrariness: just as with nature's dikē, which stands on the receiving end of social criticism for being arbitrary, contemporary forms of civic justice also rely on arbitrariness, but this is less visible because civic justice defines itself as *the* historical process whose *end* is the abolition of arbitrariness. I contend that the arbitrariness of civic justice is all the more problematic because of this built-in teleology that functions as a mechanism of self-legitimation: assuming reason itself to be an immanent human faculty alone, with no correspondence to natural referents,[23] civic justice presents itself as the result of rational deliberations, and therefore, as an indisputable improvement over nature's logos and patterns.

If I were to isolate one iconic—and more crucially, ironic—contemporary figure in which many of these conundrums converge, it would be that of the SJW, the "social justice warrior." (Despite the irony of which I speak, it should be clarified that the term itself is in no way ironic, since it has been used as a self-designation by many activists themselves as well as by their critics.) In this term, the notion of justice as predation continues unabated, especially if we consider Burkert's analysis that war is in continuity with hunting, with both being considered states of nature. The ubiquity of the SJW, and of the cultural attitudes and practices associated with this figure, show that the archaic violence of the hunt remains formally constitutive to justice—so much so that the term "warrior" (itself an archaic synonym for the more vernacular "soldier")[24] appears at the center of the language of justice at the very moment this language seeks to sanitize itself from any other possibly offensive meanings. Note also how the recourse to the war metaphor stands otherwise in sharp contrast to the predominant cultural rhetoric of compassion, sensitivity, politeness, inclusivity, and so on.

Justice remains *essentially* tied to hypervigilance, pursuit, revenge, and even vigilantism, and what is interesting—albeit unnerving—is that all this often serves good purposes. In fact, if this retributive impulse did not fuel and legitimize the demand for justice, many of our exalted revolutions (whether national or class-based), emancipatory movements, or extrajudicial but morally exigent interventions[25] undertaken by all sorts of agents should make us hesitant about condoning their violence. Yet I wager that any such hesitation would not be deemed a sign of moral advancement but of callousness, for the operative assumption is that when justice is not served by the law, and when certain intolerable limits have been reached, extrajudicial solutions become necessary, even at the cost of escalating violence. At this juncture, however, an epochal fissure appears: a self-proclaimed enlightened age finds it difficult to admit that this argument of moral exigency, of a state of legal exception, underlies precisely the logic of the Furies. Although, at present, no law-based state would overtly advocate for extrajudicial justice, particularly not in supporting causes that contravene official morality, the idealization of justice as *the* supreme moral category is often applauded when it serves, even by *any means*, whatever is considered moral under the circumstances. That we now feel that only social injustices warrant such extrajudicial violence at the limit, but not injustice perpetrated against individuals (as was customary in the ancient world), is an indicator of the moral rankings of our culture, but not necessarily an essential difference in the structure of the justice claim.

My critical intervention, therefore, questions not the necessity of this spirit of vengeance (or of war, for that matter) but modernity's misrecognition that, in supposedly condemning archaic violence, it has succeeded in releasing itself from its own necessary participation in it. This thinking effectively conceals the very idea of necessity as a constraint imposed on the human from the outside, from an *order of things* that we, moderns, believe only *appears* as inevitability, when in fact, it *is* one. In this contemporary scene of justice, where moral perfectibility admits no natural limits or tragic inevitabilities, the SJW functions as a moral enforcement agent in vigilant pursuit of transgressors. Like the ancient hunter, lurking late at night to secure food for his entire community, this new type of hunter also lurks daily and nightly behind an electronic device, camouflaged in various avatars, to catch those threatening the telos of a just society. Whereas the goal of justice is a lofty one, the irony to which I am pointing involves the disavowal, on the one hand, of a "violent theory" such as Burkert's for exposing the inevitability of human aggression, and on the other hand, the undisputed espousal of the activist dream of a "juster" world, predicated though it is on practices of aggression. Here, Burkert's definition of the *act* as (sacrificial) murder proves again terribly poignant: his theory of aggressivity, which is based on the tragic structure of necessity, is not falsified but confirmed by the idealization and infinitization of justice.

This strange continuity of the predatory aspect of justice, as well as of its originary spirit in identitarian affiliations, becomes most clearly evident against the background of the *Eumenides*. The *Eumenides* has, at least since Hegel, been interpreted as a historical trajectory during which *politics*, in its public, objective sense, overcomes the earlier tribalism of the family feud, announcing the era of universal civic justice. Freeing justice from its primitive trappings in natural kinship and identity particularism, the citizen jury ushers in civic kinship and the public square of rational deliberation, where personal intimacies and enmities are set aside for the common good: except that Orestes's trial results in a hung jury, and the supposedly civic resolution is too arbitrary to satisfy any modern notion of the city as a rational space. Consequently, instead of focusing on the political aspect of this resolution, I point to its cosmological coordinates. Arbitrary, yet in correspondence with a natural logos that obeys the Anaximandrian patterns of emergence and destruction, Athena's tie-breaking vote figures this natural cessation of the destruction that would ensue the perpetuation of the justice claim.[26] The justice that arrives at the end of the *Eumenides* is dikē as a cosmic sending—namely, the Uranian aspect of the same dikē whose chthonic underside previously demanded revenge, yet both these aspects are never exhaustible at the political threshold.

Switching to the present, social justice similarly takes up causes pertaining to *identity* politics, thus hearkening to these early kinship structures of justice, now based on in-group rather than family ties, and to the infinite and retaliatory logic that regulates them if left unchecked. To what extent the designation "social" achieves the objective universality Hegel announces, and/or to what extent the present forms of identity-based particularism compromise such universality, remains at the very least a legitimate question. Nevertheless, whether social, or individual, the radical infinitization of justice, far from the moral perfectibility it promises, seems to compile further conflicts and further injustice. To follow justice's "justest" justness risks nothing short of catastrophe: "The race is bound fast in calamity," Aeschylus warns (*Ag.* ln. 1566), and Heinrich von Kleist's "Michael Kohlhaas" repeats this, showing in a more modern context the self-destruction and social terror that the fanaticism of justice entails. It was to avoid such calamities that the *Oresteia*'s curse had to be lifted. But a curse is not a containable act on which several political actors can deliberate and then resolve. A curse stands for the incalculable concatenation of accident and intention, for the misfortune (*dustuchia*) that inheres in the order of things and that blocks human attempts at preempting it. At such times, a different sort of intervention is also needed, but because it arrives already belatedly, after *too much* injustice has already piled up, it too is bound to be both just and unjust in its coming. This is Aeschylus's belated (ὑστερόποινον) Dikē whose exorbitant arbitrariness comes to settle the score. In the *Eumenides*, it does so by exonerating the last murderer, to the chagrin of the last victim who feels unavenged.

If this antipolitical strain of reading appears so at odds with our hyperpoliticized culture, let me conclude with some brief remarks on Attic tragedy in general, which hopefully will explain it.[27] It is an understatement to say that tragic theater has elicited and continues to elicit political interpretations that read it in dialogue with the rise of democracy in Athens. There are of course many legitimate formal and thematic reasons to draw these connections, though I would not classify tragedy as a political genre of writing for the simple reason that there is nothing *programmatic* about tragic action, and politics without a program is—well—not politics in any sense that we have come to know the term. Tragedy may well have engaged politics and had things to say about it, but this does not render it a political genre, nor does it mean that it affirmed politics as the sole and undisputed way of living together. I am of the mind that when tragedy did speak about politics, it was more often as a withdrawal from it, which the politically minded critics may reimagine as protest, and thus repoliticize it. Semantic and dialectical games aside, even if there is a tragic politics, it is not of the kind we meet ordinarily in ancient Athens, and much less today. For it is the task of politics to change the world—that is its programmatic part—and it is the task of tragedy to describe it, and to describe most emphatically those moments that the human being cannot change. To describe: this is a verb that carries with it as much neutrality, objectivity, and remove as the human being could ever muster. It lends tragedy its Homeric impartial undertones during the very age where philosophy and politics decided to revise and, in fact, "unlearn" Homer, and it is because of this quality that tragedy was already a political anachronism in fifth-century Athens.

Poetic description is concerned with the nature of reality, with the things that are (*pragmata*) as they are. In Aeschylean tragedy, the cosmology of dikē unfolds as such a description of the world. Through the practice of description, the relationship between theater (as well as "theory"/*theoria*, which share the same root as "theater") and reality is set aright with theater emerging as a medium of reality, not a representation of it. Tragedy is not reality turned into theatrical artifice; this kind of conventional realism—art reflecting real social conditions—would not be serious enough. In setting nature qua reality at its origin, as Aristotle correctly discerned, tragedy does not relegate itself to a derivative status, as it might be tempting to think; rather, it aligns itself with, and becomes, those things that are in themselves of priority. Nietzsche is right that the elevation of tragedy removes it from realism qua conventional matters (and let us recall that political matters are also conventional ones). However, when he speaks of tragedy's disclosing a deeper—in his language, non-realist—truth,[28] I take him to mean that this truth is none other but the truth of the things-in-themselves, the truth of those things that Seferis's poem wove together into a "rich pattern" (πλούσια τάξις). Tragedy, in this sense, might be contemplated as the profoundest realism literature has afforded us.

Chapter 2

Tragedy and the Seriousness of Culture
Aristotle and Walter Burkert

Imitation: Nature as Priority

That tragedy may have had religious origins is a position long held and copiously documented from Jane Ellen Harrison and the Cambridge Ritualists to the philosophical postulate of the Dionysian in Nietzsche.[1] James George Frazer's *The Golden Bough*—a monumental work on comparative mythology that was contested by official anthropology for its speculative leaps but proved influential among literary circles—advanced the thesis of the dying god, which led Harrison and her collaborator Gilbert Murray to interpret tragedy as a ritual reenactment of a vegetation daimon who dies yearly (ἐνιαυτός) to be regenerated. In the world of tragedy, this suffering deity, often linked to and symbolized by sacred kings who must be ritually killed or dismembered, is identified with Dionysus. Even scholars such as Walter Otto and Karl Kerényi, who do not espouse a clear priority of cult over myth, would agree that tragedy's reliance on myth signals a simultaneous reliance on cult.[2] Indeed, tragedy draws multiply on cult: its inspiration from and elaboration of mythical material that is often etiological in nature, explaining cultic phenomena; its own agonistic presentation within the frame of cultic activity during the Great Dionysia festival; its internal formal unfolding as peripeteia (that is, an extreme change of fortune), and thematic preoccupation with the agon and fall of the sovereign—all these fulfill the sacrificial logic Walter Burkert detects in the history of Greek ritual. To elucidate this connection between Burkert's theory of sacrifice and the tragic genre, I will turn to some key terms from his description of sacrificial rites that are also crucially present in Aristotle's definition of tragedy in *Poetics* 6.

The comparison between these two sets of terms is particularly significant, given that Aristotle's interpretation of tragedy has been largely understood (and even later critiqued for that reason by Nietzsche) to be political rather than religious.[3] Here, however, I should insert an important parenthesis that, for Burkert, too, religion is not simply *related* to politics but forms the basis and guarantee of the social bond. Burkert stresses that religion is synonymous with the power of tradition and, as such, it constitutes the long-term substratum that ensures social continuity over cultural change (xxiii). The equation between tradition and religious sentiment is most poignantly witnessed before Christianity, when it was ancestral worship alone that guaranteed the legitimacy of religion (xxii), and by extension legitimized the customs of the city. Religion thus does not reflect society, but grounds and sustains it. For instance, economic phenomena are derivative of religion and not vice versa: in a footnote, Burkert highlights the Weberian thesis that Calvinism explains capitalism, not the other way around. He ventures even further, stating that only religious societies have been able to survive critical thresholds in the passage of history because religion mobilizes deep-seated, life-affirming sentiments that aid the continuation of the existing culture. These sentiments surge as a result of the symbolism of the sacrificial rite whose overall purpose is to disclose the mystery of life growing from the shedding of blood: "Religion outlives all non-religious communities; and sacrificial ritual plays a special role in this process," writes Burkert (26). In contrast, religious movements that lack such life-affirmative tenets become quickly extinct, with Manichaeism and Gnosticism as two of his corroborating examples.

Aristotle famously defined tragedy as an "imitation of a grave act." This cluster of three terms takes, in turn, a specifically sacrificial content in Burkert's anthropology, where sacrifice is consistently shown to be the ritualized repetition of the primordial scene of the hunt, the scene that from the earliest of times disclosed to the human being the stakes of life and death by setting both hunter and prey in danger. Ritual repetition serves, in fact, as Burkert's corresponding concept to Aristotle's imitation. Not only do Burkert's descriptions of the sacrificial tableau recall theatrical performances, but he also speaks explicitly of the rite as "imitation" of the hunt (26). I will begin therefore with a limited elaboration of the otherwise complex and long-studied concept of imitation mainly in order to prepare the ground for a more extended discussion of the next shared terms—namely, the act, and most importantly, its gravity.

In the *Poetics*, Aristotle assigns to poetry two natural causes (1448b5–15): first, an innate urge to imitate that arises in humans in early childhood, and, second, the pleasure human beings take in seeing successful likenesses of things, even of unpleasant and painful things such as "obscene beasts" and "corpses." The relevance of the painful and ugly representations to the kinds of truth revealed by tragedy (and sacrificial ritual) will become apparent in the rest of the chapter, but for now, I will develop further the relation between nature and mimesis that Aristotle articulates. Aristotle's accent on nature as the origin of imitation dovetails with Burkert's theory of religion, according to which it was again nature, in the guise of the survival instinct of the ancient hunting practices, that engendered the language of ritual as mimetic reenactment. The mimetic instinct is so deeply ingrained in all human beings that, for Aristotle, it accounts for a kinship between two groups of people often unlike one another: philosophers and nonphilosophers. Whereas Plato was at times suspicious, and hence cautious, of the imitative instinct, Aristotle built his theory of tragic poetry very much around this assumption of a shared enthrallment both philosophers and laypeople experience when presented with an accurate representation (εἰκόνας ἠκριβωμένας). Plato tasked the philosopher with the discernment of the acceptable imitation from the harmful one by use of an ethico-political criterion of selection: acceptable imitations are only those that enhance the integrity of the individual soul, and thus contribute to the cohesion of the social fabric. Aristotle, in turn, shifted the focus so that the purpose of imitation is not morality, at least not immediately, but accuracy: the veracious correspondence between an original and its representation. Of course, insofar as the terms "accuracy" and "veracity" belong to the domain of truth, they also involve ethics, but in a way that is mediated through the aesthetic register.

An accurate imitation is lifelike, and it attracts us precisely because of its fidelity to life as it is, or as it could probably be. In contrast, representations of a fantastical object—say, an absurd scenario that could never materialize outside someone's active imagination, or a utopia that redraws the world as it ought to but never will be—do not affect us as intensely because their object is not necessary, and thus cannot convey in full the inevitability of the real. The stakes are much higher, Aristotle seems to suggest, when we encounter incontrovertible reality. Furthermore, the pressure this reality exerts on us affects us in common, and the *Poetics* elaborates the formal requirements and techniques that allow tragic poetry, in particular, to elicit this common affect. Indeed, the commonality of affect harks back to the pivotal concept of nature. As already mentioned, nature is the source of the imitative instinct, and of the pleasure associated with this instinct. In other words, not only are we endowed naturally with the desire to imitate, but imitation also presupposes the presence of something external to us that fascinates us to the point of imposing itself as an origin—an *archē* of sorts—worthy of our reckoning with by representing it. One could even conjecture that the imitative instinct is granted us as nature's way of revealing itself through us by calling us to engage actively with it. It is crucial to underline this priority of the natural occurrence, since the concept of imitation requires a robust notion of hierarchy.[4] Such hierarchy does not entail that art is axiologically less important than its referent, but alerts us to the fact that the temporal priority of nature in inciting the imitative urge also stamps the poetic work substantively, in a way that exceeds nature's chronological precedence in the process: in short, nature becomes art's inaugural cause and privileged subject matter, thereby grounding human expression and creativity outside human immanence.

As it turns out, then, the first of the two natural causes that Aristotle indicates for poetry itself contains two parts: not only does the mimetic tendency arise from nature as a connatural (1448b5; σύμφυτον) physiological trait (1448b20; κατὰ φύσιν) of the human being who is, furthermore, the most mimetic of all animals (1448b8; ζῶον μιμητικώτατον), but secondarily, nature also serves as the prototypical object of representation, as the preferred domain from which imitation selects its themes. Aristotle's recurring examples of living persons, corpses, wild beasts, and other lifelike phenomena serving as objects of representation illustrates this. In aesthetic imitation, which is congenital and thus immanent to the human being, the mind is nevertheless compelled to go outside itself and to render the world *as it is*, unencumbered by the rival intellectual desire to tailor reality to human expectations and conventions. Imitation shows the world by following the cues of the world's appearances. It does not seek to conform the world to *artificial* human precepts, even though this does not mean that Aristotelian mimesis is reducible to a simple reduplication of nature;[5] rather, Aristotelian mimesis, especially regarding tragedy's demand for realistic scenarios, affords us a space wherein we can conceive of art without artifice, if I may be permitted this expression. In such a theory of imitation, the use of aesthetic form—while undoubtedly involving conventions of some kind—prioritizes that which it represents rather than its own self-consciousness. In subjectivity's withdrawal before an external referent, nature activates in us through imitation the capacity for description, while description, in turn, grants the potential for universality, for a "neutral" sharing and recording of the phenomenon. This mode of engagement stands in contrast to the philosophical project, which prioritizes and showcases the human construction of the world through the invention of various intellectual prototypes—be they just polities, scientific progress, or moral systematization—that aim at organizing and improving, rather than describing reality at its ontic, factual level. Nevertheless, despite the differences between the *via activa* of (imitative) poetry and the *via contemplativa* of philosophy, Aristotle maintains that all humans are to some degree attracted to the world as described by the former alone. I submit here that it is imitation's seemingly restricted capacity to *plainly* describe that accounts for this universal appeal. Just as philosophy exemplifies the human daring to organize the world and dispel nature's chaotic violence, so poetic imitation attests to a different form of courage through its faithful adherence to reality regardless of how painful or even abhorrent this reality might appear to the human eye.

Of course, Aristotle also makes clear that this reality does not have to be empirically existent in order to qualify as real. This is why poetry was writ larger than history in the *Poetics*: whereas history relates particular events, poetry relates the universal in that the reality imitated by poetry (εἰκών) does not have to actualize itself, though it must always appear as necessary and probable (εἰκὸς), thus, as convincing as if it were actual, and could one day become actual.[6] This last possibility needs to be stressed, since it is quite tempting in the current theoretical climate to fetishize an infinitely deferred potentiality over actualization. Aristotle's valuation of poetry over history must be gauged within his overall emphasis on the probable nature of the tragic plot, which implies that tragic potentiality is exemplary because it describes what is likely to happen rather than not. Though *by chance* not *yet* actual, tragic potentiality *inclines* toward actualization because it is too lifelike not to ever occur. Aristotle's theory of mimesis verges on saying that tragic plots are icons of life and this iconicity militates against their perpetually deferred nonactualization. At any rate, whether we adopt the reading of perpetual deferment or not, we must still identify this necessary element within tragic mimesis that accounts for its realness, particularly when it is not (yet) actualized. I submit that the necessity that makes the *idea of reality* real is intrinsically linked to a sense of inevitable harshness[7] often apparent in the unyielding side of nature that erects itself as a formidable opponent and limit against the human: this is a perilous albeit universal condition that tragic poetry, in particular, represents without the immediate moral urge of condemning or correcting it. Even when a plot is not actual, its imaginary prototype must obey realistic constraints.

Because it communicates a universal, Aristotle views poetry as "more philosophical and more serious" (1451b5–10; φιλοσοφώτερον καὶ σπουδαιότερον) than history, an assessment that is intricate and provocative in its implications. To better understand this phrase, we must heed Aristotle's use of the term "serious," which he had already introduced in his definition of tragedy as imitation of a serious act (1449b23–24), in the kinship he observed between epic and tragedy regarding their imitation of serious matters or personages (1449b8–10), and in his mention of Homer as the exemplary representative of epic seriousness (1448b32–34). This suggests that the seriousness involved in the general concept of poetic universality also shares in the seriousness that characterizes specifically the tragic-heroic themes, acts, and agents. Here, the alternative English translation to "serious" for the Greek σπουδαῖον is worth noting.[8] Stephen Halliwell consistently translates it as "elevated," and the verticality of this term conveys the underlying hierarchies to which I have begun pointing as well: the hierarchy between the original and its poetic imitation, which we detect in Aristotle's privileging of plot as the *archē* (ἀρχὴ) of tragedy (1450a38), where plot stands for the original event to be imitated, whether actual or imagined—albeit if imagined, still lifelike. This hierarchy, in turn, implicitly attests to the fact that tragedy is a hieratic (sacred) genre tasked to communicate a view of human life as seen from above, from the divine perspective; hence, its heroes must be preferably of higher-than-average caliber (1453a13–16). Above all, it is the sequential mention of the philosophical and the serious that remains intriguing: whereas it is evident why these two terms could be read synonymously, and at one level they should be, it is also possible that Aristotle orders them contiguously, touching on one another but resonating in slightly different registers. A stronger reading could even propose that the philosophical is not semantically adequate to capture the full effect of poetry, and so it requires the second qualifier, seriousness itself. Either way, the double predication should not be dismissed as a pleonasm but might well point to a tension between philosophical seriousness and another type of seriousness that poetry thematizes through its acts. This would be an iteration of the intimate but competing paths and ends of poetry and philosophy mentioned earlier: the seriousness of poetry involves its faithful rendering of those inhuman (and even inhumane) dimensions of reality, which philosophy seeks to explain and sublimate through concepts. Poetry, like philosophy, accedes to the universal because it can imagine the real beyond its empirical occurrences. However, unlike philosophy, which constructs its universal often by jettisoning the constraints of the real in favor of the ever-radicalizing progress of human intellection, poetry communicates reality's ineluctable aspect, against which the human being may only erect a kind of ontological courage—the courage with which tragic heroes are typically invested.

I should clarify here that tragic-heroic courage does not mean surrender to necessity; if it were simply a fatalistic acceptance of life as it is, it would not count as courage. Tragic personages become heroic in choosing to confront the most extreme of life's constraints, yet they do so without expecting reality to change and reward their defiance, without demanding that life be "fair." On the contrary, tragic heroes often have the foreknowledge that they will lose the battle but still choose to wage it. The reason for this seemingly counterintuitive decision lies in the hero's or heroine's cost-benefit analysis of their act: for the heroic consciousness, valor far outweighs the pleasures of daily welfare and even life itself. The operative term is "outweighs," because it invokes again prioritization and hierarchy. Heroic agency combines an idealism that risks everything to defy necessity with a stoic—realistic, I would say—sobriety that does not expect to change the order of things: despite the battle with fate, the hero never stoops to complain about life's unfairness or to direct blame for his state elsewhere but accepts the outcome with perseverance. It is this juxtaposition of the ideal with reality's most relentless aspect that lends tragic heroes their seriousness.[9] It is in this juxtaposition also that their moral caliber appears: had there not been the possibility of great cost in the conflict, and had reality simply bent to satisfy their demand, there would be no significant moral gain in the story.

It might then be that in another—perhaps even unintended—hierarchy, Aristotle alludes to poetry being "more universal" than philosophy, at least in its capacity to appeal emotively to all human beings through description alone, through its "realism." If so, the emotions should not be underestimated as trivial or simply subordinate to thought, since the emotions are themselves instructive and in concordance with thought in the *Poetics*.[10] Thus, if poetry is more universal quantitatively speaking, insofar as it touches everyone, Aristotle emphasizes that, qualitatively, it is the philosophers who are most affected by poetic imitation because its feeling of pleasure promotes learning. In this vein, my distinction between the philosophical and the serious does not mean to exaggerate the cleavage between philosophy and poetry but to point to their contiguity: while the seriousness of poetry acts on everyone, it affects the philosopher to a greater extent, not least because it may illuminate the difference and interaction between truth as an ideal, deontological construct and veracity as the representation of the actual nature of things.

The world is not always what it ought to be, but for Aristotle, the strange attraction of imitation, which pulls everyone into its orbit, lies precisely in its convincing rendering even of the parts of life that are not in and of themselves appealing. Imitation captivates us in abiding by what is. Aristotle uses the term πίστις, which means conviction, to refer to the manner in which imitative poetry remains faithful to the world and yields lifelike representations (1451b17–18). Through this convincingness, imitation transforms both the object and the spectator: it lifts what is detestable into something sensuously pleasing and, eventually also, morally worthy of contemplation. Put elsewise, in discussing the topic of imitation, Aristotle seizes the opportunity to reflect productively on the dialectic of beauty and truth, a dialectic Plato had already introduced in various contexts. That humans take pleasure as much in beautiful representations as in those that are ugly and painful shows that imitation does not simply quench the human thirst for beauty but also stimulates the pursuit of truth, which is conceived as an arduous process with potentially unpleasant disclosures. Consequently, this "negative" aspect of imitation—namely, its capacity to aestheticize even the abominable—also allows for its educative and moral potential. While beauty may instruct, it is truth that constitutes thought's most proper object; the truth of tragic imitation, then, consists not only in the depiction of a specific terrible event but also in the larger realization that humans *by nature* rely on mimesis to contemplate the decisions that moral thought may wish to resolve without actually suffering them. While affirming literature's quest for truth as equal and even rival to that of philosophical inquiry, Richard Kuhns begins his study of the *Oresteia* by stating that "literature has more than a mimetic interest in truth" (v). Most likely he feels obliged to cite this disclaimer because he shares the widespread assumption that mimesis is a facile didacticism. At the same time, however, the very profundity he admires in poetry's treatment of philosophical themes has to do with poetry's capacity to deliver us a world that we can take for granted—namely, a world that is patent—before it becomes subject to philosophical skepticism and doubt (7), and such grantedness spells precisely its mimeticism and iconicity.

Having discussed the importance of verisimilitude for the universality of feeling aroused by imitation, a few reflections are due on this feeling of pleasure. In both the contexts of tragic theater and ancient religious ritual, which—as I show in this chapter—are coextensive, the human being attains a strange form of pleasure after undergoing a harrowing experience. This mixed enjoyment[11] is most poignantly signaled by Aristotle's notion of catharsis (1449b24-28). However, before his mention of catharsis, which pertains specifically to tragedy, Aristotle uses two variant vocabularies of pleasure to describe the generally positive feeling that all successful imitations induce: on the one hand, the verb χαίρω, which means "to rejoice," "to take delight in something," and also "to encounter and greet someone," including a favorable encounter with a Grace (Χάρις); on the other, the noun ἡδονή and the adjective ἡδύς, which refer to pleasure arising from the satisfaction of sensuous needs and appetites. Still, despite the implicit moral ordering between these two sets of terms (χαίρω/χάρις and ἡδονή/ἡδύς), we should recall that in either of its forms, the pleasure resulting from imitation—just like the imitative instinct itself—stems from nature, and its affective impact is measured vis-à-vis nature as well. For instance, Aristotle notes that, whereas an actual object in nature such as a beast or a corpse produces distress or sorrow in us, its representation is enjoyable (1448b10-11). Accurate representations transform the negative feelings that unpleasant sights in nature produce, just as in tragedy, catharsis channels the similarly negative feelings resulting from the plot's ordeals into a sense of relief at their conclusion.[12]

As I already noted, the pleasure of imitation is felt acutely by the philosophers because this sentiment—described now as ἥδιστον (the sweetest)—is conducive to learning. With his choice of words, Aristotle mixes the higher pleasure of learning with the sweetness of taste, thus referring the intellectual component of mimesis back to the sensuousness of nature. By contemplating the image, one learns about the world and begins to categorize real things and phenomena—an activity proper to the philosophical mind. At this point, Aristotle adds a crucial detail: had we not seen the original *before* its representation, our pleasure (ἡδονή) would not involve the mimetic process itself but would be limited to the appreciation of contingent and artificial things such as technique, use of color, and so forth. Whereas we may experience sensuous pleasure at the application of colors or sounds arbitrarily, it is the comparison of an image against nature's original (against the real) that engages the feelings in their cognitive range. Here, the pleasure of imitation serves learning, since the latter proceeds from our recognition of similarities and differences between nature and representation.

This brief inquiry into the concept of imitation in the *Poetics* was meant to elucidate the first of three standard terms in the definition of the tragic genre—namely, "the imitation of a grave act"—that are also operative in Burkert's anthropology of Greek ritual. These terms, as I have shown starting with imitation, link tragedy to ritual by grounding both of them in an experience of nature, an experience that is especially central for Aeschylus. Indeed, in summarizing our discussion of poetic imitation, four determinations arise, all of which involve nature explicitly or implicitly: (a) imitation is connatural to the human being; (b) it is manifest in humans from early childhood; (c) the human being is the most mimetic of all animals; (d) imitation (naturally) fosters learning. The last clause refers to nature implicitly—hence, my parenthetical insertion of it—yet its prevalence here as well can be argued by the fact that imitation constitutes for Aristotle the most spontaneous and inherent way of learning, since it is through imitation that human beings receive their first lessons (1448b9; τὰς μαθήσεις ποιεῖται διὰ μιμήσεως τὰς πρώτας).

Much like Aristotle, who understood the human being to be the most mimetic of animals, and for whom mimesis was a natural inclination most pronounced in childhood, Burkert too links the birth of human society to the imitative practices of ritual, while noting that the mimetic impulse is strongest in children (26). Regarding imitation being the first and most constitutive mode of learning, Burkert similarly maintains that it is through "the theatricality of ritual" that a community learns about its past, just as it is thanks to its mimetic character that ritual successfully perpetuates itself (26, 29). The instructive function of mimesis in the case of religious ritual proves especially important since it reveals that imitation lies at the root of tradition, and tradition, in turn, serves as the basis of social formation and as the guarantor of cultural continuity. Without some reference to tradition and ancestry, any such formation would be unthinkable or very quick to self-destruct. As Burkert shows, ritualization is in fact the theatricalization of the natural-biological necessity of hunting as a means of sustenance; a materially motivated behavior is thus translated into a structuring, perhaps even primal, scene of tradition. "Those rituals which are not innate can endure only when passed on through a learning process," writes Burkert (26), citing as examples children's playacting of weddings and funerals. Yet for this childish roleplay to become collectively effective and transmit the culture of that community from generation to generation, the rite has to be sacralized; it has to be invested with significance or, to use Burkert's own term, seriousness (*Ernst*).

Tradition reveals its seriousness each time a culture erects its past as a bulwark against change, particularly against accelerated, or externally enforced, change that threatens to replace the culture's most venerable codes with ephemerae. In effect, the seriousness of tradition consists in the perpetual war of time against itself: time as authority and preservation confronts time as novelty and transience. Burkert explicitly links the theatricality of ritual to cultural continuity via the participants' experience of serious affects during said ritual: "Thanks to its theatrical, mimetic character and the deep impression that its sacred solemnity [*heiligen Ernstes*] can impart, ritual is self-perpetuating" (29). That these "deep impressions" should achieve a pedagogical impact is evidenced by Burkert's opportune citation of Plato's *Laws* (887d), where the concept of seriousness is considered in relation to the education of the young through traditional ritual (Burkert 28). Ironically, this passage about the importance of tradition, which introduces the Athenian's proof of the existence of the gods, is a response to the breakdown of tradition and the rise of atheist intellectuals who, apparently, were not convinced enough (οὐ πειθόμενοι) by the stories and spectacles of the rite. Nevertheless, in lamenting tradition's failure while at the same time describing its educative function, the passage anticipates several concepts that we have already encountered in Aristotle's treatment of imitation. For this reason, I cite it in full:

> Πῶς ἄν τις μὴ θυμῷ λέγοι περὶ θεῶν ὡς εἰσίν; ἀνάγκη γὰρ δὴ χαλεπῶς ἐκείνους οἳ τούτων ἡμῖν αἴτιοι τῶν λόγων γεγένηνται καὶ γίγνονται νῦν, οὐ πειθόμενοι τοῖς μύθοις οὓς ἐκ νέων παίδων ἔτι ἐν γάλαξι τρεφόμενοι τροφῶν τε ἤκουον καὶ μητέρων, οἷον ἐν ἐπῳδαῖς μετά τε παιδιᾶς καὶ μετὰ σπουδῆς λεγομένων καὶ μετὰ θυσιῶν ἐν εὐχαῖς αὐτοὺς ἀκούοντές τε, καὶ ὄψεις ὁρῶντες ἑπομένας αὐτοῖς ἃς ἥδιστα ὅ γε νέος ὁρᾷ τε καὶ ἀκούει πραττομένας θυόντων, ἐν σπουδῇ τῇ μεγίστῃ τοὺς αὑτῶν γονέας ὑπὲρ αὑτῶν τε καὶ ἐκείνων ἐσπουδακότας. (887c-d)

> Come, then; how is one to argue on behalf of the existence of the gods without passion? For we needs must be vexed and indignant with the men who have been, and now are, responsible for laying on us this burden of argument, through their disbelief in those stories which they used to hear, while infants and sucklings, from the lips of their nurses and mothers—stories chanted to them, as it were, in lullabies, whether in jest or in earnest; and the same stories they heard repeated also in prayers at sacrifices, and they saw spectacles which illustrated them, of the kind which the young delight to see and hear when performed at sacrifices; and their own parents they saw showing the utmost zeal on behalf of themselves and their children in addressing the gods in prayers and supplications, as though they most certainly existed.[13]

Here, as in Aristotle, education from the time of infancy takes place through imitation, through stories that will be later enacted in ceremonies (πραττομένας θυόντων)[14] whose terror, however, is mitigated precisely by the child's recognition in them of material processed earlier. Plato's language contains key terms that reappear in Aristotle: ἥδιστα for the delight of recognition of the myth in the ritual, and most importantly, the emphatic vocabulary of seriousness that resonates in two distinct but interrelated registers—namely, as the foreboding feeling attached to the sacred, and as a state of urgency that calls us to respond with due haste.[15] Μετὰ σπουδῆς and ἐν σπουδῇ τῇ μεγίστῃ, two prepositional formulations of Aristotle's σπουδαῖον, denote the seriousness (and in contrast, the lightheartedness [μετὰ παιδιᾶς]) with which parents and caretakers first communicate the legends, and later accompany the youth to attend to the actual ritual with great intensity and eagerness (ἐσπουδακότας).

Burkert mentions the excerpt from the *Laws* because it confirms the seriousness inherent in the fearful contents of the ritual as well as the critical importance that such ritual imitations have for the survival of a culture and its traditions. Concerning tradition, Burkert underlines that the persistence of the hunting ritual well after the end of prehistory and into the modern symbolic practices of both religion and war goes beyond the "psychological impulse of imitation and imprinting" to the function that such processes actually serve—namely, the culture's self-assertion through its collective power to kill, which is disclosed time and again in ceremony (35). In yet another context, Burkert writes: "Above all, the young must confront the Holy again and again so that the ancestral tradition will become their own" (40–41). Even after the ritual's primary function proves obsolete, its vestigial existence conveys crucial messages for the preservation of the social bond (23). For instance, hunting ritual with its predator-prey dyad was initially propped on the pragmatic need for sustenance. Later, it became symbolic of sovereign power—that is, the power to kill—and many ancient kings were celebrated as hunters (42–43). Whereas Burkert mentions the pharaohs, the kings of Persia, Babylon, and Nineveh, stopping with Alexander, his remarks apply even today, at least for kingdoms where tradition managed to preserve itself, despite modernity's relegation of monarchy to obsolescence. One need only look at the current British royal family, renowned for holding fast more than any other European royal house to the "pomp and circumstance" of tradition: its members regularly pursue hunting sports and remain loyal to the habits of country life, with horses and dogs accompanying them in their pastime as well as in their courtly portraits—these being animals that feature prominently in the hunt.

In Burkert's terminology of the ritual's "sacred solemnity," the notion of hierarchy is implied in seriousness, and this link becomes evident in the temporal and processual ordering of the sacrificial scene, which I discuss further in the next section. At this moment, it is useful to recall that hierarchy, like seriousness, is operative in the parallel plane of tragedy as well. Hierarchy not only marks the tragic-heroic comportment as shown in Aristotle's preference for the noble over the average agent but also obtains in the social and collective experience of tragic theater as a spectacle with sacred origins and with a divine audience, particularly considering that the most exalted seat in the *koilon* was assigned neither to a civic leader nor simply to any prominent citizen but to the priest of Dionysus.

Notably, despite the emphatic connections Burkert draws between ritualization and theatricalization, he insists on differentiating between them as well. He does so with the criterion of seriousness in mind, by prioritizing the intensity of seriousness during an actual state of urgency, such as in a sacrificial rite, over the symbolic seriousness of a theatrical performance. At stake, thus, once again, is the tangible reality of the situation and its inescapability. Ritual, for Burkert, cannot be simply theatrical or it would lose ground with younger generations that aggressively question tradition (43–43), a state of affairs that had already come to pass in Plato's time, as we just saw. In order not to endanger its potency, ritual must retain a heightened degree of seriousness, which means that it must always return from symbolism to concrete reality. If it is to communicate anything meaningful long after it has ceased to be instinct, ritual must still involve an unquestionable pragmatism in which the literal outweighs the symbolic.

Aristotle and Burkert both theorize imitation with reference to seriousness, the former in the sphere of theater, the latter in that of ritual. Additionally, both of them underline the necessity of realism as prerequisite to that seriousness, but they assess the nature of this realism differently even as they assign it the same task—namely, to convince the participants of the ineluctable (cosmic, we could say) conditions of existence. Burkert, citing Plato, is aware of the temporal weakening of tradition, and thus stresses that the efficacy of ritual qua representation of life-and-death processes must rely on the preservation of the actually fearful component within that representation. In other words, the experience of harm cannot be compromised by its displacement into a rhetorical figure without simultaneously compromising the degree of seriousness that the ritual purports to instill. Nevertheless, even the most dreadful—and presumably most serious—of rituals could not prevent the attenuation of tradition, as both Plato and Burkert realize. In fact, it is quite reasonable to assume that the very extremity of ritual undermined its viability over time. For Aristotle, however, tragedy's unique aesthetics of relative distance from actuality combined with its mandate to imitate realistic plots renders it a serious medium, and one that can aspire to "psychological" universality. Tragedy emerges as a middle ground where imitation does not have to duplicate real bloodshed in order to retain an elevated degree of seriousness. The tragic plot may still uphold its gravity because it remains reality-bound in its metaphysical claims about the structure of the world and the scarcity of favorable conditions surrounding human life.

It is certainly true that insofar as the sacrificial element in tragedy is symbolic, the immediate stakes of life and death appear lowered. The solemn feelings previously aroused by the spectacle of literal bloodshed in the ritual now proceed from a slightly modified experience: from witnessing the inherently dilemmatic structure of decision-making, which, precisely in being dilemmatic, expresses the *punitively* restrictive, and thus often fatally serious, conditions that bind human existence. "To be or not to be" recapitulates the critical threshold of every moral dilemma, exposing the costs one should be willing and ready to pay in making any meaningful decision. Appropriately, it is because of the enormous costs involved in moral judgment that the notion of hierarchy plays a cardinal role in any understanding of seriousness. We can grasp this "translation" of seriousness from ritual to tragedy in purely dramaturgical terms: the murder never happens onstage,[16] but through the symbolic death of the sovereign backstage, the spectator, even after a successfully cathartic ending, has been shown the unrelenting necessities that reality holds in store for all tragic protagonists. In terms of syntax, tragic-dilemmatic seriousness requires an "either/or" disjunction; conversely, this means that tragedy refuses the permissiveness implied in the conjunctive "and," which promises us to have the proverbial cake and eat it too.

Consequently, it is hardly surprising that in our current global culture—whose egalitarian impetus dictates that scarcity be not an issue, options be infinite, all desires be appeased, and all choices be accommodated at no cost—tragedy's constitutive refusal of leniency is deemed anywhere from illegible to unethical to unacceptable. Even more poignantly, the recent shift within this egalitarian vision from equality (equality of opportunity) to equity (equality of outcome) marks the augmentation of social artifice, which paradoxically legitimates its own *necessity*—having otherwise displaced necessity categorically as a "naturalist" vestige—by way of political exigency. As such, the ontology espoused by tragedy—namely, its affirmation of an ineluctable cosmic order of necessity—offends the political deontology according to which necessity/Ananke can and should *always* be successfully resolved by craft/techne. Indeed, my earlier accent on Aristotle's theory of the universality of tragedy, and its potential to instill seriousness after the advent of ritual, may no longer be a transparent premise for an age that ironizes and upturns everything, seriousness most of all. However, since this epochal disjunction is a guiding, albeit exceedingly challenging, concern behind this project, it cannot be exhausted presently, but will have to be revisited and reformulated throughout. For now, it is sufficient to emphasize that the effect of imitation in both Aristotle's view of tragedy and Burkert's theory of ritual involves the feeling of seriousness. Seriousness arises from the experience of the irrevocable constraints that reality imposes on human beings, and is the hinge around which both tragedy and sacrificial ritual pivot.

A Grave Act: Tragedy as Mysterium Tremendum

In both the theatrical and ritual performances, the object of imitation is the act, the second shared noun between Aristotle and Burkert. Drama, it has been proposed, derives from the Doric δρᾶν, which means "to act." Aristotle observes that δρᾶν is used for both comedies and tragedies (1448a), and that the Dorians claimed both, though the Megarians claimed comedy as well; the Athenian equivalent for δρᾶν is πράττειν (1448b), from which the noun "praxis" is derived. Although the constitutive unit of both theatrical genres is action, it is the kind of action presented in each that accounts for the difference between comedy and tragedy. What kind of act is then involved specifically in tragic drama? A momentary glance into Burkert's text quickly corroborates what we find in Aristotle as well. Arguing for a strong definition of the act in general, Burkert states that "to do" and "to act" are synonyms of sacrifice (3n4). The religious man is the man who kills (*homo necans*), and even more intrinsically, the man of action is the man who kills.[17] Burkert reinforces this thesis with yet another etymological link: the Latin *operari* (to act) is behind the German *Opfer*, the word for "offering," which "merely covers up the heart of the action with a euphemism" (3). "Act" and "offering" refer to the same linguistic root, and so does "opera," which most closely resembles ancient tragedy in the world of modern art.

In the *Poetics*, tragedy's difference from the other poetic genres rests on this term as well. Neither a narrative, like the epic, nor a musical expression of subjective feeling, like the lyric, tragedy involves the imitation of an act. Accordingly, it is the plot (μῦθος) that Aristotle prioritizes as "the first principle and soul of tragedy" (1450a38; ἀρχὴ μὲν οὖν καὶ οἷον ψυχὴ ὁ μῦθος τῆς τραγῳδίας), and as its "goal" (1450a22; ὁ μῦθος τέλος τῆς τραγῳδίας), for plot and act are one and the same: hence, Aristotle's definitive condition that "without action there could be no tragedy" (1450a23–24; ἔτι ἄνευ μὲν πράξεως οὐκ ἂν γένοιτο τραγῳδία). If mythos serves as the etiology of *cultus*, plot here would correspond to the linguistic explication of ritual action. Of course, it can be argued that Aristotle's use of mythos does not refer exclusively to the etiological kind and that the philosopher intends the term in its purely philological definition: mythos as a collection of words that yield an autonomous story independent of cultic phenomena.[18] Nevertheless, even if the latter were the case, the link of myth to ritual persists, especially considering the prominent position that Euripides's *Iphigenia among the Taurians* enjoys in the *Poetics*, where this tragedy could be construed as a model rivaling Sophocles's *Oedipus Tyrannus*. The example of this Euripidean tragedy is poignant since it deals explicitly with the theme of sacrifice and its sublimation from a deadly practice in Tauris to its milder version in Brauron. The Brauronian rite requires that only some token blood be drawn when the sword touches the neck of a man, in commemoration of Iphigenia's eventually averted sacrifice in Aulis.[19] Thus, the dark archaism of maiden sacrifice is now substituted with a male victim who survives, representing Orestes as the spared victim of Tauris.

While the *Tyrannus* concluded with a symbolic sacrificial ending in the moment of Oedipus's self-blinding, both of Euripides's Iphigenia plays (*at Aulis* and *among the Taurians*) confront us directly with the scene of the blood rite in its most primal and prohibitive form: human sacrifice. Iphigenia, who was herself the victim of a maiden sacrifice to Artemis in the parodos of the *Oresteia*, reappears in Euripides as a spared victim-turned-priestess of Artemis, now performing the dreaded task of human sacrifice to the goddess in the distant country of Tauris. When her brother Orestes reaches these foreign shores, emerging accidentally as her next victim, Euripides orchestrates a credible scene of recognition before the ceremony begins, thus reversing the tragic ending into a joyful reunion and escape. Christopher Morrissey has argued that *Iphigenia among the Taurians* could be raised into a model tragedy over and against the *Tyrannus* by juxtaposing the two plays along the criteria of plot and character, respectively: while *Oedipus Tyrannus* portrays exemplarily the character of the fallen hero, *Iphigenia among the Taurians* excels formally in terms of the mastery of plot. Morrissey contends that by reversing the temporality of reversal/recognition to recognition/reversal, *Iphigenia among the Taurians* can afford an atypical turn to the better—something many scholars dismiss as the "comic" element in Euripidean tragedy. Aristotle's commendation of this tragedy not only confirms his emphasis on plot structure—namely, the priority of action as masterful peripeteia over all other dramatic elements—but is especially poignant in light of the fact that *Iphigenia among the Taurians* exposes its central act to be a sacrificial one. That the bloodshed is eventually averted and translated into a harmless rite is also a focal point in Burkert's anthropology of violence, which traces the displacements of sacrifice from the earliest killing of fellow humans to the later animal and plant substitutes.[20]

In the Taurian play, it is Athena who reveals to Orestes and Iphigenia the translated rite of the human sacrifice from Tauris to the temple of Artemis Tauropolos at Halae. Notably, Athena's decree specifies the location of Halae at the farthest borders of Athens (*IT* ln. 1450; ἐσχάτοις ὅροισι), which confirms the archaeological record of temples to Artemis in defensive and contested places, as it also does Jean-Pierre Vernant's analysis of Artemis as a goddess who ensures the demarcation of boundaries and passageways. One of those passages is between the wild and the civilized, which is expressed in her manifestation as goddess of the hunt.[21] Artemis's liminality works in tandem with Burkert's thesis that the greatest evolutionary passage in human history, which led to the emergence of homo sapiens, occurred at the threshold where man became hunter, and the anthropoid evolved into the human proper (17–18). In the image of the divine huntress, we recognize the human passage through predation to civilized existence; in her gender, we may also recall that, with the exception of humans, it is the females of predatory mammals that hunt for the family.[22] Among other things, the passage to becoming human meant an inversion of the sex roles of the animal world. Thus, Artemis, herself forever arrested in the passage between adolescence and womanhood, is a trace of the animal order against which human society formed through the rise of the hunter and the concomitant overturning of sexual norms.[23]

The intertext between the *Oresteia* and Euripides's two Iphigenia plays is rich since they draw their material from the House of Atreus and, more specifically, since the myth of Iphigenia's sacrifice serves as the immediate cause of the *Oresteia*'s blood feud.[24] Artemis, who presides over the plot of both of Euripides's Iphigenia tragedies, emerges also as an important, albeit more hidden, deity of the *Oresteia*'s first play (*Agamemnon*), just as Athena operates in both Euripides and Aeschylus as a civilizing intercessor. The crucial but subtler presence of Artemis in *Agamemnon* will be discussed more elaborately in the next chapter. Here, I draw attention to Athena's "translation" of sacrifice, which aims to dispel the archaic, cannibalistic curse that haunted the Atreidae.[25] Athena's intervention concludes this curse in the *Oresteia* by transforming the blood feud into due process, and by revealing chthonic nature to be a source of prosperity and not simply blind instinct, thus in effect reforming the old sacrificial order as well. In the *Eumenides*, the *Oresteia*'s last play, she prevails over the Erinyes, turning them from canine monsters to the Semnai—the austere but temperate goddesses underneath the Acropolis, now responsible for natural fecundity as well as domestic and civic wealth.

While scholarship on the *Oresteia* often focuses on the juridical shift that replaces the archaic, vendetta-driven order of the Furies with the new, law-based reign of the Olympians, less attention is paid to the concomitant transformation of the Furies' μένος—their energy—toward nature at large. Indeed, the new form of justice coincides with the Furies' assumption of a distinctly generative role in nature,[26] and this shift is realized by means of a sacrificial exchange: the Furies must relinquish their essence as agents of *talio*, and as reward for this transformation, Athena promises them many sacred offerings from the people of her city. On the one hand, Orestes is exonerated despite the Furies' bloody demands; on the other, their vengeful office could only conclude with the assurance of future sacrifices, now performed under the auspices of the city. In a chiasmatic inversion, the Furies become civilized—that is, they literally join civic religion—by emerging as nature goddesses and foregoing their pursuit of justice, a pursuit hitherto linked with the family feud, and thus, with the realm of natural kinship rather than civic cohesion. To be sure, the Furies were always nature goddesses, both before and after their translation into the Eumenides; the difference has to do with which aspect of nature they were identified. In the retaliative spirit of ancestral justice, they exacted blood for the blood of kin, where bloodshed is seen as a mark of the violence of nature. After Burkert, I would suggest that this form of justice conjures forth symbolically the primitive age of the hunter, when the Furies literally chased after the blood stains of their victims. In contrast, civic order extends beyond the immediate cries of the family ghosts, and thus needs not only the groundwork of a conventional legal system but also the grounding in a nature that reveals itself as benign and restorative, much like the image of Athens built on the secure foundations provided by the retreating Eumenides.

This shift from blight to abundance appears in multiple contexts in the *Eumenides*. Sensing their defeat as agents of justice, the Erinyes initially threaten to depart with one last performance of the blood feud that would lead to universal barrenness: they vow to drip their bitter poison so as to rob the earth of fruit while spreading illness and childlessness throughout the city (ln. 780–87). This malediction is repeated "ritually" (ln. 810–17) following Athena's attempt to convince them that they have not been defeated or dishonored but merely reassigned tasks in the new order of things. Hard to bend by gentle promises alone, the Furies soften and become accepting of their new function only after Athena appeals to the power of Peithō, the goddess of persuasion.[27] No household will flourish without their protection (ln. 895), Athena declares, exhorting them to abandon their destructive role and serve as a new cosmic axis, linking the subterranean and aquatic depths with the lightness of the sky's atmosphere:

> Let it [your spell] come out of the ground, out of the sea's water,
> and from the high air make the waft of gentle gales
> wash over the country in full sunlight, and the seed
> and stream of the soil's yield and of the grazing beasts
> be strong and never fail our people as time goes,
> and make the human seed be kept alive. (ln. 904–9)

The Erinyes eventually yield, changing their curses to benedictions for abundance of fruits and animals as well as of mineral resources, which fittingly are extracted from the depths of the earth, where these deities have their chthonic kingdom:

> Let there blow no wind that wrecks the trees.
> I pronounce words of grace.
> Nor blaze of heat blind the blossoms of grown plants, nor
> cross the circles of its right
> place. Let no barren deadly sickness creep and kill.
> Flocks fatten. Earth be kind
> to them, with double fold of fruit
> in time appointed for its yielding. Secret child
> of earth, her hidden wealth, bestow
> blessing and surprise of gods. (938–48)

Their generosity extends beyond the natural realm to ensuring a time of peace for the citizens. Politically speaking, prosperity is often linked to peaceful times, and here the Eumenides wish for the cessation of war so that young lives are spared: "Death of manhood cut down / before its prime I forbid: / girls' grace and glory find / men to live life with them" (ln. 956–59). Orestes's final exoneration too can be seen in this light, as a young life spared. Indeed, in the passage where they pray for the cessation of revenge—the warlike activity over which they specifically preside—their language becomes most disclosive; hence, I quote this passage fully in the Greek original as well:

> τὰν δ' ἄπληστον κακῶν
> μήποτ' ἐν πόλει στάσιν
> τᾷδ' ἐπεύχομαι βρέμειν.
> μηδὲ πιοῦσα κόνις
> μέλαν αἷμα πολιτᾶν

δι' ὀργὰν ποινᾶς
ἀντιφόνους ἄτας
ἁρπαλίσαι πόλεως. (ln. 976–83)

This is my prayer: Civil War
fattening on men's ruin shall
not thunder in our city. Let
not the dry dust that drinks
the black blood of citizens
through passion for revenge
and bloodshed for bloodshed
be given our state to prey upon.

Civic sedition (ἐν πόλει στάσιν) is depicted as a greedy evil (ἄπληστον κακῶν) that *preys* on the city. The interconnection of family and state is noteworthy in this passage since civil war appears as a form of the vendetta (ποινᾶς ἀντιφόνους ἄτας)—that is, of the same desire for revenge that drives the family feud.[28] The verb ἁρπαλίζω (to prey) carries strong predatory connotations of snatching something away by force, as a thief or a wild animal would. Translator Herbert Weir Smyth allots a footnote to this passage that stresses the overdetermined links between the language of predation and that of the vendetta: "The expression of the thought 'take reprisals in a civil war,' is overloaded and the grammatical relation of the words is involved. More exactly: 'seize greedily (as a wild beast seizes his prey) upon calamities—of vengeance—to the State, calamities in which blood is shed in requital for blood'" (365n2). Earlier, Athena also explicitly referred to such feuds as cock fights, and urged the Erinyes to refrain from inflicting on the citizens "the fury not of wine" but of civil bloodshed (ln. 860–61). While as Erinyes the goddesses thirsted for the blood of young men—here for the blood of the matricide Orestes—as the venerable Eumenides they bestow wealth, and promote from their underground hollows civic flourishment above.

At the conclusion of the *Oresteia*'s sacrificial narrative, the erstwhile canine avengers become explicitly linked to fertility, just as eons earlier, the hunting era of dog and wolf,[29] with its rabid madness, had given way to the ritual substitutions of the agricultural age. Yet, as I have already noted, this passage from vengeance to benevolence was not itself bloodless any more than the ritual offerings of the agricultural age were themselves thoroughly bloodless.[30] The Eumenides' good disposition is predicated on citizens' respect, demonstrated through sacrificial worship. The chthonic world needs as much propitiation as the Olympians since it provides, after all, the very foundation of the citadel. In anthropological terms, the chthonic world supports the citadel because in its depths rest the city's dead heroes. Hence, as Burkert shows, every great shrine in Greece was divided between its Olympian and chthonic altars. The former were marked by their height, by the ever-growing heap of ashes from burnt offerings whose smoke ascended to heaven; the latter, devoted to the local hero, were pits into which the sacrificial blood was poured. Burkert offers the examples of Olympia, sacred to Zeus and dedicated to the hero Pelops, and of the sanctuary at the isthmus near Corinth about which he writes: "As often, there are two cult centers that give the sanctuary at the Isthmus its shape: that of Palaimon and that of Poseidon, the hero and the god, chthonic versus Olympian ritual, the tholos and the temple" (197). The tholos and the temple form the two spatiotemporal coordinates through which ancient human beings attempted to orient themselves in the world. Covering the space underneath the sky-earth axis, the tholos commemorates the finite, horizontal existence of mortals; rising from the upper earth toward heaven, the temple glorifies the verticality of the immortals.

These are similar coordinates to which Jan Kott refers with respect to Aeschylean tragedy's "vertical axis"—the axis mundi—of Furies and Fates. Aeschylean theogony, which Kott correctly remarks, is also a cosmogony (8), aligns the chthonic Furies with memory and the past, and thus, with mythological, cyclically recurring time, and the Uranian Fates with the future, thus, in Kott's estimation, with unidirectional historical time (12–13).[31] Nonetheless, I submit that this distinction between mythical past and historical future is rather too simplified. Present time, as it carves the future ahead and itself fades into the past, always also responds to ripples from its own remoter past; most of all, it grapples with that past's hauntedness that often takes the form of demands for justice and even explicit revenge. Myth and recurrence are at the heart of historical time; the translation of the Furies into civic goddesses—that is, into goddesses of history along with being goddesses of nature—shows that these times are not merely antithetical but supplant one another.

If the Furies once served the family by punishing crimes against the natural order and promoting vigilante justice and civil war, they now serve a larger collective, the city-state. They do so by way of presiding over the space of the city's dead heroes—that is, the ancestors of local noble families who gradually acquired a more universal symbolic status, becoming shared heritage for the city. For such a service, they still command the sacrifices of the citizens, which are now regulated acts of ritual rather than random feats of vengeance, just as Athena's court issues punishment through law not whim. Burkert aptly notes this link between sacrifice and the cult of the dead, particularly of the city's heroes, who model behavior for the future citizens: "We see here how deeply sacrificial and funerary ritual permeated one another. By joining together to honor the dead, the survivors, and especially the young, would have been initiated, integrated into the continuity of the society, and educated in the tradition all at once. . . . The myth tells of death and destruction, while in sacrifice an animal is killed. By encountering death as symbolized in word and ritual, succeeding generations are molded into successors. In this way society is consolidated and renewed" (56). The Eumenides are not simply buried and forgotten by the new patriarchal Olympian order, as feminist critiques sometimes assert. Rather, they reemerge as patron goddesses of tradition, where the combination of the masculine "patron" and the feminine "goddess" quite literally expresses their double status: once guardians of domesticity, summoned to avenge the ghosts of the household's murdered, they then become guarantors of the universal tradition of the city and protectresses of the shades of its heroes. Although the city-state is more than the aggregate of its families, and although its organization is irreducible to the family model, the translation of the Eumenides from house to civic deities supports the idea that civic identity continues to draw on relations first shaped within the family, be they congenial or aggressive.

The above examples from *Iphigenia among the Taurians* and the *Oresteia* illustrate at least on the level of the content the strong connection between tragic and sacrificial acts. However, beyond the particular themes of a play, the sacrificial nature of tragedy is attested in a constitutive level by the adjective "grave" (σπουδαία) with which Aristotle designates the tragic act in the first instance: "ἔστιν οὖν τραγῳδία μίμησις πράξεως σπουδαίας" (1449b23–24; tragedy, then, is mimesis of an action which is elevated [grave]). It is the *weighty* presence of this adjective several times in the *Poetics* that links most saliently Aristotle's theory of tragedy to Burkert's ritual anthropology, which relies equally on seriousness in order to express the irrevocability at issue in sacrifice. I use the term "weighty" not only to emphasize the conceptual importance of seriousness in the respective texts of Aristotle and Burkert, but to point additionally to the connotation of seriousness as weight. This connotation is instantly captured in English, where "grave" is a synonym for "serious," and "gravity" defines the force acting on physical weight and—by extension—refers to any situation of moral weight. Gravity of course pulls us down. The English synonym for "tomb," which also happens to be "grave" (from the Proto-Indo-European root *ghrebh- for "to dig, to scratch, to scrape"), links homonymously the seriousness of death to the downward movement of gravity. Etymologically, the adjective "grave" derives from the Latin *gravis*, meaning "heavy, ponderous, burdensome, loaded, pregnant"; of matters that are "weighty, important"; of sounds that are "deep, low, bass"; figuratively, it refers to a state that is "oppressive, hard to bear, troublesome, grievous"; from the Proto-Indo-European root *gwere- for "heavy."[32] However, the depth of this downward movement is counterbalanced by the opposite vertical dimension of elevation, the meaning of which I have already elaborated. Seriousness partakes simultaneously in depth and height, the dimensions of the axis mundi.

A grave act therefore implies severe and irreparable consequences. The inaugural drama in which this severity was shown most explicitly and dreadfully was, according to Burkert, not a theatrical play but the actual killing during ritual.[33] Such seriousness is identified with the moment of the mysterium tremendum—namely, the irrevocable moment of striking the animal to its death. In Burkert's temporalization of the ritual sequence, the mysterium tremendum reaches its apex during the second phase, which constitutes the middle part of the ritual, and which, as I will discuss shortly, discloses seriousness as the moment of irreversibility, when the narrative has no possibility of turning back and the life being spared.

"Mysterium tremendum" is a term Burkert borrows from Rudolf Otto, who used it to describe the religious feeling arising from a numinous experience, such as the presence of something majestic and threatening that cannot be fully understood by the faculty of intelligence. Burkert describes sacrificial ritual as a source of terror, bliss, and absolute authority (40; mysterium tremendum, *fascinans*, *augustum*), elements that Otto assigns to the experience of "the holy." This experience is analogous to Kant's beautiful, writes Otto, insofar as they both refer to feeling rather than understanding (5), even though Otto's holy verges on the irrational, in contrast to Kant's beautiful, which remains intelligible despite its conceptual indeterminacy. Furthermore, Otto remarks that the holy is not simply "the good"; this ethical content is a later accretion but became dominant to the exclusion of its original meaning, which involved something of the overpowering, something in excess—in fact, an excess of meaning itself (6). Such an experience requires an external presence: the numen must be objective and outside the self, and the resultant feeling of awe is not a means toward self-consciousness, as Schleiermacher thought, counters Otto (7). Yet, Otto too arguably returns this externality to being a projection of the irrational part of subjectivity. Outer reality is still a mental construction, albeit of the irrational subject, not the subject of consciousness. It is exactly this Kantian subjectification of the empirical phenomenon that another Otto challenges because it prioritizes what comes later—namely, the psychological response of awe before the stimulus that provoked it (Walter Otto, *Dionysus* 32). Walter Otto shifts the focus from the ineffable alterity of the event (the numen) that causes the subject to feel its finitude to the objective reality of the *phenomenon*: "That which confronts mankind in epiphanies is not a reality which is completely unrecognizable and imperceptible, affecting only the soul which turns its back on the world, but the world itself as a divine form, as a plenitude of divine configurations" (33). In contrast to this natural epiphany, the holy as the "wholly other" externalizes a primal human fantasy, just as Rudolf Otto's philosophy of religion can be read as a psychology of emotions. The subject is still at work even as the self is threatened; what withdraws is self-consciousness.

Consequently, Rudolf Otto denaturalizes the holy, even as he compares its originary potency to a "hidden force of nature," or "stored-up electricity" (18). He maintains that the fear felt at its presence is not of the order of "natural" fear since its source cannot be localized and thus rationalized. It is also not the fear of "natural" man—namely, of primitive, animalistic man—since beastly creatures do not possess the capacity for religious dread. At the same time, he does argue that the exposure to the supernatural induces in the human being the feeling of "creaturehood" or "creature-consciousness" (21, 10)—in other words, a fundamental helplessness and dependence comparable to the state of a natural creature before something terrifying and invincible. To be sure, the confrontation with a natural predator would provide the most apt example of such creaturely terror. Closer to our tragic context, I would argue that this feeling of religious shudder is not dissimilar to Aristotle's concept of fear (φόβος), which, along with the other tragic emotion of pity (ἔλεος), were not "inner state[s] of mind," nor did they have the "subjective tinge" they later acquired, as Hans-Georg Gadamer clarifies: "Rather, both are events that overwhelm man and sweep him away" (131).[34] In effect, the physicality of the emotion bespeaks the seriousness that we find at the core of the mysterium tremendum. The word "tremendum" signifies physical trembling, and conveys the sense of self-diminishment in the proximity of this sweeping force. In *Homo Necans*, too, the emergence of religious feeling out of the killing scene of the hunt occurs in the visceral affinity felt with the victim, thus marking the beginnings of the human as a being cognizable and capable of ethical relationships.

Let us then return properly to our focus on ritual and tragedy, after this excursion into the meaning and philosophical history of the mysterium tremendum. Despite the bodily literalness required by ritual, which Burkert differentiates from the figurative aspect of theatricalization, the formal parallelism between tragedy and sacrifice still holds, and can be further evidenced by juxtaposing the linear tripartite ordering of sacrificial action with the progression of beginning, middle, and end (1450b25; ἀρχὴν καὶ μέσον καὶ τελευτήν) that Aristotle expects from a complete tragedy. Before outlining this comparison, some remarks are due regarding the notion of tragedy as completion. Until now, I have elaborated the designation of the tragic act as "grave" or "elevated," but Aristotle adds a second adjective to his famous phrase: tragedy is "mimesis of an action which is elevated, complete, and has magnitude" (1449b24–25; μίμησις πράξεως σπουδαίας καὶ τελείας μέγεθος ἐχούσης). Just as σπουδαία invokes hierarchy in meaning "elevated," so τελεία is a word firmly embedded in a religious semantics: the Liddell-Scott-Jones lexicon shows that it derives from τελέω/τελῶ, which means "to complete," "fulfill," or "perfect" something, and is often used in the context of completing a ritual. This is also the root of τέλος as "accomplishment" and "purpose," and of τελετή, which signifies "ritual ceremony" or "celebration of a mystery"—namely, a process that must be completed and whose completion fulfills not just any purpose, but sacred purpose, while the sacred itself marks the provenance that grants purposefulness. The dialectic between the meaning of σπουδαία as urgency and τελεία as that which must be perfectly accomplished is now evident, just as is also evident the fact that a mythos/plot that is complete cannot be firmly separated from religious ritual.

From a historically minded literary-critical perspective, this requirement of having a beginning, a middle, and an end has been "surpassed" by modern forms of writing. Modern and postmodern novels as well as dramatic works are replete with temporal and narrative fragmentation, and regularly contravene the Aristotelian unities of space, time, and action. Yet in doing so, such literary works also show that, unlike in Attic tragedy, *action* is not at stake in them: had it been so, the works would have required the moment of irreversibility that is possible only within linear time. Aristotle's linear, tripartite division of tragedy makes sense when viewed in light of sacrificial temporality, which is processual and irreversible. Beginning, middle, and end do not anymore look like some pedantic prescriptions but obey the irrevocable temporality of a mysterious process (and procession) that leads from ominous preparation to an unspeakable climax to a conclusion pointing toward restoration. It is important to emphasize here that the cycle promised by the restorative ending comes after the first, linear end has been accomplished—that is, after the death of the sacrificial animal, or the ordeal of the tragic protagonist, has taken place. While each tragedy is a linear exposition of a mysterium tremendum, its cathartic end is in accordance with the cyclical time of nature that regenerates itself despite the death of its individual members. The death or suffering of the tragic agent (as that of the quarry) is experienced ontogenetically but the restoration is affirmed phylogenetically.

A closer look at Burkert's description of the three stages of the sacrificial rite—beginning or preparation, act, and restitution (3–7, 135)—confirms the parallel to the tragic temporal order. The ritual preliminaries include a mourning procession by women and girls (5, 54, 107), which often refers to the "drama of a maiden" (152, 162), commemorating archaic practices of virgin sacrifice: an Iphigenia or Kore drama. Such a gendered scene epitomizes the intimate but antagonistic links between sexuality, death, and aggression as natural forces that provided the *necessary* template for the prehistoric hunter to begin the story of human culture by first subjecting these forces to symbolization. It is worth bearing in mind that, for Burkert, human culture proceeds from and develops alongside the "nature" of the "hunting ape,"[35] rather than by negating and superseding it. Ritual beginning marks a general sense of departure from the time and space of the ordinary world: the animal and the human participants are both adorned, while sexual abstinence prior to the ceremony is often a requirement that repeats the abstinence practiced by early hunters before departing for their expedition; here, Burkert also underlines that Artemis was a virgin huntress (61). In another citation of early hunting, well after the age of the hunter had concluded, animals designated to become offerings—now likely domestic—were released to roam free for a year before their slaughter, just as the early prey was caught in the wild. Yet, whereas early prey posed significant danger to the prehistoric human predator, now the tension shifts between the religious requirement of the gruesome act and the familial attachment to that animal, hence introducing the ethical demand of renunciation of the attachment along with the symmetrical counterdemand of atonement for the crime. Because of this counterdemand, ruses are in place to secure either the animal's "willing" participation, or its "self-incrimination." For example, in the case of the Buphonia, the ox is tempted to eat grain from the altar, and then is punished for violating the sacred boundary (138) in a scenario of displacing guilt that Burkert, following Karl Meuli, calls "comedy of innocence" (16). To this expiating gesture of the preparation, the Buphonia adds a second, following the conclusion of the sacrifice: upon the ox-slayer's flight from the scene, a trial is staged with the murder weapon (the axe) standing as the culprit, but being eventually acquitted (140).[36]

This scene of trial and acquittal is not the only one that Burkert finds in sacrificial myth: the murder of Argos by Hermes, the latter henceforth being called Argeiophontes, is the founding myth of sacrifice, rendering a god the slayer and "inventor of sacrifice," and putting him on trial (165). Argos was a hundred-eyed cowherd ordered by Hera to keep watch over the captive Io, a mortal lover of Zeus who was turned into a heifer, in a myth that indicates the special role of cattle in sacrificial tradition. Hermes killed Argos on the behest of Zeus, who wished to liberate Io. Argos's heightened vigilance—he is called Argos Panoptes, the one who sees everything—points to the disciplined and guarded focus of the hunter, the evolutionary trait that rendered the "hunting ape" capable of assuming the civilizational project. For our purposes, however, it also points to the vigilance pertinent to any concept of justice, justice being one of those long-prized values of human culture. At the limit, this zealous vigilance underlying the pursuit of justice cannot but turn to vigilantism, the feeling that the necessity for justice sanctions its attainment by any means necessary. Thus, just as Argos defended vigilantly Hera's justice against Zeus's marital infidelities, so he was slain by the vigilante son who not only reasserted his father's will but also brought release to the captive maiden. Indeed, the very expression of the *pursuit* of justice belongs to the hunting vocabulary just as the term "bounty hunter" is more than a metaphorical nod to the profession of chasing and capturing fugitives. Back to the myth of slain Argos: the gods were torn by their desire to cleanse their precinct from Hermes's blood pollution on the one hand, and the mandate not to offend Zeus in punishment of Hermes, on the other. A trial was held at the end of which the gods threw their votes in the form of pebbles at Hermes, and the pebbles gathered into a pile of stones before his feet. Burkert notes that the god is thus symbolically stoned, and eventually acquitted (165). This trial and acquittal bear more than a passing resemblance to Orestes's story, which is the translation into the realm of the mortals of this divine exoneration from capital punishment for a capital crime: Orestes also murdered Clytemnestra on Apollo's command, and Apollo implements the will and law of his father, Zeus; Orestes's case too provoked a split between two divine orders, chthonic and Olympian; finally, his acquittal required divine intervention that broke the stalemate of the human court.[37] Above all, the trials of Hermes, who kills a vigilant guardian, and of Orestes, who is pursued by the vigilante Furies, reveal that, among the cultural advances incipient in the naturalist figure of the hunter, the institution of justice carries within it most uncannily the violence of those "benighted" ages, particularly through its militant relation to vigilance. We will revisit this uncanniness, however, at the conclusion of this chapter.

In tragic drama, the corresponding stage to the ritual preliminaries is the prologue, which summarizes the background of the myth and reveals the generational curse or individual fault that haunts and hunts the protagonist, becoming the reason for the impending ordeal. Symbolically speaking at least, the prologue reiterates something of the animal's "misconduct": just as the animal must "falter" in order to justify its gruesome end, so the tragic protagonist is chosen to suffer on the basis of some fault, often unconscious, that propels the action forward. In fact, some plays construct the fault to be identical to that of the sacred animal since the human agents are said to have trespassed, unbeknownst to themselves, sacred grounds. Thus we find the wounded Philoctetes, in Sophocles's play by the same title, suffering for having unknowingly entered a sacred grove in Chryse (ln. 1326–28); and in Sophocles's *Electra*, Agamemnon happened to hunt in Artemis's grove, killed her sacred stag, and boasted afterward, incurring the wrath of the goddess, who asked for the sacrifice of his firstborn daughter in return (ln. 566–70). Notably, these sacred spaces are unmarked, trapping mortals within their invisible boundaries much like the sacred animal is trapped during the ritual; thus, hunters are turned into prey for the gods. This principle is expressed in the Oedipal transgression as well, however more symbolically: Oedipus too was innocent of a certain knowledge, and it was precisely his innocence that led him to violate the boundaries of his own family. That he was destined to find eternal rest by the grove of the Eumenides, which he reached and sensed as the right place to die, reveals not only the eventual redemption of the guileless victim but also Sophocles's reiteration of the Aeschylean translation of the Eumenides into goddesses of civic prosperity and unity: from their grove, the exiled Theban king blesses Athens in *Oedipus at Colonus*, becoming its symbolic founder while claiming its land as his grave.

Moving to the middle stage of the ritual, it comprises the *act proper*, the scene par excellence of the mysterium tremendum, which commands utmost seriousness, and which Burkert identifies as "unspeakable" (135; ἄρρητον). This is the climax of the ordeal, arrived at after a sequence of "small" beginnings (ἄρχεσθαι), each of which leads ever closer to the fatal act when the axe is raised for the blow, and which marks the moment when "the inviolability of the sacrificial animal has been abolished irreversibly" (5). Before this moment, there were other beginnings, such as sprinkling the animal with water and flinging barley grains, but the cutting of hairs from the animal's brow signifies the last and most serious beginning that seals the animal's fate (5). Note here the use of ἄρχεσθαι, which combines temporal beginning with sacred principle. Like τέλος and τελετή, ἀρχή has religious provenance evidenced in the word "hierarchy," the importance of which was discussed earlier. The seriousness of irreversibility belongs to the penult: the moment before the blood is spilled, but the moment that announces that there is no other option available. In that lack of choice, the heavy assertion of necessity reveals its seriousness as inevitability, and so it holds for the tragic plot as well.

The middle in the tragic plot corresponds to the sacrifice of the sovereign, sometimes related as an actual dismemberment (Pentheus), other times as symbolic (Oedipus). Here, as in the sacrificial sequence, the important point proves again to be the irreversibility of fate, which is communicated through the mention of oracles and, in Sophocles in particular, through the stage presence of Teiresias himself. The utterance of Teiresias is like the raising of the sacrificial knife: in his prophecy, which speaks the order of things, hang the life and death of the tragic agent. In this sense, his speech always partakes of the unspeakable: in effect, it announces the irreversibility of the tragic process, even when it appears as a helpful guidance that could lead to an alternative outcome. While theoretically he could redirect the course of events, this *philosophical* possibility is nullified by the inexorable demands of reality. Reality asserts itself where thought speculates over possibilities. The wise counsel is never heard by the mortal ears, and it is likely that its inefficacy stems from this very dimension of the unspeakable that it attempts to convey. Tragedy is that which could not happen otherwise, but not because the agent lacks will or intelligence. On the contrary, he/she may be well gifted with both.

Nonetheless, this gift is either too excessive and becomes its owner's liability, or it is imperceptibly—thus, all the more tragically—insufficient to the task. If the animal has no rational faculty, and is thus fated to die for lack of resources, the human being is fated because it has many resources that, however, cannot overcome the forces conspiring against it. Aeschylus captures this in his *Prometheus Bound*: "Craft is far weaker than necessity" (ln. 514; τέχνη δ' ἀνάγκης ἀσθενεστέρα μακρῷ).

Writing about the role of the jury in Aeschylus's *Eumenides*, Judith Fletcher notes its silent conduct. This type of jury conduct was specific to Athens's homicide courts, and showed their seriousness in contrast to the noise of popular courts that later assumed capital cases. Contrary to Euripides's version of the trial in his *Orestes*, which is set in this later backdrop of a popular assembly with its boisterous noise lending it a mob-like quality, the court of Aeschylus harkens to the earlier institution of homicide courts that were sacrosanct, met at special times of the year, and upheld their dignity by the silence of their jurors and the secrecy of their votes (Fletcher 70–71). This removal of the homicide courts from the ordinary socius reflected the seriousness of the cases they judged. That their seriousness proceeded from their sacred foundation is emphasized in a defense speech written by Antiphon for a non-Athenian client accused of killing an Athenian citizen. The defendant complains that he is not granted due process by not standing trial in a proper homicide court: "The laws, the oaths, the sacrifices, the proclamations, in fact the entire proceeding in connection with trials for murder are so very different from other types of proceedings simply because it is of supreme importance that the facts at issue, on which so much turns, should themselves be rightly interpreted. Such a right interpretation means vengeance for him who has been wronged; whereas to find an innocent man guilty of murder is a tragic mistake, and an impiety, against both gods and laws" (Antiphon qtd. in Fletcher 70–71). Murder and capital punishment are exceptional events, just as the sacrificial altar and the festive calendar form exceptions in space and time. The homicide court, ritual altar, and tragic stage are spaces bound together by the feeling of seriousness since in all of them an "act" sets life and death always at stake.

Lastly, the conclusion of the sacrifice involves an element of restitution through which the community atones and asserts its continuation. Burkert offers various examples of restorative symbology from several mystery cults, of which the Eleusinian initiation is the most commonly known. However, the example that seems most compelling of all—perhaps because it reaches us from a time much earlier and foggier than that of Greek myth—is the prehistoric hunter's own gestures at symbolic reparation after the kill. Drawing on Emil Bächler and Karl Meuli's studies of the Upper Paleolithic, Burkert notes the "striking similarities" between Greek sacrifice, with its prevalence of thigh bones, and prehistoric hunting customs such as the Neanderthal "burial of bears," where "bears' skulls and bones, especially thigh-bones, [were] carefully set up in caves," and the Siberian custom of depositing skulls and bones of quarry in sacred places (13).[38] Although the distant antiquity of Bächler's claim has been disputed, archaeological remains from the Upper Paleolithic, during which the ceremonial character of hunting society became clearer, seem to confirm the hypothesis regarding the symbolic intention of the earliest hunting customs (14). Burkert responds to the objection that the hunter's killing is not ceremonial, but rather profane and utilitarian, by appealing to these similarities between hunting and sacrificial customs. Indeed, I think that a chief theoretical corollary of his anthropology—one that, however, recedes behind the wall of his empirical evidence—involves the realization that human beings pass to the ethical through this violent but redemptive threshold that nature presents them in the scene of the hunt. In one of the select passages where this translation of nature into the ethical comes to the fore, Burkert describes the restorative function of hunting ritual:

> The shock felt in the act of killing is answered later by consolidation; guilt is followed by reparation, destruction by reconstruction. Its simplest manifestation is in the custom of collecting bones, of raising the skull, the horns, or the antlers, thereby establishing an order whose power resides in its contrast to what went before. *In the experience of killing one perceives the sacredness of life*; it is nourished and perpetuated by death. This paradox is embodied, acted out, and generalized in the ritual. Whatever is to endure and be effective must pass through a sacrifice which opens and reseals the abyss of annihilation. (38; my emphasis)

Symmetrically, tragic drama, according to its Aristotelian definition, lays claim to a cathartic function. Whereas the interpretation of catharsis has a long and contested history that exceeds the scope of this chapter, even the most divergent positions agree on this point: catharsis implies some sort of restoration or balance. In other words, something lost can be restored symbolically in and through something else; more pointedly, even in the face of irretrievable loss, something else can still emerge, just as in the human experience of the natural cycle, death is followed by new birth. Aristotle could not be insouciant to this life-affirming, naturalist aspect of tragedy, given his emphasis on tragic action being lifelike. The convincingness of tragedy rests for him in its resemblance to real life, and it is self-evident that the most *real* concern about life involves its relation to death—a relation that on the individual level is always felt as a great interruption, yet on the cosmic level appears as part of an uninterrupted continuity of the change of states.

It is perhaps not sheer coincidence that the earliest form of dramatic presentation was trilogic, thus carrying within its structure the tripartite sequence of ritual. Tragedies, of course, continued to be presented in a sequence of threes (plus a satyr play) in the Great Dionysia competitions throughout the classical age, but beginning with Sophocles, the cohesion of a single plot from a single mythical cycle was broken in favor of a common theme across three independent plays. The *Oresteia* remains the only surviving trilogy from the great tragedians that is a trilogy in the strict sense of the term. Therefore, even though we can never draw an exact correspondence between the predetermined structure of ritual and that of a freer literary exploration, some patterns repeat themselves visibly enough for us to speculate about the deeper links between ritual and tragic sequences. With its background of maiden sacrifice as the cause that propels the *Oresteia*'s impending murders, *Agamemnon* contains elements of the preparation along with the first act of murder, the regicide. The *Choephoroi* begins with libations to the dead, a scene similar to those Burkert has in mind when speaking of the sacrificial character of chthonic cults. The play then culminates in the murder of Clytemnestra, which may be viewed as the central act of the entire trilogy in that it defines most palpably the destiny of the main personage, Orestes.[39] Finally, albeit somewhat precariously, the *Eumenides* concludes with a sense of resolution of the blood feud into due process.

Seriousness, Hierarchy, and the Justice of the Hunt: *Homo Necans* as *Homo Gravis*

By its own methodological admission, *Homo Necans* proposes an anthropology of ancient Greek ritual that draws on evolutionary-biological theory.[40] I suggest, however, that this is also a book about something else, about a concept that may have arisen out of natural history to become fundamental for the building of human culture: seriousness. The complex significance of Burkert's reliance on evolutionary biology notwithstanding,[41] I do not focus on the technical merits of the science he presupposes. My interest lies in the attendant concept of seriousness that develops out of his engagement with evolutionary biology, insofar as this concept remembers and preserves nature as the prototype of necessity that human existence must confront. Put differently, Burkert's choice of evolutionary theory as a naturalist template for his cultural narrative remains for me somewhat of an accidental, no matter how scientifically compelling or suspect an accidental it has proved for modernity. Such a disclaimer is neither easily taken nor does it aim to dispel various problematics that the Darwinian paradigm has ushered in. Instead, the urgency to reflect on nature once again as a formative element of culture has outweighed other considerations at this moment. Subsequently, I frame my choice to read Burkert in terms of a necessity that has obliged me to take *seriously* modes of thought that give pride of place to nature and to its continual inscription in civilization building. This necessity arises from epistemic and disciplinary concerns as much as from certain historical, and thus, axiological urgencies.

In regard to the disciplinary context, working on tragedy invites quite organically the discussion of nature, since, along with its much-lauded explorations of matters of the polis, tragedy is replete with cosmogonic assumptions and statements. In the tragic universe, cosmos and polis are often coextensive, and thus, the genre may well be viewed as one of the earliest attempts at showing that individual and political freedoms do not result from a negative transcendence of nature's brute necessity but rather arise from it and, to an extent, obey its rhythms. This is likely the reason tragedy enjoyed a central place in the wake of Kant's thought, which claimed the unity of moral freedom and nature—an antinomial unity, however, shown exemplarily through aesthetic judgment. Hence, the age of Kant became the age of tragedy, while the effort to grapple with this antinomy continues. Nevertheless, I submit that tragedy can contribute to this effort not only by illustrating the antinomial character of this unity—as, for instance, through its catastrophic outcomes, which scholarship often ascribes to the competing demands of freedom and nature—but also by giving us a glimpse into the latent and deep accord between those demands. Regardless of their particular outcomes, and in spite of many such outcomes being admittedly disastrous, tragedies do not show freedom only as antagonizing and superseding nature. Rather, tragic agents *freely* accept the necessity of nature as an originary condition—above all, as an originary element of their own constitution as moral beings. Hence, tragic freedom is about the fulfillment of nature, and of heroic nature, more specifically. This is a recapitulation of a previous point regarding the stoicism or "realism" with which the tragic hero faces necessity. This is also what Antigone and Ismene both have in mind when they resort to their *phusis* in order to explain to each other their respective moral choices (*Ant*. ln. 37–38, 61–62, 78–79).

Turning to historical and ethico-political concerns, my engagement with Burkert results from a protracted and perturbing feeling that it is modernity's gradual divorce of politics from nature and the cosmos that accounts for much of the unfreedom underlying its various self-described liberatory discourses and movements. Cosmopolitanism is such a current, much-touted discourse that explicitly includes in its name the notion of the cosmos. Yet, the repression of nature's formative contribution to human life, ranging from our rarefied lives in overpopulated urban milieus to the conception of science as dominative rather than explicative of nature to the radical revisionism even of human physiology, ushers in cosmopolitanism as an exclusively anthropocentric artifice with its attendant exceptionalisms—for instance, the sense that humans, contrary to all other mammals, are allowed special permission to create even their embodied reality at will. As such, the contemporary appeals to cosmopolitanism, though louder than ever, sound all the more redundant since the *cosmos* in cosmopolitanism is invariably reabsorbed into political artifice, into a pure technic, leaving no space for the cosmological—let alone the cosmogonic—to inform politics. Much like its twin concern of environmentalism, cosmopolitanism relies increasingly on a technocratic rather than cosmological platform.

One can see this philosophical deflection mirrored in certain semantic transpositions within the Greek language itself. *Cosmos* early on meant "jewel," connoting a precious but majestic beauty, and was used by Pythagoras to describe the harmonious order of the universe. Already by Plato's time, however, κοσμιότης [*cosmiotēs*] (temperance, sophrosyne) had come to signify the civic virtue of moderation. Plato concludes his *Statesman* by arguing that the good statesman achieves, through a kind of weaving, the right admixture of two antithetical civic temperaments, both of which are necessary and beneficial to the civic tapestry: *cosmiotēs*, linked to gentleness, quietude, and restrained consideration, and *andreia*, linked to courage, acuity, and swiftness of thought and action (306e–310e). The softer and peace-loving *cosmios*-type is aptly translated by Harold N. Fowler as "decorous" (307b), which highlights the qualities of being conciliatory, polite, and well-versed in manners, qualities related to the ornamental or decorative—thus hinting at, but also severely diminishing, the splendor of cosmos as jewel.

In keep with Plato's mature philosophy, the *Statesman* pursues through the exploration of statecraft the onto-epistemic question of the overlapping of the virtues and the interference by their opposites. Thus, the Stranger in this dialogue admits to the negative expression of *cosmiotēs* as leading to "cowardly or indolent" character (307c). *Andreia*, in contrast, untethered by matters of etiquette, may for its part descend to an "excessive and even maniacal" character (307c) of beastly nature (309e). The *andreios* fits incidentally the tragic-heroic type. Without going much further into the *Statesman*, I will simply indicate three relevant points. First, both these temperaments as well as their receptivity to being mixed with the good part of their opposite are discussed in terms of native and generational inclinations;[42] even the decorous type, who excels in manners and artifice, owes this inclination to his "nature." Secondly, with respect to our topic of seriousness, it is notable that the acuity and swiftness ascribed to the courageous echoes the urgency and hastiness of action required elsewhere of the σπουδαῖον (the serious). Thirdly, and most revealingly, in his proposal of maximizing the civic good by mixing the virtuous sides of both temperaments while eliminating their negative potential through education, Plato ends up with a subtle asymmetry: whereas the decorous improves by refraining from excess into cowardice, the courageous can actively cross over and behave gently, channeling his erstwhile brutality into civil service and commitment to a just society. The decorous improves by decreasing his negative manifestations, but the courageous leaps and alloys himself with the opposite virtue so as to respond to the circumstances (309d). We could interpret this as the decorous needing less of a correction, but I think a more convincing reading yields that the courageous is more capacious in producing certain unexpected harmonies within himself. Eventually, what emerges out of Plato's juxtaposition is that *cosmiotēs* qua decorum describes no longer primarily the vast brilliance of the universe but a quieter sort of beauty, the ornament-like virtue that fosters civic propriety. This shift is even more pronounced in Modern Greek usage, where the vernacular *cosmos* refers to "the world" not as a celestial entity but as an aggregate of people: it stands as synonym for a crowd—namely, for human beings in their decidedly mundane, undifferentiated, secular capacity; people as an indistinct social mass. Its derivative adjective κοσμικός now signifies both secular laity in general, and the frivolous ostentation of the socialite and celebrity class. In short, cosmology is reduced to sociology; seriousness to lightheartedness.

A discourse such as Burkert's, precisely in the discomforts it raises, not least in the present author, acts as a kind of caesura from the way we have been accustomed to think away from nature and the cosmos. The naturalist imprint on the human narrative, which few tried to register after Nietzsche, calls for a turn in the reading of culture that has predominantly focused on artifice. Moreover, I wish to accent yet again that the priority of nature, in my argument, shows itself chiefly through the figure of seriousness it bestows on human culture. The seriousness nature imparts to the human being stems from a space that cannot be reduced to the absolutist aspirations of techne—namely, to human artifice as infinite license and permissiveness—but involves necessity as a continuous pressure that first *necessitates*, and even emboldens, human artifice as an expression of freedom. Hence, we might recall Aristotle's priority of nature in instigating the artistic process of imitation. For its even more explicit relevance here, we should also cite again the Aeschylean verse: "Craft is far weaker than necessity." The historical and ethical necessity to admit a discourse that prioritizes nature instead of considering it merely as an effect of culture thus rendered *Homo Necans* an important resource for this study.

Homo Necans assumes seriousness to be the indispensable requirement for the establishment and development of any culture, and at moments, the book reads as a phenomenology of seriousness, describing the ways in which seriousness appears in ritual, and the affects it produces in the participants both individually and collectively. In Burkert's theorization, seriousness is intimately tied to aggression, which he deems a fundamental life-instinct whose expression is reflected in, and can be redirected through, ritual, particularly in the case of humans.

Markedly, Burkert's definition of ritual is first biological, before it becomes cultural-anthropological, and is indebted to the work of Austrian zoologist and ethologist Konrad Lorenz. Despite the politically problematic figure of Lorenz, the concept of aggression as constitutive to human behavior is not unique to him but enjoys prominent position in Freudian analysis and in Nietzsche, among others. Since the interconnection of biology and culture is crucial to Burkert's methodology, it is worth citing in full his remark about the relative precedence of the biological to the cultural: "The concept of *ritual* has long been used to describe the rules of religious behavior. Biology's recent usurpation of the term appears, however, to confuse the concept, mixing the transcendent with the infra-human. But perhaps these two do indeed meet within the fundamental orders that constitute life. Thus, we deliberately start from the biological definition of ritual, and from there we will soon be led deep into the nature of religion" (23). Biology usurped ritual, Burkert admits, but the usurpation, which would imply something derivative and false, turns out to be genuinely disclosive: it shows that the transcendent and the infrahuman, the high and the low, meet at the beginnings of life, and it is thus his deliberation—not unlike Aristotle—to give precedence to the biological as not only origin but also conduit of religious, cultural, and symbolic practices. Of course, one can easily dismiss this method through the predictable twist of saying that biology and nature are themselves cultural narratives with no truth of their own. However, such an objection stands on rather shaky ground since it is open to a counterobjection much of its own kind—namely, that the reduction of everything to cultural narrative is itself a cultural narrative, which thus relativizes and diminishes the impact of the initial objection, as it empties everything else for that matter. In short, the sophistry game, which interests me no further than its simple mention, involves precisely a lack of seriousness.

In various places throughout his study, Burkert leaves remarks that consistently lead to this prominence of seriousness as a negative—in effect, hostile—attitude that is yet responsible for the rise of culture as a social edifice. He cites findings from ethological research that suggest a number of gestures we now consider sociable to have had origins in aggressive behavior: laughter and the waving of branches, for instance, were initially gestures of aversion, not of welcome and sociality (24, 35, 278). Laughter, now an expression of amiability, "is thought to originate in an aggressive display of teeth" (24), in a grimace likely directed against a threat.[43] Culture is a serious business, and to achieve the cooperation and cohesion of the social bond, the human being had to first traverse the negativity of aversion and exclusion: "A smile can, of course, establish contact, and a crying child touches our hearts, but in all human societies 'seriousness' takes precedence over friendliness and compassion" (Burkert 35). Harrison's theory of ritual had earlier traveled along the same arc: Homer's rational banquets and their *do ut des* form, where the mortals exact a sharing in the divine feast in return for their due sacrifices, was preceded by the *do ut abeas* form of darker rituals of aversion, and by cannibalistic feasts of the sort we find in the background of the *Oresteia* (Harrison ix).

This constitutive negativity of seriousness is well attested also in the psychology of the tragic emotions of pity and fear, which are *serious* emotions, as Aristotle defined them in the *Poetics*. The negativity is obvious in the case of fear, but as David Konstan argues, pity too is a painful emotion produced by the cognitive disturbance of seeing someone suffer even though innocent (*Pity* 49, 128–36). Here I would append that Aristotle's sharp differentiation between pity and philanthropy, which disqualifies the latter from the sphere of proper tragic feelings, can be further elucidated in terms of this underlying negativity: whereas *philia* in philanthropy describes a positive form of connection, just as *anthropos* implies it being a humanitarianism—namely, a feeling directed "intraspecifically" from humans to other humans, as Burkert would say—pity is more complicated. Pity involves judgment regarding this "injustice" of fate, but does not require of the one who pities to feel exactly the emotion of the victim as compassion would (Konstan, *Pity* 8).[44] In this sense, it is arguable that pity would be less concerned with the species of the recipient and more with the witness's registering of the conspicuous distance between the fate the victim "deserves" and the fate it is dealt. Although Aristotle does not explicitly state this point, the recipient of pity could be possibly someone other than human: an animal, perhaps, whose innocence dictated the ruse of the "comedy of innocence" in order to justify its sacrifice.

Nevertheless, if we follow Burkert's vein of thought, such extension of pity to nonhuman recipients does not signal an ethics of alterity because the animal quarry is already a substitute for what was originally there, and to which the quarry bears a strange resemblance: a human being. As Burkert describes, during the prehistoric struggle for survival, before men gathered to work communally, and with only rudimentary weapons, it was easier for a solitary hunter to target and kill another human rather than a large animal, or an animal that could speedily escape (18). Later, in the sight of the dead animal prey, the now-cooperating human hunters recalled the early scene of human slaughter and cannibalism, seeking to expiate their guilt through religious atonement: "Hunting concentrated on the great mammals, which conspicuously resembled men in their body structure, movements, their eyes and their 'faces,' their breath and voices, in fleeing and in fear, in attacking and in rage. Most of all, this similarity with man was to be recognized in killing and slaughtering; the flesh was like flesh, bones like bones, phallus like phallus, and heart like heart, and, most important of all, the warm running blood was the same. One could, perhaps, most clearly grasp the animal's resemblance to man when it died. Thus, the quarry turned into a sacrificial victim" (20). Importantly, in Burkert's story, guilt and atonement as inaugural ethical moments arise from resemblance and identification, not alterity, the latter concept having enjoyed much prominence in recent ethical theory.

The ritual substitution of the human by the animal that hence took place now reverts in tragedy where the human sovereign is destroyed. If ritual is symbolization of the hunt, and tragedy is a further aestheticization of ritual, the second-degree aestheticization puts the terms back into their original equation: it is the human being who is once again at stake as it was in its forgotten natural prehistory, when it underwent its evolutionary leap of becoming predator. It was this transition that, for Burkert, marked the quantum leap from bestiality to humanity proper, as homo sapiens is first and foremost *homo necans*. Paradoxically, the scene of predation, the transformation into a carnivorous creature, turns the human being for the first time toward ethical life. To put it elsewise: the question of "to kill or not to kill" constitutes the backbone of ethics and of culture. We do not start from *philia*; we start from the kill, and even ethical life has inscribed in it this aggressive prehistory of aversion.

Since "to kill or not to kill" is a matter of utmost seriousness, it imports into our discussion the notion of authenticity, and its ancient meaning. Though authenticity has long been overlaid with the cheerful meanings of the "true" and "genuine," the ancient *authentēs* (αὐθέντης) was someone who acted on—that is, killed—oneself or one's own kin. In "La Main d'Antigone," Nicole Loraux offers a philological account of αὐθέντης in terms of the act of killing, and, like Burkert, defines "act" first and foremost as killing. Because of this violence, however, Loraux develops an ideological critique of action and, in a thoroughly anti-Aristotelian gesture, removes agency from tragedy. Eventually, her ethico-political stakes become more central to her interpretation than is the case for Burkert, but they both recognize that the act is synonymous with killing, and consequently, the concept of authenticity is enmeshed with the scene of killing. Remaining rather neutral in his description and analysis, Burkert instead suggests that there is something necessary to the violence through which human beings process the serious question of life. To quote him again, "In the experience of killing, one perceives the sacredness of life" (38).

To further consolidate this convergence between the notion of seriousness in regard to the precarity of life, and the negative emotions this precarity arouses, let me briefly return to the fear and awe accompanying the mysterium tremendum—a scene that in Kantian thought emerged as the locus of the sublime.[45] Kant's elaboration of the sublime and of its moral possibilities hinge on the *serious* feelings of awe and respect that it provokes—feelings somewhat equivalent to Aristotelian *phobos*—by posing an imminent threat to the subject's integrity, albeit threat at a distance. Unlike the pleasure felt at the sight of the beautiful, respect is a *negative* feeling born of the confrontation with infinity that disturbs the accord of our faculties though it does not pose an actual physical risk as an aesthetic experience. Notable here is the hierarchy implied in such serious feelings, with hierarchy being a concept also pivotal to Aristotle's theory of tragic mimesis, and a concept that I will revisit shortly in my concluding comments regarding some intriguing contradictions of our own cultural situation. Indeed, not only is Kant's theory of the sublime replete with the deferential feelings of awe, reverence, fear, and respect both in his precritical *Observations on the Feeling of the Beautiful and Sublime* and in the *Critique of Judgment*,[46] but his formal definition of the judgment of the sublime requires the hierarchical subordination of our cognitive faculties to the supersensible faculty of Reason. His preferred examples for eliciting respect show hierarchy in their use of scale, power, and magnitude; hence Rudolf Otto's mobilization of Kant in his effort to describe the archetypally hierarchical relation—that is, the relation to the holy. Instances that command respect include imminent (natural) disasters because they imply a threat to life even if they do not actually pose it in the aesthetic register, and it has been duly noted that the 1755 Lisbon earthquake provoked Kant's turn to scientific thought in the precritical period as well as fueled his later reflections on the sublime.[47]

The risk to life, or at the very least, to the physical or mental integrity of the human being, proves the common thread that links together the concepts of seriousness and authenticity along with those of hierarchy and respect, while nature and the holy offer themselves as inaugural sites where these concepts are rehearsed. Were we indeed to entertain a provisional list of examples of seriousness, we would detect that they all share these "negative" sentiments of hierarchy and respect directed toward something that imposes itself over us. For instance, we behave solemnly as we pay our respects to the dead in moments of silence; we bow in salute of an office and, in many non-Western cultures, in front of an elder. These are instances of self-diminishment and subordination to an idea that is larger than ourselves; hence, the emphasis is not on deference toward the individual (the particular king, general, judge, tribal chief, and so on) but toward the office each represents. Meanwhile, the threatening aspect is preserved in the linguistic pragmatics of seriousness. Thus, to convey that something is a serious matter, one may instead use the expression that "it is a matter of life and death." When one is "seriously injured," one is said to be "in critical condition"—meaning again that the integrity of one's life is at stake. "Critical," deriving from "crisis," which means "judgment," is thus synonymous with seriousness. The adjective "serious" accompanies words like "emergency," "accident," "offence"; it does not qualify words like "amusement," "vacation," "play"—at least, not outside of attempts to be oxymoronic or funny. Hence, also, serious crimes and often serious punishments both involve the life and death of the victim and the perpetrator, being called "capital," which refers to the irreducible necessity of the head on a living body.

Seriousness is embedded in the negativity, and thus also the exclusivity, that marks any hierarchical relation. In turn, the notion of exclusivity belongs to the structure of dilemmatic thought, which, as I discussed earlier, characterizes tragedy both as a theatrical genre and as a mode of being historically in the world. A tragic act owes its seriousness to the scarcity of options to which it is called to respond. A tragic agent must abide by the inherently hierarchical, exclusive, and binary syntax of an "either/or" because necessity, by definition, is that which deprives us of the privilege of options, while at the same time revealing our freedom as the capacity to decide in spite of the poverty of options. To put it shortly, tragedy is not possible within the frame of permissiveness.

Coming closer to our reality, it is precisely this logic of hierarchical priority that contemporary culture repudiates, and in so doing perhaps even contravenes the very determinants of what would qualify it as a culture for Burkert. Naturally, hierarchy has no place in a culture that posits unrestrained egalitarianism as its thoroughly unquestionable, critically immune, and completely transparent ideal, indeed as its *exclusive* political virtue, even if such egalitarianism in effect yields *sameness* rather than equality of differences. Yet, strangely, hierarchy hardly disappeared from our world, and I submit that this is because it cannot, because it belongs to the order of necessity. In other words, culture may well weaken some concepts by relegating them to a foggy prehistory, or may attempt to redefine them to suit new perceptions and experiences, but this does not make them vanish, nor does it even mean that their translation is as seamless as intended. More often than not, the concepts remain unwieldy, and as a result, the dissonance between their initial meaning and their (often instrumental) translation exposes the latent paradoxes accompanying the narrative of their translational progress. They become, in other words, jarring *ritual* vestiges for a culture that has allegedly demythologized all ritual.

Let us consider for a moment how this paradoxical tension works in the example of respect, a feeling (and a moral value) grounded in hierarchy and belonging to this nexus of concepts linked to seriousness. Respect indeed turns out to be a highly prized category in our contemporary political culture, though it remains a question whether the appeal to it is merely nominal. For instance, well beyond the strict purview of equality before the law assured by any democracy to *all* its citizens, contemporary culture attempts to enforce a social code of respect—*particularly* for "marginalized identities"—through its official ideological outlets: beyond the clear juridical necessity of universal equal rights, the social pressure exercised by this demand is built around the language of respect. At the same time, respect's structural reliance on hierarchy is either elided, because its admission would challenge the culture's egalitarian principle as such, or is selectively justified as a means to bring about a just and necessary inversion of power, thus ironically proving the point of hierarchy's inevitability. The contradiction emerges as one appeals to respect by implicitly relying on, but not acknowledging, its hierarchical structure, because hierarchy is viewed as an anachronistic, theological remnant that disturbs the horizontal plane of democratic equality. Hence, even though respect's grounding in authority and hierarchy is eroded, the vestigial appeal to respect as a moral value is harnessed to serve various sociopolitical ends. Such instrumental usage, however, only points to the inconvenient fact that hierarchy is still operative, albeit in reconfigured expressions of power that are now deemed ideologically preferable. It may be, then, that authenticity, in its later meaning of genuineness, becomes a crucial gauge for assessing such historical and ethico-political translations, obfuscations, and instrumentalizations of cultural concepts. After all, it is possible that the reason why authenticity itself has been translated into "genuineness" has something to do with the *deadly* seriousness involved in the act of taking a life (which was its original meaning), for such an act cannot be faked (neither in real life nor in sacrificial ritual, though it is in theater!), nor played around with, nor "ironized," nor "subverted," because its truth is irreversible. While the darker ancient meaning of the authentic has been forgotten, it is upon its terror that the more affirmative meaning of the genuine is built.

Concluding these remarks on seriousness as the formative impetus behind all cultural norms and institutions, I would like to return to an earlier point regarding justice, the concept around which eventually both the *Oresteia* and this study pivot. Discussing Hermes's trial for the murder of Argos in tandem with Orestes's pursuit by the Furies, I have noted that both myths thematize how justice recites *uncannily* evermore the archaic violence of the hunter. It is time to address this remark more concretely, and if not explain it, at least illustrate it. I said "uncannily" because justice as the ideal end of sociopolitical progress from Plato onward is chiefly considered to be the overcoming of ancestral nativism: the universal, rational idea that drives human relations toward a peaceful civil society and away from the primitive, natural demands of the blood tie. Viewed in this philosophical light, justice appears significantly different from the image Walter Otto gives when describing the vengeful Furies as the objective forms of an instinctual human demand to exact due payment for its losses, of the cry of blood for blood: "Human blood, which obligates every man to his neighbor, cries out to them [the Furies] and obtains their response. This obligation has nothing whatever to do with charity or selflessness. It is based on no philosophy or doctrine; it results from life's powerful need to convince and unite. The objective order to which it belongs is precisely coextensive with the primal revolt of the human soul when in fear and affliction it unburdens itself of its preternatural pressure by a curse and appeals to the obligation" (*Homeric Gods* 24–25). In this passage, justice begins not as a concept, least of all as an altruism, but as a living, native, spontaneous cry proceeding from the claim of blood, which binds one first and foremost to one's own, or to one's neighbor—namely, to one's most immediate proximity. The appeal to unity is not a matter of civic inclusion but of cosmic necessity that impinges on the sufferer and his immediate witnesses from the order of things, from "life's powerful need," in Otto's exact words. Accordingly, the demand for justice takes its archetypal objective form in a cosmological, rather than institutional, legal image: in the injured person's laying of a curse meant to shatter not only a particular culprit but the whole world. Let us recall here the blight of sterility and famine sent by the Furies to entire cities in retribution for a crime. More than two millennia after Aeschylus, another Greek poet, Odysseus Elytis, conjured up the same cosmological image in an appeal to the "sun of Justice" not to forget his country in the aftermath of its national battles for independence and its World War II resistance that culminated in civil war: "My bitter hands circle with the Thunderbolt to the other side of Time, / I summon my old friends with threats and running blood!" (35). Like Burkert's account of guilt, which posits its origin in the hunters' identification with their quarry's blood, Otto's origin of justice is not located in an abstraction but in the innate grip that the sight of familiar blood had on human beings.

As I have hinted, such language appears understandably jarring and even dangerous to an outlook that insists on the unquestionable primacy of the civic bond, and on the belief in social progress as the overcoming of nature through the ever-increasing use of artifice. Yet the point I also made above about the violent nativism that grounds the concept of justice, and the uncanniness with which it periodically erupts, could not be more timely. At present, the colors of the hunting tableau shine afresh, as social activism grows into a global industry of prosecution alongside the admittedly less-vivid procedures of official courts: a decade-long survey of the threats, accusations, and retaliations by social media's cancel culture should illustrate both the hypervigilance in identifying and the vigilantism in pursuing the prey until formal punishment or public humiliation is exacted.[48] Focus, patience, and discipline were, according to Burkert, the evolutionary traits that the human predator successfully translated into culture-building tools. To be able to wait patiently alert amid life-threatening conditions until he caught his prey: that was the virtue of the hunter, then of the warrior strategizing his enemy's defeat, and of humans in general as steadfast builders of long-term projects and institutions with long-term goals to be achieved. Thus, particularly intriguing is the social justice activists' self-designation as "warriors" at a time when warlike traits are otherwise disparaged as vestiges of patriarchy and of toxic masculinity. War, to cite Burkert again, was another outlet for the aggressivity of the hunt, and the self-identification of the activist with the warrior points precisely, though most likely unwittingly, to this disconcerting fact. (And of course, the violence behind the term "act" in activism should by now be clear, after both Burkert's and Loraux's analyses.) A new form of Argos Panoptes, the social activist stands vigilant guard over others' ideas and expressions, and once the latter are deemed unacceptable, the activist—attuned like the ancient hunter to every sound and movement—strikes the prey, real or imagined.

That the relentless vigilance and vigilantism of the Fury are at the heart of the pursuit of justice can be seen in another current term that bears more than an accidental lexical kinship to vigilance. I am referring to the term "woke," which has come to summarize, with no other rival term in use, our global political culture. To keep vigil means not only to stay generally alert but to keep awake in the dead of night—that is, to occupy a state of acute readiness at a time that is considered especially dangerous. Of course, such alertness has been and continues to be almost universally commended as a personal and civic virtue for obvious reasons. Consequently, it is not surprising that parallel to the left-leaning (and suitably grammatically unconventional) virtue of "woke," one can find the right-leaning, and suitably old-fashioned and religiously inspired, equivalent of "awakening," though the latter has not really gained currency. Virtues, however, can turn into their opposites when pushed to their extreme, as Plato and Aristotle both observed. Thus, hypervigilance—whether of the woke or awakened variety—risks derailing into paranoia, conspiracy, and even vigilantism, particularly if the vigilant gaze deems that the existing legal processes are not sufficient for delivering *just* justice.

More importantly still, the nativism of justice does not exhaust itself at the level of the figure—that is, at the level of the formal similarity between the vigilance and aggressivity of the hunter and that of the modern justice seeker. It also extends to the very content of the justice claim, a content that is increasingly identitarian. Ironically, the louder the call for cosmopolitanism and for the critique of all forms of nationhood grew, this nativism—logically expected to decrease—has also grown ever more pronounced through the global rise of identity politics. The figure of the social justice warrior serving this kind of politics emerges as an allegory of the Fury insofar as it utters otherwise—that is, with new words, new artillery, and new audience—an old but strangely familiar (and familial) battle cry. Classical philosophical or political apologetics that insist on the universality of justice are regularly counteracted by this deeply sectarian reality of justice movements; this sectarianism, I submit, is not merely a historical contingency reflecting particular—hence resolvable—power differentials but a moment structurally and originarily germane to the concept of justice as illustrated in the objective form of the Fury and its hunt.

Starting at least from the famously countercultural 1960s and up to recent, contested events, violent acts in the name of justice worldwide, themselves erupting from competing spaces in the social and political spectrum, have been described as anything from "liberation fronts" and "people's revolutions" to "riots" and "insurrections," depending on one's ideological inclinations. Yet, regardless of these inclinations, or of the official interpretations of such events in different historical contexts, they all expose the militancy of justice as a long-standing translation of an old, menacing ritual: of that Dionysian surging impulse that fostered conspiracies and unrest, leading to assassinations, mass arrests, summary executions, and lawless overthrows, and that, according to Loraux, often took place during the extraordinary springtime of theater festivals in Athens, exploiting precisely its interruptive character. The myths and the tragedians, it seems, have understood something about the darkness of justice better than the philosophers: the pursuit of justice cannot be separated from the hunt.

This realization does not mean that the pursuit of justice must be abandoned; rather, as the *Oresteia*'s conclusion implies, justice may have to be bracketed, or even suspended, at the very moment of grounding the law, by being itself *grounded* (in both a punitive and honoring manner) under the earth with the Furies. Thus, what might appear problematic to some—the burial and forgetting of the Furies as justice agents—is in fact a pointer toward a more humane existence, insofar as it allows both the individual (Orestes) and the polis (Argos) to begin again without the oppressiveness of indelible memory that is the trait of the Furies, and that breeds perpetual vengefulness, holding all time hostage to the crimes of the past. The Aeschylean conclusion suggests that there is justice in forgetting justice. Moreover, this forgetting is not simply the dialectical *cultural* antithesis to the *naturalist* thesis of retribution. Instead, I suggest that it is itself naturalist as well, and at best only quasi-conscious, having its origins in the life-need for the world to go on, "to move on," as the saying goes. Here, it is crucial to foreground this competing life-need as the other pole of the cosmology to the one expressed by Otto's Fury: the need to forget the blood cry when its insistence becomes untenable—namely, when the need to satisfy its justice claim becomes a life-denying solipsism, creating new injustices and accruing ever more blood. In this sense, the law that resolves the *Oresteia* is less a civic law, though it proceeds from a court setting, and more of a realization of a cosmic demand that appears through the jurors' exercise of a new "common sense." I would also add that it is by introducing this Uranian pole of the cosmology to its chthonic counterpart that we can move from nativism to the cosmological, for there is a distinction to be made between these two notions: the cosmological refers to the human attunement and accordance with nature, whereas nativism tends to lead to selective political *naturalizations* of claims about oneself, or one's group membership.

The Furies at the end of the *Oresteia* continue to dwell below, but Aeschylus has shifted the weight from the predatory and perpetual demands of justice to the life-sustaining function of the law in helping us mediate our daily existence. It is certainly true that the law may not catch every injustice committed or every sleight perceived, but this, Aeschylus seems to imply, is still a predicament preferable to the hypervigilance and life-denying infinity of justice claims—for, as the generational feud shows, nothing is ever just *enough* for the justice seeker; there will always be hurt parties, often produced unwittingly as collateral damages of justice delivered, and easily a just demand turns infinitely unjust for others. This said, I recognize that shifting the focus from the demands of justice to the mediating rule of law can be seen as conceding something of great importance. Moreover, it can even be argued that we can keep *both* the Furies and the court simultaneously—and Aeschylus is indeed keeping them both—but not both above the earth, for the Furies, even as Eumenides, are not made to belong under light. Were it possible to keep both these forms of dikē above ground, there would be no need for the *Oresteia*, or for tragedy at all. In other words, the kind of critique that expects all options to be available at all times is not immanent to tragedy, which, as I hope to have shown in this chapter, is a genre structured by the principle of sacrifice, regulated by the logic of constraints and hierarchical priority, and elevated by the feeling of seriousness that attends great loss.

Chapter 3

Like a Dog, or in Artemis's Night

Dikē in *Agamemnon*

Starry Night: Dikē as Destiny

The first play of the *Oresteia* trilogy opens with a guard atop the palace roof, keeping his night vigil, and looking for beacon fires ordered by Clytemnestra to relay messages from the distant war front. He describes vividly his toil, which involves him crouching on all fours "like a dog" (ln. 3; κυνὸς δίκην) so that—while alert to everything around him—he himself may remain imperceptible in this lowered position. Oliver Taplin notes this strange but impressive choice of stagecraft: with no official entrance, and already in watchful position, the guard epitomizes the secrecy, fear, and anxiety that have befallen Argos in the absence of its lawful king. What Aeschylus loses in the solemn act of an entrance, continues Taplin, he gains in this innovative introduction, where the sleepless vigil of the guard is subtly communicated through his having already been on his post. Spending long and lonely nights, with no dream allowed to enter his world, the guard keeps watch with fear and pain as his only companions. Aeschylus suggests that the endlessness of the Trojan War is experienced equally on the home front through the agony of the guard, who worries not only about the war's outcome but also about the sinister atmosphere of his own city and the ominous future that awaits the return of his king. This foreboding scene has been astutely compared to the ghostly opening of *Hamlet*, whose equally foreboding events begin with the change of the night guard (Taplin 276–77).

Though not noble by status, Aeschylus's watchman speaks eloquently, transforming his loneliness into a nocturnal philosophical exercise. If fear and trepidation were his psychological companions, both being markers of human limitation, they are offset by the vastness of the night sky that is also present in his vigil and that inspires his speech: "I have learned to know aright the conclave of the stars of night, yea those radiant potentates conspicuous in the firmament, bringers of winter and summer unto mankind" (ln. 4–5).[1] Having studied the constellations above him, he has also endured the cycles of change from summer to winter on the ground, those cycles that taught ancient people the meaning of human transience. His patience proves a supreme discipline with which he has not only served Argos—namely, the civic microcosm—but through which he has observed and reflected on the larger workings of the cosmos. Nonetheless, this is a task from which he prays for relief, presumably because it is physically burdensome, but possibly also because doglike loyalty to a tyrannical regime is oppressive. "Κυνὸς δίκην"—the "way" or "manner" of the dog—constitutes a magnificent Aeschylean wordplay that foreshadows the famous canines of the *Oresteia*, whose dikē is justice-as-hunt. These canines are the Erinyes, who hunt especially murderers of kin, demanding retribution. Before their explicit appearance in the third play, these vengeful deities are anticipated figuratively in *Agamemnon* with Cassandra, the unlucky prophetess whom the chorus calls "doglike" because of her ability to sniff the past and future corpses of the Atreidae (ln. 1093–94), and with the guard who opens the play in his doglike crouch. The guard's monologue, interrupted by the beacon that signals the fall of Troy, concludes with a reserved optimism about Agamemnon's return and the restoration of civic order in Argos. Thus, the dog, sacred companion of Artemis Kynegos (Artemis the Huntress), appears figuratively at the very start of the trilogy, which then unfolds literally as a hunt for justice.

The importance of nature in Aeschylus's drama and the interconnections he draws between justice as a moral idea and fate as a cosmic necessity have been long attested in classical scholarship. In this vein, Helen Bacon observed that the cosmic order in the *Oresteia* is "the system of Justice (Dikē) enforced and administered by Zeus and the Furies, an order that includes, but is not confined to, the moral order on which human society is based" (110).[2] This remark deserves further elucidation so as to make its implications as explicit as possible: dikē, which is typically translated as "justice," but which most fundamentally means "the manner" or "way" of something, is not reducible to the human moral order nor to the constructedness of the latter's institutions. Dikē with a capital D, as it were, includes but exceeds, and may even contravene, whatever our historical views or expectations of justice may be. As the "rightful manner," dikē is sent to human beings from the cosmos, and it is rightful insofar as it reflects the order of that cosmos—namely, natural necessity. Human conventions of justice, in contrast, respond to this necessity, and thus must also be held accountable to it beyond serving their own narrow, immanent purpose of ameliorating social relations. Put differently, cosmic necessity (Ananke) cannot be manipulated to fit human expectations and social experiments, and nothing would qualify better for hubris in Aeschylean tragedy than the assumption that necessity must yield to human voluntarism. This robustly cosmological view of justice that Aeschylus puts forth no longer obtains, at least not with the same clarity with which it once registered in the critical commentary, because justice is discussed today solely as a cultural construct—that is, in terms of the furthest possible distance from anything cosmological, or nature-related. However, as I have already suggested in the conclusion of the previous chapter, this divorce between nature and justice does not necessarily signal a "juster" society. Instead, the refusal to admit this "sending" of dikē has coincided with an increase of cultural exercises in nativism, where the native does not signify the natural but the hijacking of the natural—namely, a paradoxical and even belligerent tactic of *naturalization* taking place at the very moment that the natural is recast as an offense to the constructedness of culture.

Therefore, in this chapter, I attempt to return to this suppler notion of dikē that calibrates the human order in terms of the natural necessity to which it eventually belongs. To do so, I focus on the theme of the hunt, partly because it seems to structure the plot of the *Oresteia*, and partly because it has not been sufficiently mined for the insights it yields about the link between cosmic forces and ethical principles that earlier scholarship had already noticed in Aeschylus. As such, it is obvious why Walter Burkert's *Homo Necans* has proved an important source, and why I will keep returning to its insights both implicitly and explicitly. For now, I will just begin with a general observation about the *Oresteia*'s sustained parallel between hunting and morality—a parallel that, as we will be seeing in this chapter, is most poignantly elucidated through the mantic art of reading dreams and portents since, there, the animal functions both as a natural creature and a religious cipher.

We could in fact say that the *Oresteia* reads as a bestiary of sorts, with dogs, hares, spiders, bulls, snakes, vultures, eagles, and even nightingales and swans[3] communicating powerful symbolic correspondences between the pursuit of hunting as a prerequisite for survival and the moral demand for justice as a prerequisite for civil society. In the first play, Clytemnestra ensnares Agamemnon in a net that is compared to a spider web, killing him to avenge their daughter Iphigenia, who was sacrificed by him for the sake of his Trojan campaign. In the *Choephoroi*, Clytemnestra's dream, which anticipates her demise at the hands of her son Orestes, tells a savage story of birth and predation: in the dream, she births a poisonous snake that suckles not only her milk but her blood as well. At the scene of her murder, both she and Orestes correctly interpret the snake as a symbol of the avenging son. Clytemnestra and Orestes are both snakelike, using deceit to catch their prey, and in this dream, it is as if maternal milk and blood transmute into the venom that nourishes the son but that he will also use to kill his mother. Indeed, Orestes had earlier described himself and Electra as the orphaned brood of an eagle-father who died "entangled in the binding coils / of the deadly viper" (ln. 247–49), thus pointing to Clytemnestra's serpentine nature. Meanwhile, in yet another canine simile, Electra emphasized her grief at watching impotently her father's murder, having herself been sequestered in the palace like a feral dog (ln. 445–47; κυνὸς δίκαν). Notable in the simile structure is the repetition of dikē as the term used for the likening, for the way something is: in short, dikē conveys the "troping" of things, the *how* of their manifestation, the *as* in "as they are." "Like a dog": the simile that described the guard's sense of duty and Cassandra's prophetic gift in *Agamemnon* passes then through Electra's feeling of impotent rage to culminate in the enduring image of chthonic justice spoken from the lips of the condemned Clytemnestra. Moments before her death, she bids farewell to her son by reminding him of the hounds of wrath that avenge mothers: "Take care. Your mother's curse, like dogs, will drag you down" (ln. 924; φύλαξαι μητρὸς ἐγκότους κύνας).

Additionally, the image of the animalistic predator is reinforced in the *Choephoroi* by the symbolism of the archer-hunter. Upon hearing the deceitful story of Orestes's death from the vagrant Orestes himself, the unsuspecting Clytemnestra is devastated, comparing the news to an archer's "well-aimed shots" (ln. 694; τόξοις εὐσκόποις). Orestes's murderous capacity is snakelike, but he doubles also as a weapon of Apollo—a shaft—since, after all, it is the archer-god's command that Orestes follows in avenging his dead father. Fittingly, εὔσκοπος, which means "keen-sighted" and "watchful," is a Homeric epithet applied to both Artemis and Hermes. This double attribution is significant because, apart from the obvious association of archery and hunting with the twin deities of Apollo and Artemis, the vigilant watch expected of a hunter-predator is also a trait of Hermes,[4] the god who presides over the chthonic atmosphere of the *Choephoroi* with its ritual incantations and funerary devotion. As god of passage, Hermes forges a formal bridge in this middle play from the prophetic Apollo of *Agamemnon* to Apollo's reappearance along with Athena as the adjudicating powers of the *Eumenides*.

The Parodos: Beasts That Mean

Even though Apollo and Athena—two civic, rational gods—frame the plot of the *Oresteia*'s ritual and juridical resolution, the numerous beasts that feature in the trilogy honor the presence of the darker and more elusive Artemis, who equally deserves our attention. Artemis appears in the parodos of *Agamemnon*, but her name does not occur again in the trilogy; still, even as her name recedes, her symbolic efficacy remains. In the parodos, she is linked to a scene of predation, which is first interpreted as portent but is subsequently grafted onto human moral terms. Here, the seer Calchas sees Zeus's eagles attack and devour a pregnant hare, an animal sacred to Artemis.[5] The divine rivalry between Zeus and Artemis—Father Sky and his virgin daughter—is then displaced onto the unholy sacrifice of a human daughter by her father, which the offended goddess demands so that she may be propitiated.

Since I consider the omen incident to be of structuring significance for the trilogy, I will take some time to contextualize my analysis in view of John Peradotto's seminal essay on it, in which he also remarks that its critical importance can be gauged "by the fact that in most cases a critic's interpretation of this portent turns out to be a capsule-version of his total view of Aeschylean moral and religious thought" (237). Arguing against scholars who downplay Agamemnon's personal choice of sacrificing his daughter and of heading a war that will be disproportionate revenge for Paris's violation of hospitality because they see both these decisions as divine compulsions, Peradotto presents a different image of the gods. His Artemis, in particular, is less a hunting goddess and more a protectress of the young,[6] who is therefore angry both historically and proleptically at the Atreidae's aggression against them. She is angry at Atreus for having killed his brother's children, and at Agamemnon who will choose to sacrifice his daughter in order to proceed with a military campaign that will assume genocidal dimensions. Contrary to the standard interpretation, Peradotto's Artemis does not *demand* the sacrifice of Iphigenia (249), any more than his Zeus Xenios *obliges* the Greeks to avenge the violation of hospitality in such a cruel and disproportionate manner (251), as the chorus nonetheless suggests. The language of requirement is not strong enough in the play, according to Peradotto, nor does the tradition show anywhere that killing is mandated as recompense for improper conduct of guest-friends. As for the lack of winds that Artemis brings about, Peradotto interprets it as an opportunity for Agamemnon to exercise his free choice: "Artemis compels Agamemnon to nothing. She merely creates a situation in which he may either cancel the war, or else pursue it by inflicting on his own household the kind of slaughter he will perpetrate at Troy"; and "Agamemnon is *free* to sacrifice or not to sacrifice Iphigeneia, to pursue the war against Troy or not to do so" (250; original emphasis).

Although I agree that tragic heroes act of their own choice, and that a chaste goddess would be particularly angry at a father willing to kill his virgin daughter for the sake of an adulteress, I think that Peradotto overestimates the freedom allotted to the hero. In fact, I would argue that his proposal of ethos as the sole cause of agency—and thus, as counterweight to divine compulsion—works precisely to delimit these degrees of freedom. In Peradotto's argument, the lack of winds caused by Artemis lets Agamemnon show who he is: his ethos as an unscrupulous man and destroyer of the young, just like his father. But in this resemblance with Atreus, we find something key, to which Peradotto also points when he cites Aristotle's definition of ethos and its vestigial aristocracy: "The constitutive elements of ἦθος are varied, but the early aristocratic emphasis on heredity as an important (*if not its prime*) factor never quite disappears. In the *Oresteia* the idea of inherited ἦθος is a motif of major significance" (Peradotto 256; my emphasis). If we think of heredity as the inscription of nature within the human—the within that is really a *without*—then my interpretation meets Peradotto's via a different route: I show that the way in which a mortal being responds (the ethos) depends on *how* the deity shows itself to this being. In other words, the gods madden those whom they choose, and there is a correspondence between what we may call "theology" and "psychology."[7] In this case, Artemis, a par excellence nature goddess, may not have given a direct mandate one way or another, but in creating the adverse circumstances, she represents the initial constraint to which persons of the *nature* of Agamemnon could respond only within a limited range.

Peradotto's analysis emphasizes that Agamemnon *could* have escaped his predicament by responding differently to the circumstance of the weather, that there was a harmless alternative not chosen, thus evoking the metatheatrical question of evitability as tragic possibility. It is exactly with respect to encountering this question that my analysis swerves from his. In a sense, evitability is always *theoretically* possible, and Agamemnon could have done otherwise (if he were someone else, perhaps), but I rather think that tragedy unfolds as the exposition of the *actual* impossibility of escape, at least when the divine interventions of Euripides are unavailable. We could conclude that this impossibility is due to a remediable human fault—thus implying that Agamemnon's "betters" would do better, though we cannot be sure of this either—but my counterargument remains that the part of the human being that works against itself is also the same part that is distinctly bound from the beginning by the circumstance as well as by its own partially unmalleable and irremediable nature, by Aristotle's moral heredity. In this view, Ananke does not only appear retroactively as the terrible consequence of a terrible decision taken by a completely free agent, as Peradotto suggests (252); Ananke also stands as a constraint within the initial circumstance, which means that there may not be a fully harmless alternative to choose from. Peradotto adduces Heraclitus's saying that one's character (ἦθος) is one's daimon (257) to support his thesis of Agamemnon's personal choice. What I surmise from this saying, however, is something analogous to Aristotle's heredity of ethos. The daimon is this accident of nature that inhabits the human being as a certain trait—one not necessarily of the person's choosing—a trait that then marks the inception of every decision, and against which tragic freedom takes its proper meaning as a rather *narrow* exercise of choice. Agamemnon is certainly free, and yet he is only as free as those traits of the Atreidae (which he himself did not choose at birth) allow him to be.

That this natural inexorability, however, should never become an excuse for moral misdeeds is something that tragedy also imparts. In this aspect, I am completely sympathetic with what I detect to be the moral motivations behind Peradotto's reading—namely, to circumvent precisely this type of excuse not only as ethically dubious but as unfitting to tragic ennoblement.[8] The human being cannot control the circumstance, and as a result may even opt for the more terrible of the available alternatives; however, once the consequences arrive, the tragic personage gets a second chance to show his/her moral worth by way of responding to these consequences, and blaming others for one's predicament is not the way of tragedy. It is for this reason that I conclude the present study with a brief excursion into Sophocles's *Oedipus Tyrannus* because this tragedy stages paradigmatically this question of tragic (in)evitability: Oedipus made the responsible, and deeply ethical, choice to remove himself from the vicinity of his parents once he learned of the dreadful prophecy. His precautions did nothing to prevent what was in store for him. Yet, when the consequences arrived, never once did he blame anyone but himself, despite all the mitigating circumstances to which he could appeal for his innocence.

Let us now return to *Agamemnon* and to the precise words of its prologue, meant customarily to offer an explanation of the events preceding the plot, which in this case amounts to providing background on the Trojan War. Two sibling Achaean kings, Menelaus and Agamemnon, both throned and sceptered according to Zeus's will (ln. 43–45), responded to the Trojan violation of their hospitality by launching a thousand ships to retrieve the abducted wife of Menelaus, Helen. Their anger and warlike cries are likened to the screams of vultures (ln. 49; τρόπον αἰγυπιῶν)[9] who have lost their young and who circle furiously over their empty nests. Once again, the simile, this Homeric device to which Aeschylus and the other tragedians pay regular homage, is employed as *the* trope that discloses the correspondence between the human and animal worlds. That the simile is a trope about tropes—namely, about modes of being—becomes here explicit with *tropos* being used in lieu of dikē to establish the equivalency between Agamemnon's army and the predatory birds. The Trojans' conduct offended not only their mortal hosts but the gods as well, the chorus continues, describing the reach of the Achaean complaint to the divine abode in terms of avian flight: "Yet someone hears in the air, a god, / Apollo, Pan, or Zeus, the high / thin wail of these sky-guests, and drives / late to its mark / the Fury upon the transgressors" (ln. 55–59). This is the first instance of the name "Erinys" in the *Oresteia*, and the gods are said to have sent her late. With this one adjective (ὑστερόποινον), Aeschylus introduces the inevitably retroactive, always belated, temporality of justice. "Time is out of joint," another bard will say again about dealing just revenge. Even the omniscient gods miss the precise moment of the crime, delivering their justice after the fact and with all the injustices this belatedness entails. Apollo (the sun who sees all), Pan (the all-encompassing), and Zeus (the all-sovereign) are mentioned specifically by the chorus as the potential senders of the Erinys of a long-drawn war that will cost lives well beyond those immediately responsible for the offense.

Out of these three divine candidates, however, the chorus concludes that it was Zeus Xenios (ln. 60–61) who was most offended by the Trojans' dishonoring of their host, and thus released the Fury. Right before, the description of the birds/Achaeans in the simile as μέτοικοι to heaven ("sky-guests" in Lattimore, "sojourners" in Smyth's translation) reinforces the point of Zeus's justice. At this pivotal moment of the Fury's release, Aeschylus puts in the mouth of the chorus two lines that encapsulate his tragic poetics as a philosophy of being: "ἔστι δ' ὅπη νῦν / ἔστι· τελεῖται δ' ἐς τὸ πεπρωμένον" (ln. 67–68; It goes as it goes / now. The end will be destiny). Smyth translates the same lines thusly: "The case now standeth where it doth—it moveth to fulfillment at its destined end." I offer a more literal rendering: "It is the way it is / now. It will be completed in destiny." The verses resonate with the type of seriousness I discussed in the preceding chapter as they also recall the notion of completion involved in the sacred domain of both ritual and tragedy: ritual and tragedy are defined as complete acts, both moving toward a final purpose. This purpose is now revealed as πεπρωμένον, the passive participle of πόρω (to give, to furnish), from which πόρος (a way, a means of passing) also derives. In the Aeschylean tragic vision, τὸ πεπρωμένον belongs to the same class of nouns as dikē insofar as they both convey the way things are and are *already given* to us: something or someone is *by way* of dikē, at whose end lies τὸ πεπρωμένον, awaiting for its fulfillment.[10] Fast-forwarding briefly to the *Choephoroi*, Aeschylus resorts to a metallurgical image to impress the notion of Right (Dikē) being forged by Destiny (Aisa) and concluding in Vengeance (Erinys): "Δίκας δ' ἐρείδεται πυθμήν· / προχαλκεύει δ' Αἶσα φασγανουργός· / τέκνον δ' ἐπεισφέρει δόμοισιν / αἱμάτων παλαιτέρων τίνειν μύσος / χρόνῳ κλυτὰ βυσσόφρων Ἐρινύς" (ln. 646–50; Right's anvil stands staunch on the ground / and the smith, Destiny, hammers out the sword. / Delayed in glory pensive from / the murk, Vengeance brings home at last / a child, to wipe out the stain of blood shed long ago).

Back in *Agamemnon*, the chorus reiterates the link between dikē and destiny in its reflections on the aftermath of Iphigenia's death: "Δίκα δὲ τοῖς μὲν παθοῦσιν μαθεῖν / ἐπιρρέπει· / τὸ μέλλον δ', / ἐπεὶ γένοιτ'" (ln. 250–52; Justice so moves that those only learn / who suffer; and the future / you shall know when it has come).[11] The chorus here does not define justice in the usual terms of a fair resolution of a crime or dispute but as a force that compels us to learn through suffering. Such an enlarged notion of justice sounds rather troubling to anyone who instead expects a formal procedure that rewards and punishes those "just" and "unjust," respectively, according to the ever-existing norms. Though such procedures may well be part of dikē, and though some culprits may well become wiser through punishment, neither of these conditions exhausts the scope of this justice: this same justice first came to innocent Iphigenia and taught her extreme suffering at a tender age only to return as curse and destiny in the House of Agamemnon, demanding the expiation of her death through more death and, apparently, more wisdom. Thus, the chorus intimates that the legitimacy and efficacy of dikē do not derive from sociopolitical categories but from the cosmic order to which a balanced and beneficent society should try to attune its ethical norms and judicial institutions. It bears repeating what I mentioned before: dikē is not decided by mortal beings, whether individually or collectively, but conveys the rightful mode of being whose very rightfulness consists in its being sent to us from the cosmos, which is personified by Aeschylus in Zeus and the Fates.

Experientially speaking, such truth is much more easily gleaned by those familiar with the constellations and the cycles of seasons than those devising social experiments, and this is why the guard's opening words reverberate with a lofty eloquence atypical for lesser tragic personages. To live with nature's indifference to our demands and expectations, to be open to the possibility that one's harvest may be destroyed by blight, or to plan one's daily activities according to the solar clock and thus be limited by it, means to fathom a radically different way of being (and way to being) from the one that clings to the seemingly unlimited options and protections offered by immanent political institutions. Though himself employed by the machinery of state power, the palace guard at the beginning of *Agamemnon* embodies the former type of existence: he understands that justice qua dikē is first and foremost the order of things, and that according to this order, his individual dikē is to serve "doglike" his purpose, to stay steadfast at his allotted place—his jurisdiction, we might even say—and to fulfill his portion (Moira/Destiny) as his duty. Consequently, when he speaks of his doglike nature, the simile is not merely a subjective perception or a poetic contrivance. Aeschylus assigns to κυνὸς δίκην the potency of dikē, turning the simile into a constative assertion. The figure becomes literal not only because the guard presents himself physically in a four-legged position: many animals are four-legged, but the dog is chosen because of its attendant qualities that the guard also inhabits by way of another dikē, his (moral) destiny. Like the dog who has been a trusty friend to humans from early times, serving as a loyal companion to hunters in moments of danger, the guard's task is to be friend of his fellow citizens, protecting them with his vigilant gaze; and like the dog who excels in obedience, the guard must submit to his larger task—the defense of his city—even as he tacitly may record his fears and objections to the tyranny looming over this city. Discerning the position of the stars turns out to be the way to discern one's own proper way: to orient oneself, to locate one's proper place in the world. Conversely, this also means that hubris would largely consist in the swerving from that place, in the blind misrecognition (hamartia) that obstructs the appropriation of one's allotted place, which then disturbs not only one's own boundaries but the harmony of the world as well. Thus, Aeschylean tragic freedom lies not in the infinity of choices offered by existence but in the sharp discernment needed to circumscribe, appropriate (make one's own), and fulfill, to the highest degree possible, one's nature.

Having solidified the connection between dikē and destiny—namely, the manner of being that is assigned to each of us by the cosmos—I will now return to the description of the fateful portent that started the Trojan War so as to draw out further this interaction between nature and moral comportment. According to the chorus of Argive Elders, it was Zeus Xenios who drove the Achaeans to seek just revenge by sending them an auspicious sign: two eagles—symbols of Zeus's kingship in the skies—appeared before the palace, killing a pregnant hare and eating it along with its unborn. The seer Calchas interpreted the hare to be the fallen Troy and the eagles to be the victorious Achaean kings. Whereas the predatory birds in the chorus's opening simile (eagles, too, in Lattimore's translation) had lost their nestlings to another predator, those of the portent devour their prey and its young. This double figuration of the eaglet as prey and the eagle as predator exploits the naturalist aspect of hunting to showcase the inexorable change of fortune and degree of arbitrariness that pertains to human conflict and to the implementation of justice as well: Achaean and Trojan, each has occupied the position of both prey and predator at different points of their dispute. Indeed, the chorus makes this equivalency explicit in the release of the Fury, which is said to have inflicted evils on both Greeks and Trojans: "Danaans and Trojans / they have it alike" (ln. 65–66; Δαναοῖσι / Τρωσί θ' ὁμοίως).[12] To the adjective "belated," which indicated the temporal disjoining of justice from the deed, Aeschylus adds the adverb "alike" to reveal the "unjustifiable" symmetry of justice at the moment of its appearance. From a modern perspective, this looks like a strange type of justice. Even though the Trojans bear the responsibility for the offense, the Fury sent in the service of justice distributes her effects unsparingly to both sides, and while vindication eventually comes to the aggrieved, they have suffered too many collateral damages for this justice not to be deemed unjust. The equivalency between victim and culprit registers as a moral scandal to readers who are understandably horrified at seeing victims suffer further violence, and more horrified still at admitting that victims themselves can be culprits—or, at the very least, may be bound to commit unintended casualties on the way to attaining their justice. Yet Aeschylus suggests that this moral scandal is part and parcel of the arrival of justice: with the first mention of the Fury, the chorus intimates that *before* justice becomes a matter of rational adjudication, it is grounded in an instance of inscrutable necessity, chance, or even blind rage—something shown by the fact that even the most rational delivery of justice rarely occurs without a resultant injustice somewhere else, in a cosmic economy that drives the correction of one asymmetry into the propagation of another.

Mantic art is the paradoxical art of reading the unreadable: it gives nature intent and makes it signify, not only for humans but for gods as well. Thus, if the birds of prey—which as mere nature do not signify anything—are read by Calchas to be the Achaean kings, then, in turn, the offended goddess exacts for her slaughtered animal a sacrifice that is overdeterminedly meaningful since it involves a human life, that of Agamemnon's firstborn daughter. Artemis is of course the goddess of the hunt, of mountains and forest wilderness, and particularly of all young life—animal and human. Though herself fiercely chaste, she is the goddess of birth and midwifery, called on by women during labor and the birth pangs. The chorus appeals to her precisely in her capacity as motherly protectress of "ravening lions" and of "sucklings of all the savage beasts" (ln. 141–43) to fulfill the Achaean victory without the sacrifice of the human maiden, though intimating that this hope is immaterial since human meaning does not replace sacred (read also: natural) happening. In other words, the chorus's is a fragile, civilizational hope: the abolition of maiden sacrifice on the premise of Artemis's *universally* protective function of feral creatures and human children.[13] Such mortal hope, however, based solely on human logic, cannot compel a change in the workings of dikē. After all, this protectress of the forest young is also the huntress of their parents, and in her *particular* capacity as friend of wild beasts, she may well show fatal indifference to the children of reason, even though she presides over human childbirth as well.

Burkert addresses her virginal sexuality in relation to maiden sacrifice as a preparatory ritual before war, where war itself can be viewed as a symbolic extension of the hunt (61, 65). Still according to Burkert, "hunting is . . . fueled in part by the powers of aggression, which had their original function in mating fights" (59). Two aspects must be pointed out concerning this age-old link between hunting and sexuality: first, both hunting and sexuality refer back to the most elemental beginnings of humanity—namely, the survival instincts of eating and reproduction; and second and more importantly, of the two instincts, it is sexuality that, despite its ubiquity, claims an aspect of strangeness, an excessiveness that lends it a signifying capacity beyond its biological directive: "There is no social order without a sexual order; but, even so, sexuality always retains the quality of something extraordinary and strange" (58). Strangeness accounts for the liminal character of sexuality, which turns aggressive tensions into sexual enthusiasm and vice versa, blurring boundaries between violence and pleasure and thus risking the very clarity of the signifying categories it engenders, and which are also intended to delimit it. Hence, Burkert cites the contradictory yet intimate manner in which sex and aggression are shown to be connected by ethnological evidence: on the one hand, "in hunting rituals, sacrifice, warlike fighting, and even in funerary cult, there are frequent periods of license" (59), but on the other, "precisely because the act of killing is sexually charged, sexual abstinence is frequently a part of preparing for sacrifice, for war, and for the hunt" (60–61). The chaste Artemis gives form to the link between male aggression and virginal renunciation.[14] Hence, the myths abound in which the chaste goddess harshly punishes hunters either because they offend her chastity with their lust (Actaeon) or because they are boastful about their hunting skills (also Actaeon, Adonis, Broteas, Orion). Apropos, according to several myth variants, Iphigenia's sacrifice was payment for Agamemnon's conceit upon killing one of Artemis's stags, the very animal that becomes Iphigenia's sacrificial proxy in some of these variants.[15] In her virginal hunting aspect, Artemis performs an important function in the plot of the *Oresteia*, as I have noted before, even if her name does not appear central to the action. As the chorus tells us, she presides over the start of Agamemnon's campaign, and in precipitating his daughter's sacrifice, she serves as cause behind the acts of revenge that plague the

House of Agamemnon and that are themselves described in the language of the hunt. Even the location of the *Oresteia*'s conclusion on the Areopagus figures mythically the juncture between maiden sexuality and war, and eventually, the juncture between justice and war: the Areopagus, the "hill of Ares," was the tribunal where the war god was tried for murder and acquitted, having avenged the rape of his virgin daughter by a son of Poseidon (Apollodorus, *Library* 3.14.2).

Artemis is also a deity of the night. In her lunar aspect, for instance, she is akin to Hecate, a chthonic goddess of witchcraft, passageways, and liminal spaces, associated with a threefold direction and often represented as three-headed and three-bodied. Like Artemis, her sacred animal is the dog, though again, Hecate's dogs are portrayed as three-headed. The nocturnal, canine symbolic forms of Artemis correspond to two serious threats: darkness and the chase. How to hunt in conditions most adverse and foreboding? Conversely, what are the threats of being attacked when vision and visibility are limited? How to survive in inhospitable nature? These are some of the insurmountable conditions met by early humans, and the tragic genre commemorates and honors the way those humans struggled to master and even extricate themselves from this order of necessity by organizing it in structures of meaning, something Nietzsche also notes about the function of the semi-animalistic satyr in the tragic chorus.[16] Subsequently, the hunter's alertness furnished a model for both military and moral vigilance precisely because it was required of him to exercise his vision most acutely at the moment where visibility was at its lowest. The heightened vigilance of Artemis's night, attested by the secretive demeanor of Aeschylus's guard, reaches modernity intactly in the custom of naming surveillance weaponry after the goddess.[17]

In the parodos, the natural capture of prey is read first as portent, and then translated into a real war, but there is more to it: the raptors' hunt stands not only for the Achaean attack on Troy but also for a power battle within the divine family—that of Father Zeus and Daughter Artemis. In other words, it marks a split within the moral order itself at the very moment the moral order (the divine Fury) is summoned to rectify the imbalance created by Paris's violation of his host. The civil conflict between two mortal kingdoms can be communicated only through the event of another sacrifice that is intrafamilial and occurs on a simultaneously naturalistic and sacred register. To correct the injustice between two human societies, Zeus had to offend his own daughter; to reassert her divinity in her power struggle with the father of the gods, Artemis had to tear apart Agamemnon's family. The omen's symbolism shows necessity (Fate/Ananke) as the regulating principle even of the divine relations themselves: a divine hare for Helen's abduction, a mortal virgin for the hare. The human and the divine spheres interact through this common medium that is called "Fate," which, as Homer had already hinted, may rank even higher than Zeus.[18] Fate or necessity—what I also designate by "nature" or "the cosmological"—marks the plane where the *crossing* between mortals and immortals happens. This crossing signifies not only a rare overlap between these otherwise separate spheres but also the moment in which Dikē (with capital D) must inevitably *cross*—in the sense of "betray"—human understandings and expectations of justice in order to bring some justice to human beings. To repeat this idea in slightly different terms, Dikē is not exhausted by the moralism of social expectations. It belongs to a register beyond sociopolitical contracts, a register whose a priori may sometimes elide, and other times directly contravene, the ever-changing and historically contingent norms of human justification. Notably, however, though Dikē arrives from a space beyond human techne, the text permits it to be disclosed through one special type of techne: mantic art. I suggest that this is because mantic art, as I mentioned earlier, is a strange kind of art—not an artful, or "artificial," art but the art of communicating (with) nature, the art that lets nature qua necessity dictate, thus giving it due precedence.

Dikē's crossing of human expectations expresses the same necessity of which I wrote earlier, and according to which the arrival of justice signals an arbitrary equivalence between offender and offended, and even its implementation most likely concludes with a portion of injustice left as a remainder. Hence, the same seer who predicted Achaean victory over Troy understood that no aggression goes unpunished, regardless of how justified the motive behind that aggression might appear to human reasoning. The story of the Trojan War indeed shows that the victory of the wronged party could come only at an almost equal cost to the defeat of the perpetrator. As one force of nature wages itself against another, the playfield is human destiny. In a triple incantation combining prophetic hope with lament, the chorus records this ambivalence that accompanies the emergence of justice as well as the meanings that this concept gradually accrues: "Sing sorrow sorrow: but good win out in the end" (ln. 121, 139, 159). In its first instance, this refrain concludes the description of the eagles devouring the hare. It then follows the seer's interpretation of this attack as signaling both Zeus's call to war and Artemis's wrath at what she perceives as the hare's sacrifice (ln. 137; θυομένοισιν); here, Calchas's Artemis invests moral meaning in what would otherwise be a natural act of predation. Lastly, the refrain seals the story of Calchas's plea to Artemis to send winds for the Greek fleet without exacting payment through another "unlawful" and "untasted" sacrifice (ln. 151; θυσίαν ἑτέραν ἄνομόν τιν', ἄδαιτον)—namely, without the need for an immoral (because cannibalistic) feast that would be Iphigenia's slaughter.

What do, then, such conflicting divine demands and such ambivalent translations from animal meals to vengeful signs reveal? They reveal overall that when the law of nature (one animal falling prey to another) is transposed to the human domain, it means something different—precisely *in that it means at all*, and in that the human is the *animal* of meaning production. We can thus apply Nietzsche's remarks about the liminal hybridity of the satyr to tragedy as a whole: tragedy as a genre performs the satyr's figuration of the passage from mere animal to the signifying human being who remembers nature at the very moment of attempting to overcome it, and who, at times, even mourns the distance produced by that overcoming. Tragedy shows the investment of nature with meaning by also conceding that such an investment must occur without the neutralization of nature, for even our capacity for meaning production and our impulse to transcend nature are themselves not outside but within nature's matrix. Thus, even though we are by now more convention than nature, more desire than need, we cannot simply erase those beginnings, a point that becomes later solidified in the subterranean but continuous existence of the Furies as Eumenides.

The moral order must remember its origins in nature's indifference not least because in this indifference to cultural markers of status and identity, nature's dikē offers unexpectedly a prototype for the rational justice of *isonomia*—namely, of equality before the law regardless of status. The emphasis here is on "prototype" as originary but not complete template. I do not suggest that cosmic dikē amounts to a transparent paradigm or blueprint for conventional law, nor conversely do I neglect that socioeconomic status can work to mitigate or exaggerate the effects even of natural disasters on human beings: for instance, economic prosperity can shield certain populations from the damages of the earthquakes and hurricanes that more significantly impact the poor. The point, however, still holds that nature's way—indomitable despite efforts at technological domination—reveals itself as a profound indifference and arbitrariness, as a strange kind of unintended impartiality that can both instruct human conventions and expose their limits, particularly when these conventions, in their zealous moralism, violate the very principles of equality and universality they themselves seemed to initially seek.[19] I submit that in Aeschylus, who was obviously reflecting on Athens's legal advances at the time, this aspect of cosmic neutrality is shown to inform quite richly the concept of equality before the law. Without the seminal contribution of cosmic dikē, without the disclosure of nature's *way*, it is not guaranteed that justice as pure rationalization and institutional artifice will be any juster than nature's fierce but neutral and equalizing necessity.

It is this intricate juncture between the cosmic and the human, between the arbitrary necessity of nature and the dangerous ambivalence of meaning production, that the story of Calchas's portent thematizes: Artemis's divine revenge on her divine father consists in taunting the humans to behave animalistically. To revenge the violation of hospitality and thus uphold lawful custom, the kings must commit savagery and sacrifice their own child. In doing so, they return to the cannibalistic practices of the early hunters, practices that another myth of the Atreidae cycle directly commemorates—namely, the cannibalistic meal Atreus prepared for his brother Thyestes.[20] Given that in human societies cannibalism constitutes the taboo within eating, and incest the taboo within sexuality, Aeschylus exploits this double prohibition to overdetermine Clytemnestra's revenge. While her illicit relationship with Aegisthus may compromise her claim against Agamemnon, her choice of this particular lover—incidentally himself a meek character in the play—could instead be construed to strengthen the legitimacy of her claim for the following reason: Aegisthus, Agamemnon's first cousin, is also the surviving son of Thyestes with his own daughter Pelopia, the son not eaten by his father. In presenting Aegisthus openly as her lover and co-regent, Clytemnestra not only matches Agamemnon's parading of Cassandra as his concubine but, most importantly, confronts Agamemnon with the "cannibalism" he perpetrated against their daughter as part of his familial history of abomination.

Since this cannibalistic myth is not treated explicitly in the prologue, however, I will conclude my discussion of the chorus by returning to the implications of the power battle between Zeus and Artemis that frames the *Oresteia*'s blood feud: if Zeus sacrificed his daughter's totemic animal at the altar of human indiscretion, as a sign to awaken just retribution against Paris's misdeed, Artemis in turn demands a human sacrifice to the altar of wild nature, for human hubris offends not only other humans and Zeus's high principles but wild nature as well. In requiring Iphigenia's sacrifice, Artemis does not simply revenge the death of the hare, but symbolically anticipates the payment of the Greeks for what happens to Troy: the collateral damage of innocents and the desecration of Troy's nature are themselves unjust results of a just war, and they cannot go unpunished. (This moral aspect of Artemis is central to Peradotto's analysis as well.) In the mortal sphere, Clytemnestra will claim her justice by trapping her victim, but being herself tainted, she too will die trapped by her son. In turn, though the son commits matricide following divine command, he will be hounded by the agents of retaliation. The quest for justice, often undertaken with excessive zeal and purposeful determination, develops indeed as a hunting pursuit. Filled with peril, darkness, and extreme vigilance, Artemis's night dissolves into next day's vigilantism, which in this play belongs to Clytemnestra's dikē.

Clytemnestra's Sea, Clytemnestra's Fire

Just as Iphigenia's sacrifice served as preliminary to the Trojan War, so it prepares the domestic war in this play—the mother's revenge, which Aeschylus describes through tropes of hunting, sacrifice, and excessive sexuality: Clytemnestra the spider who seductively attracts and catches her prey, the unsuspecting husband and king. Cassandra's vision, for instance, mentions deathly nets (ln. 1115), while the chorus's lamentation for the slain king twice describes his corpse identically as being caught in a spiderweb (ln. 1492, 1516). In the *Choephoroi*, Orestes will use the hunting verb (ln. 493; ἐθηρεύθης) for the capture of his father as animal prey. Back to *Agamemnon*, and in keeping with the notion of the bestiary, Cassandra also foretells Agamemnon's death as the death of a bull through deceit of its mate (ln. 1125–26). Because the bull stood for virility and kingliness—Zeus transforms into a bull—it was one of the most majestic but gruesome victims of sacrifice.[21] The slain bull/Agamemnon/Zeus stands opposite the slain hare/Iphigenia as the sacrifice *of* and *to* Artemis instigated by the father's aggression. The Buphonia, a particularly grotesque ox sacrifice, was dedicated to "Zeus of the City," as Burkert describes (136), and this detail should highlight the contrast between the kingly aspect of Zeus/Agamemnon, for whom justice is a *political* problem of Achaeans and Trojans, and wild nature as the precinct of Artemis, where dikē's arbitrariness reveals justice as an extrapolitical necessity. As spider, Clytemnestra succeeds at the "manly" deed of regicide by lending this act a domestic and feminine guise through the metaphor of weaving. This web metaphor imports unexpectedly the image of Athena Ergane (the weaver), but in a way that distorts the domestic, virginal aspect of the goddess for whom Athenian maidens wove the peplos of the Panathenaea procession.[22] Aeschylus is proposing a partial reversal of another famous weaver of ancient Greek poetry: Penelope. If Homer's shrewd Penelope actually used her loom to delay the suitors while waiting for her husband's return, Aeschylus's equally shrewd Clytemnestra excels metaphorically in weaving a plot to entrap and destroy her spouse for his deeds. The former wife shows weaving as a civilized, domesticated endeavor; the latter exposes it as a mode of predation, as nature.

Nonetheless, Clytemnestra is much more than the feminine cliché of the deceitful seductress. Like the guard who intuits truths well above his station in the opening scene of *Agamemnon*, she is a woman who knows something profound about cosmic dikē. In her famous speech in which she taunts Agamemnon to walk on a red carpet for his victory—a redness that condenses pride, opulence, passion, rage, and blood all at once—she must first disabuse him of his scruples about behaving hubristically, and about wasting the kingdom's riches, those purple-red textiles dyed in a precious substance from sea snails (ln. 957; πορφύρας). Before considering her speech, and in light of our focus on dikē, it is worth reviewing Agamemnon's own use of dikē during his short-lived defense of the value of self-restraint.

Like the guard again, Agamemnon uses dikē in place of the "as/like" of a simile, albeit now of a negative simile meant to convey his rejection of a mode of being that is foreign to the Greek sensibility. He rejects being "like some barbarian" (ln. 919; μηδὲ βαρβάρου φωτὸς δίκην)[23] who would indulge in pride and ostentation—values that the Greek king considers unseemly and overweening for mortals, though they were habitual in Priam's court. Historically and sociologically speaking, Agamemnon's distinctions can be understood and critiqued as cultural assumptions and prejudices that are and should be completely mutable in their constructedness. At the same time, it is crucial to underscore the *how*—namely, the *mode*—through which the ancient king relates to his own being (and to what he does not wish to be) as something *connatural* and *rightful* to him, where "rightful" is precisely the meaning of dikē: the appropriate way, one's *phusis*. Of course, the fact that he is easily convinced by Clytemnestra's speech to change his ways supports the culturalist argument that reduces all ontological and cultural difference to matters of social prejudice and mutable power relations. However, this type of critique must either eschew the plot's fatal next turn, or relegate it as well to Aeschylus's own sociocultural blind spots: Agamemnon's swerving from his Argive/Greek nature seals his death sentence, which the poet emphasizes by using the same word (ὑφάς/ὑφάσματι) both for the luxurious tapestries of his hubris and for Clytemnestra's trap, her spiderweb, that catches him (ln. 949, 1492, 1516). Aeschylus advances an ontological argument that is admittedly challenging to—if not irreconcilable with—exclusively constructivist interpretations, but that might prove all the more intriguing because of this irreconcilability: the moment that Agamemnon forgets his nature and his place in the order of things is the moment that necessity qua cosmic dikē takes over, using Clytemnestra as its vehicle, its Fury.[24]

Let us now move to Clytemnestra's speech and her dismissal of Agamemnon's hesitation about squandering wealth: "ἔστιν θάλασσα, τίς δέ νιν κατασβέσει; / τρέφουσα πολλῆς πορφύρας ἰσάργυρον / κηκῖδα παγκαίνιστον, εἱμάτων βαφάς. / οἶκος δ᾽ ὑπάρχει τῶνδε σὺν θεοῖς ἅλις / ἔχειν" (ln. 958–62; The sea is there, and who shall drain its yield? It breeds / precious as silver, ever of itself renewed, / the purple ooze wherein our garments shall be dipped. And by gods' grace this house keeps / full sufficiency / of all).[25] Even though such response aims chiefly at luring Agamemnon to a mortal fault, its imagery and tone disclose a vision of nature that will become all the more meaningful in light of Clytemnestra's impending act. Her statement expresses the inexhaustibility of nature's abundance, the generosity with which it gives, and in front of which human demands pale, thus dispelling Agamemnon's fear of scarcity. Seen from the secular-technic perspective of contemporary environmentalist, climate, and sustainability discourses, such view sounds ignorant at best, irresponsible at worst. Nevertheless, this is not Clytemnestra's frame of mind: her statement is cosmological, rather than environmental or ecological. She is not concerned with technologies of resource distribution or government policies that secure equitable access to these resources, legitimate as these issues are on their own. By praising the sea's inexhaustibility and eternal self-renewal, she points to another, truly perilous economy of abundance: the sea's formidable capacity not only to provide for but also to destroy everything while it itself remains indifferent and in remove from human control.

This perilous possibility is somewhat lost in translation, which does not render fully the catachrestic verb with which Aeschylus confirms—via a rhetorical question—the inability of any human agent to exhaust the sea. Whereas both Lattimore and Smyth speak of "draining" the sea, a verb appropriate to liquids, Aeschylus's κατασβέσει refers to extinguishing (quenching, putting out) fire.[26] This makes perfect sense in relation to the ensuing metaphor of the self-renewed sea as κηκῖδα, a word otherwise used for the gushing forth of juices in a sacrificial fire (as in *Choephoroi* ln. 268, and Sophocles's *Antigone* ln. 1008), or the bubbling blood of murder (as in *Choephoroi* ln. 1012). Destructive fire and generous water fuse into one another, while human agency recedes at the very moment that Clytemnestra prepares to commit the "grave act." The sacrificial subtext is made manifest after Agamemnon's death in Clytemnestra's announcement that she was not really his wife but an alastor in spousal guise, an ancient spirit of revenge sent to settle payment. For the young deaths of the past, that of Iphigenia *and* of Thyestes's children, she came to sacrifice (ἐπιθύσας) the adult but also the perfect and complete (τέλεον) victim (ln. 1497–1504).[27] The language of τέλεον, linking the fulfillment of time with the perfect ritual offering, confirms Clytemnestra's act to be sacrificial, while also recalling the sacrificial logic of Aristotle's theory of tragedy as a complete act (τελεία). Much like the dikē of the constellations and of the repetitive cycles of seasons to which the guard paid heed, the sea's inexhaustible flow provides the authority behind Clytemnestra's dikē: she is the Fury, for whom there will always be enough blood for blood previously shed,[28] always enough fire to expiate past crime, just as there is infinite seawater to yield royal purple. Clytemnestra's sea is hot red fire or, to think of Homer's colors, "wine-dark" like the bath she prepares for Agamemnon.

Such destructive abundance is aptly illustrated in her punishment of Cassandra as well, the young girl Agamemnon brings as slave-concubine from Troy, and whom he demands arrogantly be given a proper welcome by his wife.[29] Early in this chapter, I mentioned that along with the guard, Cassandra too is called "doglike." Whereas his animality was shown in his crawling posture, hers is shown through a kind of vigilance particular to hunting dogs: the smelling instinct of the bloodhound in pursuit. Priestess and prophetess of Apollo, she appears in a half-crazed state, smelling the trails of blood that flow from Agamemnon's house and foretelling the impending deaths of Agamemnon and herself as well as the revenge that will follow. The scene of her ravings offers a perfect dramatization of the summoning of the Fury as cosmic cry, which I related through a passage from Walter Otto in the previous chapter: gripped by her suffering, Cassandra releases the palace curse, the memory of past murders and cannibalistic banquets, and raises the Fury of future revenge. In this world of the Fury, however, the innocents are never innocent enough, and vigilance to every slight soon turns to vigilantism. Hence, she too—though unwilling companion and victim of Agamemnon—has by virtue of her circumstance alone a share in offending Clytemnestra. While this runs counter to our normative concept of justice, it remains a fact of life that Cassandra's mere presence, let alone her prophetic audacity, is an affront to Clytemnestra, who, despite having been unfaithful to her husband and despotic to her subjects, nonetheless claims the authority of her daughter's blood. Let us recall that the arrival of cosmic dikē often entails strange equivalencies between victims and culprits from which the modern reader recoils, assessing them to be inadmissible to the thinking of justice precisely because such thinking now limits justice to the deliberative and immanent horizon of politics.

Whose dikē is more just? Who is caught unawares in Artemis's night? If Iphigenia was killed by her own father for no fault of her own, why should a foreign concubine before whom Agamemnon humiliates his lawful wife, and whose prophecies wreak havoc on the household, receive a better treatment? Apollo, Cassandra's god who abandons her, is an archer like his twin sister, a hunter of sorts, and as this play's cause is the death of an innocent virgin to the hunting goddess, so it ends with two deaths in repayment: one of the unscrupulous father, the other of an equally innocent girl who came to substitute both daughter and wife at once, and thus *by necessity*—which really means *by chance*—became culpable. To repeat, this sort of moral judgment that relies even remotely on fortune and chance is considered illegitimate by the modern view of justice. According to modern ethics and legal thought, this type of necessity is something quite "unnecessary" outside of its politically sinister function of denying justice to some while ensuring it for others. It is, in other words, merely a mythological construct invented to cement existing power relations, and thus it can be profitably eradicated by technical improvements in the judicial process.

I contend, however, that Aeschylean tragedy not only shows the insufficiency of human craft to outweigh necessity but anticipates the unexpected ways in which the structure of necessity betrays, or crosses, the human project: ironically, necessity manifests itself all the more arbitrarily in the legal efforts to circumvent it than it does when it happens as unpredictable and indifferent nature. A brief glance at our cultural efforts to eliminate chance from moral considerations by overdetermining social structure might be helpful. As I suggested above, precisely because she is an enslaved foreigner and war victim, Cassandra elicits overdeterminedly our modern sympathy,[30] and the added fact that she has no say in her fate, just like Iphigenia, whom she doubles, makes her culpability-by-circumstance all the more unacceptable to us. Yet, could not the counterargument be made that many a social justice claim relies heavily on the logic of chance and arbitrariness that our culture elsewhere disavows—namely, that one must still account for an accident of birth, particularly if born into a group deemed oppressive by the social consensus? Is not the notion of historical privilege (regardless of one's actual privilege in life) for which one must be made responsible/guilty the mirror image of the tragic responsibility toward a genealogical curse (regardless of one's actual participation in the original crime)? My point here is not to argue the details of the legitimacy of specific social justice causes, nor the reasons why each of them in its particularity may merit a thorough and thoughtful consideration. My point is to alert us to the *general* principle behind an ideology of anti-individual, *systemic* justice that tacitly relies on this concept of necessity, of culpability-by-chance, but whose very structural *arbitrariness* the same culture otherwise claims to demythologize.

Nevertheless, there is a difference between the modern and the tragic representations of this arbitrariness that should not go unnoticed since it reflects two divergent conceptions of being and of being responsible in the world, thus cultivating two divergent ethical stances. In the modern context, it is ironically the meticulous construction of social categories that exposes the individual to arbitrariness. Having rationalized all chance to be a product of social determination—that is, having reduced existence to a set of *technical* criteria for social membership—current politics treats individuals abstractly and arbitrarily: not as persons, but rather as automatic effects of the symbolic position to which they have been assigned along a spectrum of power relations, ranging from the privileged to the marginalized. By contrast, tragedy insists on arbitrariness via reference to the inexorable arrival of cosmic dikē, which proves more impartial in that it can befall equally unpredictably any mortal being. If anything, it remains tragedy's special prerogative to highlight the evils that visit particularly the privileged ones. The former stance aspires to a social idealism propped on an individual ethics of victimhood that explains virtually all personal, and even accidental, faults as effects of social structures. The latter's naturalism is certainly harsher, cultivating what I previously described as the stoic realism of the tragic hero, who also engages in an idealist struggle against necessity, but who grasps that reality is not *necessarily* fair. Another expression for this naturalism is Nietzsche's amor fati, which directs one toward affirming the world as it is rather than wishing it to be otherwise.

Along with the issue of dikē's challenge to human justice, this play, as well as the trilogy overall, rehearses a set of questions about the implications of vigilance. For instance, what kinds of vigilance do not eventually intend, or at the very least risk, the act of vigilantism? Whose vigilance strikes the right measure of alertness without turning into paranoia and derailing into full-scale bloodshed? The guard kept watch to protect his city, though his efforts proved inadequate to preventing the war from within. Clytemnestra, the vigilant queen, ordered the lighting of fires that relayed messages from the front so as to be ready for her husband's return; her revenge plot succeeded, but only temporarily. Cassandra, alert to the curse and reveling at the smell of revenge, fell victim to them both. Agamemnon, having trapped his daughter with marriage promises,[31] treated her as quarry for the purpose of his war but received the same treatment by his wife, who caught him unawares, and exalted in delivering poetic justice upon his corpse (ln. 1521-29).

Burkert argued that vigilance and its attendant traits of discipline and patience, which were once required of the hunter, formed the cornerstones on which any civilized society would be later built. Waiting for the right moment to catch the prey, under threat of starvation and animal attack, sometimes already hungry and exhausted, the ancient hunter learned the skills of restraint and endurance, and thus became a prototype of the perseverance necessary to complete any long-term project, and of the readiness to respond to emergencies. The exposure to *immediate* risk, and the simultaneous *necessity* to struggle against that risk for one's survival, contributed to the seriousness that natural existence taught to human beings. Thus, vigilance has been imprinted from early on as a moral virtue, and though modernity brackets off the naturalist underpinnings of culture, vigilance remains such a virtue, as evidenced again by the hyperawareness pervading the discourse of social justice and by the proliferation of watchdog organizations surveying all sorts of activity, from human rights violations in select countries (usually a left-leaning cause) to cultural controversies in the US academy (usually a right-leaning cause). More interestingly, while vigilance is praised as a virtue,[32] vigilantism induces horror, at least as far as mainstream legal rhetoric and official cultural feelings go.[33] The assumption seems to be that vigilance strengthens social cohesion while vigilantism threatens it; hence the former can be endorsed but the latter refuted.

However, at the very least, the identical Latin root of these two words referring to vision and wakefulness should confirm that they are strongly linked. Interestingly, in the original Greek of the *Oresteia*, there is no overt lexical connection between the corresponding terms, which sometimes are rendered periphrastically. For instance, the etymology of φύλαξ (the guard) is unknown, but his vigilance is described through his state of fearful sleeplessness (ln. 14).[34] Furthermore, there is not one fixed term that denotes the vigilante but several, some of which refer to the divine powers of revenge, such as the Erinys, while others narrate the acts of the feud. One of these terms, "alastor," a revenge daimon Clytemnestra claims to embody (ln. 1501), does potentially bear an etymological connection to watchful vision: a derivation suggests *lan*/λάω (to look) as its root, akin to Sanskrit *lasati* (to shine, to appear in full strength).[35] For the most part, however, tragic heroes who resort to vigilantism are said variously to have committed "the act," or to have taken justice into "their hands."[36] Clytemnestra and the chorus, for instance, use the vocabulary of "act" and "hand," respectively, to describe her revenge: "οὕτω δ' ἔπραξα" (ln. 1379–80; Thus have I done the deed), and "δολίῳ μόρῳ δαμεὶς δάμαρτος / ἐκ χερὸς ἀμφιτόμῳ βελέμνῳ" (ln. 1495–96; struck down in treacherous death wrought / by a weapon of double edge wielded by the hand of your own wife!). Nevertheless, even though there is no overt etymological continuity in Greek, as there is in Latin, between the wakefulness of the vigilant and the self-enforced justice of the vigilante, there is instead a sensory continuity from the sleepless eyes required of the former to the murderous hand that drives the latter. This physical sequence stretches back to one of the earliest anthropological scenes where it was exemplified in the eyes and hands of one and the same figure: the hunter.

Of course, the *Oresteia* has been read as a work that thematizes the end of vigilantism and the successful passage from the violence of the hunt to the peace of civil society; this is mainly why the trilogy forms such a seminal contribution to the thinking of justice and the law. Such progressive reading is well within the horizon of the *Oresteia*, however always and only with the qualification that the linearity of this "progress" cannot be guaranteed infinitely or uninterruptedly even after the *divine* establishment of the court by Athena. In fact, from the vantage point of recent history, it could be argued that precisely because the secular court has long shed the memory of its sacred origin and legitimacy, and relies now solely on the technical and fragmentary character of conventional statutes, the aperture for instant grievances and for the return of various kinds of Erinyes has gradually grown wider.[37] The *Oresteia*'s conclusion may civilize Artemis's wild forest, but it does not and cannot eradicate it. The universality of Aeschylus, which still reaches us today, rests nonetheless partly on the specificity of his religious and political landscape. What I mean by this is that the translated Erinyes *remain* Eumenides under the *Athenian* acropolis: they do not only sustain this polis as its new goddesses of civic prosperity, but they are also assisted by that same polis—because of the kind of polis that it is—to continue being so and not to revert to their previous status. There is, however, the alternative scenario that these deities may not have performed as promisingly under a different burial ground where the political claims from the city above would taunt and encourage their reversion. A foundation can only do so much below if winds from above threaten the edifice. It is not only Athens that needs the Eumenides; the Eumenides also need Athens. And when Athens soon failed its grounding—that is, when Athens in its pride forgot its allotted place on the Greek map, or metaphorically speaking, in the harmonic constellation of city-states—the Erinyes did return.

How Now? Kafka's Dog

Franz Kafka's famously pessimistic vision of justice in *The Trial* contains a revealing image: after many forays to the court and meetings with wayward characters,[38] searching in vain to reach an actual judge, Joseph K. comes across a painting that is an allegory of justice.[39] Yet the unusual wings at the figure's feet suggest justice to be fleeting and unstable, and K. wonders how a running justice could be trustworthy. The court painter clarifies that, in fact, it is a portrait of Victory and Justice combined in one. Normally, the idea of victorious justice would garner general approval, but the text suggests otherwise. "That is not a good combination," counters K., who is unsettled by this mixed allegory, which could imply that Might is Right. Therefore, he reinterprets the painting as depicting "a goddess of the Hunt in full cry" (147). K. makes this critical remark because he assumes that justice and the hunt are, or at least should be, mutually exclusive, even though the entire novel thematizes his vulnerability under this *unnamed* and *infinite* law's constant surveillance and his own zealous pursuit of the court. Nevertheless, the novel's strange ending tends to vindicate the painter's seemingly incongruent representation. Incessant vigilance and relentless chase after even imaginary slights and inexistent culprits (as seems to be the case against K.) are not misapplications of justice but the grounding impetus of its very ideality. In effect, it is not a law that hounds K.; it is justice—or more likely, his own wise but "unconscious" internalization of justice—as a predatory, life-denying infinity. Militancy of commitment, unwavering memory, and constant readiness to hunt down something or someone: these are the predatory traits, though not always explicitly acknowledged as such, that distinguish justice as a virtue of the "uncompromising" ones, of those who aspire to a virginal, Artemis-like purity to which K.'s comment unwittingly alludes.[40]

The Trial closes with K.'s last words during his execution, which takes place at the end of an exhausting, meaningless, and shameful process, and which is carried out clandestinely, more like a murder than a lawful operation. "Like a dog," he mutters to himself: from the noble vigil of the guard and the justice-seeking bloodhounds of the *Oresteia* to the degrading death of Joseph K., this simile appears to bookend the literary imagination of justice and the law. Perhaps *The Trial* can even be read as a modern retelling of the *Oresteia*, moving, however, in the opposite direction. Whereas the Aeschylean court managed to suspend, if not transcend, the terror of the bloodhounds and spare the matricide Orestes, Kafka's inscrutable legal machinery executed K. for a crime that neither the accused nor the readers are ever made aware of. In another reversal, the dog, once a fearsome predator, becomes in K.'s demise a wretched prey, the animal whose proverbial disposability now symbolizes a human life so unworthy as not to deserve even a good death. While brilliantly reciting moral and theological topoi, Kafka's story also points to a terrifying political vision that lies at the other end of the *Oresteia*: the implied morality of structural guilt with no concrete crime behind it—a morality hitherto described theologically as "original sin," and now exemplified in the nominally secular but actually religious discourse of social justice—is the dialectical underside of a polis where everyone is guilty who is not presumed innocent.

Kafka's reflections on law and justice traverse the entirety of his corpus and have rightly prompted a lengthy commentary that, however, extends beyond my present scope. For the purposes of my study, I will tentatively suggest that what separates, but also unites by contradistinction, Aeschylus's and Kafka's conceptions of justice is the role nature had for the cultures each author represented. Revealed in Aeschylus as portent, nature ascends for the ancients to a "language"—that of myth—whose initial violence transforms into, but never disappears from, the institution of the court of jury, which now attends to the individual case and is capable of leniency. By Kafka's time, nature and the language of myth have been maligned as violent deceptions with no other interpretative filter available to disclose their alternative possibilities. Disparaged for its indifference to human purposes, modern nature emerges as a hurdle not only to the morality of revealed religion, which is understandable, but, most tellingly, to the religion of secularism, which sometimes cites natural necessity in order to justify its social campaigns but mostly suspects nature whenever its facts threaten the dream of social immanentism. Indeed, while secular culture periodically appeals to nature, it does so only expediently and selectively in order to serve the infinite extension of "human rights," vilifying nature all the same when its necessities contradict the assumptions behind such rights. The thorough shift from the language of natural rights (negative rights) to that of human rights (positive rights) in legal discourse is the most obvious sign of this worldview. Nature, in other words, is disposable in itself, but manipulable for us according to its usefulness for our sociality. It is no longer a prescriptor of the limits and possibilities of the human being and its polis, as it was for Aeschylus, and consequently, human justice does not supplement but replaces dikē. Yet by abandoning this cosmological dimension of dikē, modern justice becomes totalitarian in its infinitization.

This last point is the reason why the militancy of modern social justice, though seemingly akin to tragic-heroic seriousness, resembles it only superficially: insofar as it relies on human techne alone, without reference to dikē's uncontrollable dimension, this type of justice compromises its claim to seriousness because genuine seriousness appears in the choice one makes when all techne fails. Put differently, the ideality of justice as a project of social perfectibility by definition excludes the ethical posture of amor fati, whose seriousness consists in courageously affirming existence not only despite but also *in* its afflictions. Investing great confidence in human artifice, the project of social justice thus appears increasingly at odds with tragic seriousness. The latter requires that human beings and, by extension, their political and cultural forms allow for an understanding of reality as chance and constraint; or, to put it in the Nietzschean formula that best captures tragic seriousness as an effect of nature, they must allow for the fact that "all that exists is just and unjust and equally justified in both" (72).

Unwittingly, when nature becomes disposable, and thus unworthy of our imparting meaning to it as myth once did, it marks all the more our institutions with its primal violence, as is shown in Kafka's regressive signifying chain that leads from the court to absent judges to an inexistent justice that is simply the stuff of legend to the hunt and to K.'s animal-like death. The doglike guard of Aeschylus was afforded an unusual nobility because he was a student of the constellations, but there are no constellations to behold in the crammed tenements of Kafka's court, and most of all, there is no equivalent language to do what mantic art did, and which might well be the quintessential human activity: bestowing meaning even there where it may not exist.

Chapter 4

Hermes of the Axis Mundi

Gē and Dikē in the *Choephoroi*

By the sacred earth on which I kneel, by the shades that wander near me, by the deep and eternal grief that I feel, I swear; and by thee, O Night, and the spirits that preside over thee, to pursue the daemon, who caused this misery, until he or I shall perish in mortal conflict. For this purpose I will preserve my life: to execute this dear revenge will I again behold the sun, and read the green herbage of earth, which otherwise should vanish from my eyes forever. And I call on you, spirits of the dead, to aid and conduct me in my work.

—Mary Shelley, *Frankenstein*

Argos as Cosmos: Fathers, Hunters, Heroes, Ancestors

Whereas mantic art served as the language of nature in *Agamemnon*, prayer and dream-interpretation do so in the *Choephoroi*; whereas Artemis's sacrificial demands caused the revenge plot of the former play, another liminal deity—Hermes—officiates at the chthonic rites of the latter. In this chapter, I elaborate on the cosmology underpinning the cult of the dead. This cosmology also grounds the profound relation of chthonic justice to war, hate, and the capacity for generation as they obtain particularly in the play's first half. I also attend to the references to animals and entrapment that continue to frame the notion of just revenge through the vocabulary of hunting.

Spoken by a returning Orestes, the first words of the *Choephoroi* appeal to chthonic Hermes and set its funereal and incantatory tone against the background of a father's (and a hero's) cult. Translator Smyth notes that Hermes is invoked in his capacities as "conductor of souls" and "herald between the celestial and infernal gods" who mediates between Orestes and the spirit of his slain father (158–59). Apollo will explicitly define him as such (πομπαῖος) in the *Eumenides*, sending him as a "shepherd" to guide the wanderings of the hunted Orestes (ln. 90–92). Hermes Chthonios travels along the axis mundi from the heavenly Fates residing near his own father, Zeus, to the underworld Furies chasing after bloodstained mortals. Electra's prayer to him draws this itinerary explicitly—"κῆρυξ μέγιστε τῶν ἄνω τε καὶ κάτω" (ln. 124; Almighty herald of the world above, the world / below)—but we will return to this passage later for its insights on vigilance and its linking of earth and justice. At the moment, the focus will be on Hermes and the cosmological elements his myth evokes in the setting of Argos.

To his role of messenger, or angel, between the upper and lower worlds, which in this play also demonstrates once again that dikē is a message *sent* rather than only sociopolitically produced, it is crucial to add another of Hermes's functions. He is, as Walter Burkert points out, a divine exception—the first homicide among the gods, a criminal who is eventually acquitted and whose crime forms the template for sacrificial killing according to the *Homeric Hymn* dedicated to him (Burkert 165). Hence, he is a god whose transgression teaches humankind the ways of atonement. Not only does his exoneration anticipate Orestes's own, but his victim—the guard Argos—by lending his name to Orestes's native city, manifests an ancient bond between the polis as a legal entity and the earth's chthonic aspect, thus also anticipating the necessity of the Eumenides' continuous tenancy underneath Athens. Two separate but interrelated sets of remarks by Burkert illuminate this relationship between chthonic earth and the polis. The first, more specific in its scope, addresses the symbolic implications of the shared name between Argos the guard and Argos the city in myth; the second involves his more general, historical observation about the paramount importance of religion qua tradition for the survival and continuity of a culture. Both of them hinge on the constitutive priority of the chthonic over the political, and, in parallel, of religion and family over civic life. To draw out more fully the theoretical corollaries of these remarks, however, we must briefly familiarize ourselves with the mythic and cultic details Burkert engages, particularly around the semantics of Argos.

Among several end-of-the-year rituals, which Burkert calls "rituals of dissolution," he discusses a Buphonia rite at the city of Argos, the aition of which he finds in the myth of Hermes Argeiophontes, also called ox-slayer (βουφόνος) in the *Homeric Hymn* to him (Burkert 166). Ox-slaying falls under such end-of-the-year rituals, and at Argos, the cult of Hermes would prepare for the new-year festival honoring Hera, the cow-eyed goddess behind Hermes's murder of Argos who guarded the cow/Io, Hera's mortal rival and double. Burkert cites evidence that identifies Argos the cowherd with a bull: having killed a bull that ravaged the area, Argos wore the bull skin—a hunting motif in which the hunter becomes his victim by putting on its hide (166). In the dissolution ritual, the slaying of the ox/cowherd marks the year's end as well as a new beginning with the release of the cattle that now, unguarded, can roam free, only to be caught for next year's hecatombs to Hera, thus encompassing a seasonal cycle of release and return to death (166–67). Hermes stands trial for his deed but is acquitted at the end of a narrative that unfolds from a hunted animal (the bull killed by Argos) to a sacrificial victim (Argos-as-bull killed by the god) to a tribunal, where the first murderer is a hunter/sacrificer while his victim is precisely what this word originally meant: sacrificial quarry.[1] The myth works to conjoin three distinct spaces—the open pastures, the altar, and the court—and just as the altar is located between wild nature and civic institution, so Burkert discerns a parallel intermediary figure who condenses the mythic roles of slayer (Hermes) and victim (Argos), of hunter and guard, in the civic function of military defense. This is the figure of the warrior-hero, and it features in the adjacent ritual of the Argive ephebes who carry a shield made of oxhide during the Heraia. In the tradition of the hunter Argos, who became the slain bull/cowherd, the Argive youth will become the city's guardians, keeping continuous vigil over it even after their death.

We should recall that Agamemnon, to whose grave Orestes pays homage, and whose posthumous protection Electra also seeks, was such a "bull" killed by its "cow," in Cassandra's prophecy (*Ag.* ln. 1125–26). The city's identity proceeds from these heroes whose memory was lavishly honored in funeral cults. The hero as a dead man—namely, as *ancestor* and protector—bestows coherence, consistency, and continuity to the city, and it is in this context that we may later gauge Apollo's strange, and otherwise objectionable, argument in the *Eumenides*, which assigns parentage only to the father. To this effect, it will also be important to keep in mind the ancients' polar view of sexuality that, on the one hand, suppressed the feminine but, on the other, allowed for unexpected reversals and compensatory relations between rival sexual attributes. (Another phrasing of this would be that their worldview relied on *sexual difference*, acknowledging the ways nature informs and interacts with culture, rather than on *gender identity*, which, in obviating nature as deterministic, replaces it with its own form of determinism—an infinitely unrestrained self-determination that demands its subjective categories be granted objective metaphysical validity.) Thus, Hera/cow/Clytemnestra/mother kills Argos/bull/Agamemnon/hero at the same time as the very word "hero," deriving from *hora* (hour), refers him back to Hera as goddess of seasonality and source of his glory.[2]

The earliest forms of religion consisted in ancestral worship, observes Burkert (xxii), and insofar as religion played a foundational and preservative role within culture, it follows that family left an indelible trace on political life. I should outline here the reason why I think ancestral cult shaped so strongly the early religious feeling and, by extension, civic identity. In the context of the family, one experiences most intimately and most absorbingly the generational pattern—namely, existence as a problem of time. Because family endures the *recurring* cosmic cycles of *change* most directly and concretely, it is in a suitable position to reveal the ontological premises on which the city too rests, but which this same city antagonizes in its technical aspect. The slain hero-ancestor, whom Agamemnon embodies in the opening of this play, is thus part of a civic-foundational myth because he is first and foremost part of a cosmology: his life and, most importantly, his sacrificial death provide the interface between the natural macrocosm and the civic microcosm, showing how the cycles of the former are reflected and, at times, refracted in the latter. This is precisely what Burkert outlines in the following passage that, though specific to Argos, contains in effect his greater insight about culture deriving its legitimacy from religion. The shared name of Argos between the animal/guard and the city thus denotes the sharing between the cosmos and the human polis:

> In a way, then, the power and order of Argos the city are embodied in Argos the neatherd, lord of the herd and lord of the land, whose name itself is the name of the land. In the myth, Argos is Zeus' opponent, but it has long been seen

that he is nonetheless closely identified with Zeus. Just as Argos is called panoptes, the one who sees all, so Zeus, the omniscient sky-god, is invoked as Zeus Panoptes. . . . In the countless, starlike eyes of Argos, poets saw an image of the universe—just as Zeus himself was the universe. Moreover, this two-faced quality of Argos recalls the myths of double beings who had to be killed and cut up so that our world could come into existence. Indeed, *in the context of the city Argos, the mythical Argos was virtually the embodiment of the cosmos, the all-embracing order.* This order, so as to endure, had to be secured with a death; it was dissolved for the sake of being reestablished. Argos died in the unspeakable sacrifice of the bull so that the youthful warriors might carry the sacred shield on their shoulders, thus carrying the city's order on into the future. (167–68; my emphasis)

Accordingly, cosmological categories appear prominently at the start of the *Choephoroi*. Just as in the opening scene of *Agamemnon* the guard understood his predicament in terms of the constellations above, here Orestes frames his return in terms of the surrounding nature, albeit turning his gaze downward. He speaks neither of his house nor of the Argive throne whose rightful heir he is but of "this land" (ln. 3; γῆν τήνδε). Soon after, the chorus of women mourners and Electra will alternately describe it as all-nurturing and ever-drenched by the blood of the murdered, as Gaia/Gē (Γῆ) and as netherworld (χθών).[3] Orestes's first offering, a lock of hair, goes to Inachus, the river of Argos. The land, its river, the father's tomb, and the bodily offering are the elements of the first order, before any mention of his political role as an Argive prince. Even the mention of might (κράτη) in the first verse does not refer to political power but to the powers of Hermes in relation to the underworld, which are delegated to him by his father, Zeus; alternatively, the term may refer to the power of Orestes's ancestors, however not so much as kings but as ancestors—that is, as the dead.[4] Even though Orestes's father was also a king, and even though the double citation of πατρῷ᾽ and πατρὶ repeats the twinship of Zeus and Agamemnon as father-kings—the eagle-kings of the first tragedy—paternal power registers first not as political power but as sacrificial deposit and generational pledge.

This talismanic function of the dead father is not an ordinary anthropological contingency that can be easily disposed of as a phantasmatic metaphysics without grave consequences in its absence.[5] The chthonic father expresses through a sexualized dynamic something essential to human experience: the ancient and very much lived struggle for survival and continuity, which recognized in the imperiled existence of the hunter/father/hero a living defender and a dead guarantor of the community. Electra points to this sheltering function of the paternal ancestor when she describes Agamemnon's tomb as a sanctuary for suppliants and fugitives (ln. 336–38). That Agamemnon failed at his fatherliness vis-à-vis Iphigenia can certainly be interpreted by the modern reader as a flaw sufficient to debunk the idea of fatherly protection as myth. Yet to afford such critical "demythologization," and furthermore, to do so without the urgency of proposing another metaphysical structure in its stead, one must also tacitly assume that there is either no such thing as an existential threat, or that the threat is negligible enough as to obviate the need for protection. One must assume, in other words, that existence can take place without adversity, without hazard, without tragedy. On the contrary, I submit that the tale of Agamemnon's failure is not meant to destabilize the talisman but to corroborate all the more the demands and the losses that necessarily endanger any attempt at sovereign existence, including—most intensely, of course—the existence of the sovereign qua king. For clarity's sake, by the term "sovereign existence," I mean primarily the very human (and very tragic) desire to overcome nature as inexorable necessity and to attain freedom, and only secondarily the political connotations it has accrued. Whereas the hitherto predominant association of sovereignty to paternity has now been problematized for obvious reasons, this problematization occurred not without the concomitant erasure of the particularly gruesome fate to which the male warrior-hunter was exposed.

Beyond the various textual accounts of war in antiquity, this terrifying fate is most vividly illustrated through the symbolism of ritual practice itself. In the sexualization of sacrifice, we have seen that the maiden victim belonged to the preliminaries, but as Burkert's literary and material evidence indicates, the larger animal offerings reserved for some of the most notable festivals were male due to their association with prowess and phallic fertility—chief among them the bull, to which Agamemnon was already compared. Other examples include a he-goat offered to Dionysus, a donkey to Priapus, and, in the Roman context, the October Horse to Mars. Because of their powerful physique, their deaths were not only the most spectacular but also the most dreadful, as was in some cases the brutal treatment of their reproductive organs.⁶ Poignantly, excessive brutality and sexual aggression are noted during sacrifices intended to secure alliances between families, guilds, or larger political organizations: "The closer the bond, the more gruesome the ritual. Those who swear an oath must touch the blood from the accompanying sacrifice and even step on the testicles of the castrated victim" (Burkert 36). In other words, the physical and symbolic castration of the male animal was literally an *overkill*, just as in actual life, the warrior-hunter was exposed to an overdetermined deathliness and dismemberment.⁷ Agamemnon does not feature prominently as an iconic figure of dismemberment in the tragic repertory—at least not as Pentheus or even the unburied Polyneices do—yet a passing detail by the chorus suffices to point to this overkill: posthumously, he was mangled (ἐμασχαλίσθη), "a savage custom," explains Smyth in his footnote, "by which the extremities of the murdered man were cut off, then hung about his neck and tied together under the arm-pits." One reason for this practice, continues Smyth, "was to disable the spirit of the dead from taking vengeance on the murderer" (201).

This sexual drama, in which the father stands as defender and guarantor through his sacrifice, is rehearsed in Electra's first of a series of prayers to Agamemnon, where she binds most expressly the notion of justice (Dikē) to that of the earth (Gē). Like Orestes earlier, Electra too first requests Hermes's intercession in raising the dead, and Earth along with them (ln. 126–28), before addressing the spirit of Agamemnon. The ancestors are said to "watch over" her father's house (πατρῴων δωμάτων ἐπισκόπους) in accord with ancient belief that grants the power of vigilance to the dead. Earth's split description as birthing and all-nurturing but also consuming of its own surplus as return is, of course, illustrated dramatically by Electra's pouring of the libations; it is also echoed in the prayer's split from a benediction asking for the father's protection to a malediction wishing for the father's avenger. Itself as opaque as the dark ritual it introduces, the prayer addresses the spirits at once as guardians of the living *and* as dependent on the living for exacting the justice due that, nevertheless, only those dead can provoke into rising. Hence, the blessing that Electra wishes for at the conclusion of this incantation requires the favor of all the gods (σὺν θεοῖσι) but hinges most specifically on the pairing of Earth with victorious Justice (ln. 148; Γῇ καὶ Δίκῃ νικηφόρῳ). Hence also, her final entreaty by the tomb stresses the offspring's redemptive role in ensuring the patrilineage and lifting this intrafamilial and intergenerational curse:

> Hear one more cry, father, from me. It is my last.
> Your nestlings huddle suppliant at your tomb: look forth
> and pity them, female with the male strain alike.
> Do not wipe out this seed of the Pelopidae.
> So, though you died, you shall not yet be dead, for when
> a man dies, children are the voice of his salvation
> afterward. Like corks upon the net, these hold
> the drenched and flaxen meshes, and they will not drown.
> Hear us then. Our complaints are for your sake, and if
> you honor this our argument, you save yourself. (ln. 500–509)

While the image of the children as nestlings recalls the avian omens of *Agamemnon*, their erstwhile powerlessness is now slowly reconfigured. Though still under threat, the offspring may transform via their alliance with the dead father into instruments of a reckoning. A kind of phylogenetic immortality (οὐ τέθνηκας)[8] joins the promise of salvation (σωτήριοι, σῴζοντες, σῴζῃ) through one's children, which really means the securing of heritage: the individual father will not be resurrected, but the family and adjacent community may endure. Once again, in anticipating the generational argument of the *Eumenides*, the exclusive patrilineality of which has proved a hermeneutical scandal, it is instructive to note that Electra's above-quoted plea already firmly directs its promises of salvation to a dead *man*: "παῖδες γὰρ ἀνδρὶ κληδόνες σωτήριοι" (ln. 505; children are the voice of *his* salvation; my emphasis). Given that ἀνδρὶ > *anēr* designates not just any "man" but a hero or man of civic stature,[9] I would argue that the funeral cult of the hero-father in the *Choephoroi* sets the background against which to understand the otherwise counterintuitive claim of the exclusively patrilineal descent in the *Eumenides*. Electra's lines contain effectively the reverse formulation of this argument in the *Eumenides* in that the children's "resurrectional" promise is directed by way of existential reciprocation to him who made possible not only their birth but their *continued* survival as well. Indeed, Apollo's insistence on the father as the only true parent relies on the hermeneutic of the *Choephoroi*'s cosmological framing of paternal sacrifice as guarantee of familial and civic continuity. Approached from the perspective of biological reproduction alone, the Apollonian argument sounds hyperbolic at best, suppressing as it does the maternal part in the process due to its passive receptivity. Despite the legitimate objections it has raised, however, this argument is not devoid of logic either. First, its overdetermination of the father, as I have mentioned above, draws on and illumines the quasi-biological need for protection and defense that typically was the task of the early hunter, and later, of the father-warrior. Second, and more interestingly, while propped on such a naturalistic necessity, the narrative of paternal generation aims at and reaches a logic beyond mere bio-logic: its focus on the father's vigilance and defense recasts parentage from simple birthing—notwithstanding Apollo's biological emphasis on the seed's *active* role in reproduction—to the duty of safeguarding life, a duty associated with another type of *activity*, that of the warrior, for he who kills is also meant to defend and protect. Apollo was, after all, the god who furnished the heroic prototype. That (military) defense was a matter not simply of a tribe of kin but of the city as a whole is a good reason why the *Oresteia*—a play as much about the restoration of a family as of a throne—privileges paternal generation qua guardianship.[10]

Richard Kuhns also proposes a cosmological basis for Apollo's patrilineal argument (42–49). In his view, however, the prominence of the semen does not carry associations of the chthonic but of its contrasting realms: reason (logos) and spirit (pneuma). These, he notes, were aligned with the male sex not only in Aeschylus but in the philosophy of Plato and Aristotle, who also combined biology with cosmology in order to theorize procreation as a process bestowing on human beings a reasoning capacity instead of blind passion. In the aftermath of feminist scholarship, such a thesis sounds both problematic and outdated, since its author does not critique the discursive assumptions of the cosmology and biology he meets in these ancient writers. Yet, Kuhns's effort to understand the logic behind Apollo's argument—a logic that commentators unrelated to feminist criticism notably also viewed as absurd or inconsequential[11]—is worthwhile. It is worthwhile because it is through this patriarchal cosmology that *Oresteia*'s important moral passage takes place from a justice of blood to the court of civic deliberation. As Kuhns explains, starting with a long citation from Hegel's reading of the trilogy in *Lectures on Fine Art*, the "seminal" logic of Apollo answers the important judicial question of which familial murder takes precedence—that of the husband by the wife, or that of the mother by the son? In placing the former above the latter, the final decision emblematizes the supersession of the family *from within* the family, a supersession that forms the first necessary step for modernity's positing of civic justice above natural justice. Whereas these issues will become clearer in the next chapter on the *Eumenides*, and whereas I swerve from the linear-historical approach, according to which natural cosmology develops into a political cosmology (what now goes by the name of "cosmopolitanism"), I wished to interject Kuhns's insights because they recognize Aeschylus's attempt to articulate a coherent relation between biology, cosmology, and political culture.

Justice and Hate

Returning to the play itself, I will elaborate further the theme of chthonic justice as it develops through a tension between hate-filled retaliation and generative promise. Besides their conceptual coupling in Electra's prayer, earth and justice are paired linguistically via the alliterative sound of χθών (netherworld) and ἔχθος/ἐχθρὸν (hate, enmity), especially in the first half of the play, where the incantatory mode prevails. Indeed, "hate" is a term frequently used in lieu of "justice," or at the very least it names both the motive and prerogative of justice (ln. 101, 123, 240, 309, 460–61).[12] Poignantly, it is the chorus of foreign women slaves who most strongly advocates for and encourages Electra in the ways of this hate-driven justice, siding with the dead king and wishing punishment for his wife, whom the chorus views as a tyrannical usurper. In one such passage, the women identify explicitly the justice of reprisal with hatred as they also intimate that the *talio* is sent by Zeus and the Fates, presumably through the agency of Hermes Chthonios: "ἀλλ' ὦ μεγάλαι Μοῖραι, Διόθεν / τῇδε τελευτᾶν, / ᾗ τὸ δίκαιον μεταβαίνει. / ἀντὶ μὲν ἐχθρᾶς γλώσσης ἐχθρὰ / γλῶσσα τελείσθω: τοὐφειλόμενον / πράσσουσα Δίκη" (ln. 306–11; Almighty Destinies, by the will / of Zeus let these things / be done, in the turning of Justice. / For the word of hatred spoken, let hate / be a word fulfilled. The spirit of Right / cries out aloud and extracts atonement due).

Though it is tempting to interpret the chorus's patriarchal loyalties solely as an ideological blind spot or as outright misogyny on Aeschylus's part, the women's commentary on the "Lemnian crime" (ln. 631–36) allows for their identification to be more complex psychologically, morally, and formally, in terms of the internal correspondences of the trilogy.[13] Above all, their reference to this particular crime serves to reinforce the connection between hate and justice that grounds the play. The Lemnian crime is a tale of revenge following the spousal betrayal of some wives who were punished by Aphrodite with a foul odor for neglecting her worship. Having been rejected by their husbands in favor of Thracian captive maidens, the women of Lemnos killed those husbands and their new wives—an act mirrored in Clytemnestra's murder of Agamemnon and Cassandra, though the Aeschylean chorus laments only the destruction of the men without mentioning the fate of their imported mistresses. For this omission, the chorus can be expectedly charged with misogyny. Yet their citation of the myth also omits an additional detail whose absence actually mitigates the women's crime, but which, I suspect, was responsible for why this legend became a singular moral topos—indeed, a cautionary tale and an exemplum for new horrors—by the classical era. This detail hinges on the gender dynamic of the myth but goes well beyond it: along with their husbands, the Lemnian women were said to have killed all male inhabitants of the island indiscriminately, an act that proves crucial for reflecting on the extremity of hate that may motivate justice.[14] In short, to focus on the misogyny alone is also to obfuscate the moral scandal of the indiscriminate nature of justice that makes this story particularly repugnant and establishes it as an example to be avoided by the time of Aeschylus.

On the one hand, such a myth showcases the intimate connection between sexuality and death; on the other, it amplifies the chasm separating the life-principle of Aphrodite from the hatred that fuels the justice-principle and that punishes not only the perpetrators but even those associated with the crime by chance, such as the old men and infant boys who become culpable by sharing the same sex as the offenders. In the tale of the Lemnian crime, the slave women of the *Choephoroi* find a traditional framework within which to contemplate their own moral and existential conundrum, their own choice of what counts as the greater evil of their fate: honoring a foreign master who appears at least to have treated them lawfully after their captivity, or serving a scorned and wrathful woman who has relegated her own daughter to the status of an enslaved exile in her own land. Interestingly, the lesson the chorus draws from the story does not involve the moral validity behind the justice claim itself—namely, whether or not the Lemnian women were justified in seeking revenge. Even though it is self-evident why the chorus's disinterest would be construed as misogyny, such interpretations gloss over the most sinister implications of this tale: the dangerous extremities to which the self-righteousness of justice can lead, and which, in the post-Aeschylean renderings of the myth, appear as a gendercide, but in the Aeschylean chorus escalate to a genocide instigated by the gods against the Lemnian race now considered accursed for the crimes of their women.[15] All new horrors (τὰ δεινὰ) are henceforth measured against this one, concludes the chorus, confirming what appears as a distinct moral topos also in Herodotus.[16] The myth of Lemnian justice as a coordinated mass action against a class of people exposes the horror that lurks potentially behind any claim of justice, most notably those claims now filed under the rubric of "systemic injustice" that require an equally systemic, thus often predetermined and abstract,[17] response.

Gendercide is answered with genocide as the chthonic type of justice escalates along the mortal-immortal axis. Even though the chorus women sense the annihilative impulse of chthonic justice, they remain bound to its implementation not only for the sake of the slain king's memory but, paradoxically, for the future of his children as well. I will return to this futural promise of chthonic justice later in the chapter; for now, I wish to stress that with paradox, Aeschylus both complicates the predictable ideological criticisms and manages to interlace formally the themes of the trilogy by balancing out the various viewpoints. For instance, if in *Agamemnon* he painted a sympathetic portrait of a scorned Clytemnestra in her jealousy against Cassandra, he now, through the slave women's account of the Lemnian crime, redirects the rage against the same woman despot who also kills indiscriminately. Let me insert a parenthesis to further clarify this partly sympathetic depiction of Clytemnestra that, as I noted in the preceding chapter, presents a stumbling block to our current ethico-political sensibilities, but that also serves to show in its dialectical relation to the Lemnians how both individual- and group-driven justice relies on hate. Whether some obligation of feminist solidarity or "allyship" should have prevented Clytemnestra from revenging herself on Cassandra, and led her to punish only Agamemnon for both women's sufferings, is beside the point for a poet who chooses to *describe* humanity in terms of its *nature*—that is, as a comportment with a degree of spontaneity that cannot be *artificialized* at will. From this naturalist perspective, which is at basis the tragic perspective, the political desideratum to unconditionally legitimize the sexuality of all enslaved concubines while vilifying the reactions of the lawful wife (*despoina*) looks morally obfuscatory, let alone psychologically obtuse, in diminishing and dismissing the harm done to the wife—all in the name of improving social morality by weighing and calculating "power imbalances" as if they were transparently measurable quantities.[18] Hence, such allyships often risk the accusation of being "performative"—namely, contrived public signalings of political orthodoxy rather than internally necessary *and* free realizations.

This type of programmatic thinking avoids any ethical context outside the social "power differential" it sees in the agents involved so as to reach its predetermined conclusion. Its conclusion, in turn, requires that the psychological and pragmatic threat suffered by the *despoina* and her resultant feeling of jealousy vanish and be replaced by the more "enlightened" cultural principle, according to which the socially disadvantaged are automatically absolved of any responsibility, complicity, or agency—and thus, strangely, of any subjectivity or humanity as well.[19] The hierarchical tension between nature and artifice underlying Aristotle's emphasis on the naturalness of tragic art, which I outlined in chapter 2, replays itself here: civic morality risks being artificially induced, and this artificiality appears more acutely against the tragic background because it severs the spontaneous accord Aristotle saw upheld in tragedy between the logic of natural emotions and the logic of the moral order.[20] Notably, both these logics maintain that a person wronged is a person wronged, just as an offender is an offender, *in excess of* the rank they occupy in society at the time of the offence. I do not mean to imply that there are not varying degrees of harm and blame, some of which depend on social markers; rather, I wish to stress the limits of the unreserved politicization of morality that insists on absolving and incriminating the agents involved according to social markers alone.

Contra this artificial morality that suppresses the logic of emotions, the natural feeling of jealousy arising from sexual and familial betrayal is corroborated between Aeschylus's two plays: in their protofeminist delivery of a systemic kind of justice, the homicidal Lemnian women engage in the same behavior that Clytemnestra, the rogue tyrant, exhibits against Cassandra. Both types of avengers kill bystanders with relatively distant degrees of proximity and complicity to the initial crime. Hence, the formal philosophical point about the hatred that incites justice runs deeper than the contingent power differentials and social structures embedded in particular crime scenes. The point is that the demand for justice, which by definition assumes a basic power differential—that of the wrongdoer over the harmed above and before all else—is constitutively linked to hate. Hate is an inaugural sentiment for justice.[21] This idea would not be so contentious were it not for our culture's rather tenuous double commitment: on the one hand, the celebration of anything pertaining to (social) justice, and on the other, the censure—and increasingly, censorship—of a perceived, or even suspected, private sentiment of hate. My thesis is, however, that the notions of justice and hate are far too closely linked for our political comfort; not acknowledging this link might be the result of a conceptual oversight, or simply itself an ideologically driven necessity.

Either way, the currently respected virtue of righteous indignation as motive for justice tends to divorce anger from hatred, considering the latter irrational.[22] Yet Aeschylus's account of chthonic justice reveals that it is precisely from the realm of hatred that righteousness (dikē) emerges. Here are the verses expressly drawing the vector from anger (θυμός) to hatred (στύγος) in the chorus's demand for justice: "πάροιθεν δὲ πρῴρας / δριμὺς ἄηται κραδίας / θυμὸς ἔγκοτον στύγος" (ln. 390–92; Full against the prow of my heart wrath blows sharply in rancorous hate).[23]

That dikē is inextricable from hate in this play can also be gleaned from its association with Ares, the "most hateful" (ἔχθιστος) god of war.[24] Accompanying Electra's libations to the tomb with appeals to a future alastor, the chorus imagines him as Ares, coming to free the house with his Scythian bow (ln. 159–63). Later on, speaking as the alastor, Orestes fulfills the chorus's wishes in one of the most Aeschylean of verses. I call it "most Aeschylean" because it embodies his typically solemn, condensed style that juxtaposes compactly a pair of nouns in a montage-like syntax, where the action is shown within the same word as between the pair through use of declensions: "Ἄρης Ἄρει ξυμβαλεῖ, Δίκᾳ Δίκα" (ln. 461; Ares will collide with Ares; Right will collide with Right).[25] Nominative to dative shows the action of same-against-same, while the comma joins paratactically Ares to Right, in a link that exposes two disconcerting aspects of justice. First, the link of Ares to justice points to the proximity between claims of Right and war—notably, not even "just war," but war as senseless killing, of which Ares is the embodiment. Secondly, the syntax of Dikē against Dikē suggests that in juridical antagonism, both justice claims pose as equivalents, opening a space of indistinction similar to that of lawless warfare of Ares against Ares. This indistinction dovetails with the notion of cosmic arbitrariness that I discussed in chapter 2, and that unwittingly also marks the human experiments with justice as a sociopolitical project. As I had pointed out there, it is strangely this arbitrariness that offers a prototype for the neutrality prerequisite to any genuine *isonomia*, particularly at times when the notion of equality before the law risks being undermined. Similarly, I would note here that it is this space of warlike indistinction that, albeit problematic, also guards against the equally problematic societal deliberation to promote one justice as "juster" than another, pending on ever-contingent and ever-changing norms.

Dikē in the *Choephoroi* is war; thus, justice comes always with sword in hand (ln. 639–41), a sword, moreover, forged by fate: "Δίκας δ' ἐρείδεται πυθμήν· / προχαλκεύει δ' Αἶσα φασγανουργός· / τέκνον δ' ἐπεισφέρει δόμοισιν / αἱμάτων παλαιτέρων τίνειν μύσος / χρόνῳ κλυτὰ βυσσόφρων Ἐρινύς" (ln. 646–51; Right's anvil stands staunch on the ground / and the smith, Destiny, hammers out the sword. / Delayed in glory, pensive from / the murk, Vengeance brings home at last / a child, to wipe out the stain of blood shed long ago). Aisa, or Moira, does not simply antagonize the Erinys, as Jan Kott's past-future temporality exaggerates, but they work in tandem at least in this play, where the one arms and sends the other to complete the task of past justice through the future generation. Thus, shortly before the murder of Aegisthus, the chorus wishes simultaneously for the expiation of old blood and for the ceasing of the blood feud in the future (ln. 800–805). Fate resonates here in a double register: as necessity—namely, as the law of the pattern, whereby committing wrongs entails by natural probability that the culprit will be answered at some point by another wrong—and as arbitrariness, in the sense that, once released, this destinal probability, though set in motion by human deeds, cannot be controlled by the craft and will of human beings.

Next to war, dikē also resembles the hunt, and as such, the play continues the thematic of feral beasts and entrapment opened up in *Agamemnon*. For instance, the canine imagery of *Agamemnon* now gives way to lupine similes, passing from the vigilant eyesight of the guard and of Cassandra's smell into the more savage task of hunting prey. Electra compares her and her brother's temper to that of a wolf (ln. 421), though she was earlier subjected to the humiliation of a "kennelled dog" (ln. 447) by her own mother. Wolves and dogs belong to the same family, but they represent opposite qualities as beasts. As I have already mentioned, Burkert elaborates on the antagonism between wolf and dog (83–93, 109–116), indicating that the initiation of young men as hunters consisted in a time of exile from peaceful society when they joined feral groups to train "in the ways of the wolf" (89). The wolf simile, however, also foreshadows the arrival of Apollo in the next instalment of the trilogy, with whom this animal is connected in myth and cult, particularly at Argos, where the god was worshiped as Lykeios (Burkert 108; wolflike).[26] The *Oresteia* indeed plays on this doubling of wolf and dog: wolflike Orestes summons his father's Furies to aid him in his revenge, yet he will end up prey to the same canine deities he himself awakens as a matricide. Orestes is keenly aware of the double hunt to which he is prey when he counters his mother's warning that he will be chased by her doglike curses, her Erinyes: "How shall I escape my father's curse, if I fail here?" (ln. 925). The hero is caught between two claims of justice that are equally legitimate and yet at odds with one another. His words expose the aporetic, yet constitutive, moment in which every justice turns upon an injustice. With this devastating question, Orestes enters for a long while the realm of justice as indistinction—that is, the realm of justice as pure principle without law and limits, or perhaps of justice as a terrifying ideality beholden to a single law, according to which every drop of blood demands more blood still, ad infinitum (ln. 400–403).

The metaphor of predation as significative of the quest for justice is most fully visible in the dream of Clytemnestra, which is narrated by the chorus in the very middle of the play (ln. 527–33), and whose interpretation by Orestes coincides shortly with its fulfillment. Since this part of the play is rather well known and commented on, I will limit my remarks to the ways in which its "zoology" ties in with the cosmology of the chthonic hero cult, the latter notably being a civic vestige of early hunting ritual. The dream depicts Clytemnestra's birthing of a snake (δράκων), which she suckled as it bit her nipple, drawing blood along with milk. Orestes interprets it as the prophecy of his coming for his father's revenge (ln. 540–50). Near the end of the play, and while reflecting on the matricide, Orestes identifies with his mother, to whom he ascribes a snakelike nature as well. He imagines her as a sea serpent or a viper (ln. 994), and calls the robe/net with which she trapped Agamemnon an "animal trap" (ln. 998; ἄγρευμα θηρός). Let me underline the distinctly chthonic character of the serpentine imagery that the *Choephoroi* adds to the bestiary of dogs, eagles, hares, and spiders of the first play. Numerous myths of autochthony are populated with snakes, whose crawling movement associates them quite obviously with the earth. The dragon that Cadmus had to slay, and from whose sown teeth the native race of Thebes was born; the legendary kings of Athens—Cecrops, Erectheus/Erichthonius—who were depicted as snakes to denote their autochthony and that of their Athenian descendants;[27] the Delphic python that Apollo killed to claim the "navel of the earth" as his own—these are but a few examples that attest to the chthonic nature of the serpent. In this play, too, the chthonic Erinyes approaching are imagined by Orestes as Gorgon-like creatures entwined with snakes (ln. 1050).[28]

Pertinent to my discussion of the *Choephoroi*'s hero cult is Jane Ellen Harrison's observation that "all over Greece the dead hero was worshiped in snake form" (20)—namely, as part of the chthonic world. Similarly, Burkert divided Greek sacred spaces into Olympian and chthonic, the former being dedicated to the gods, and the latter to local heroes. An etymological detail gives us an additional glimpse into this cosmology, in which the hero combines the past's "deep time" through his chthonic dwelling with the future of the city-world through his protective, talismanic abilities: the Greek δράκων for "serpent" derives from the verb δέρκομαι, which means "to see clearly," and moreover, "to guard," "to keep vigil." Hence, dragons protecting sacred treasures is a favorite mythical motif, such as the Colchian dragon guarding the Golden Fleece, the Hesperian dragon in charge of the golden apples in the garden of the Hesperides, and the Pythian dragon defending the center of the earth at Delphi. We thus return to the earlier remark that the dead hero, represented now as snake, keeps vigil over the city. Snakelike Orestes comes to worship at his father's tomb, and through the dream of Clytemnestra enthrones himself as the guardian of his father's legacy and, by extension, as a future Argive hero.[29]

That Apollo, the Pythian god, is appealed to increasingly in the second half of the play, ushering in the end of the *Choephoroi* opposite his brother Hermes, who begins it, reinforces the relation of the hero to the serpent. The axis mundi has been traveled from the depths of the earth to the heavenly heights, from Orestes's earlier entreaties to Hermes and Gaia to send his father as watcher (ln. 489; ἐποπτεῦσαι) of his battle, to his plea to Helios, and eventually Apollo, as spectators to the justice of his matricide. Orestes believes that the evidence of the shackles that bound his father's extremities, preventing his spirit from pursuing revenge, will turn the sun—now father and surveyor of all (πατήρ ... ὁ πάντ' ἐποπτεύων)—into a favorite witness (μάρτυς) in the judgment (ἐν δίκῃ) that will decide the son's justice against his mother (ln. 984–89; ἐνδίκως μόρον). Aeschylus foregrounds this chthonic-Uranian verticality through the repetition of *epopteia*, the all-seeing capacity that links the vigilant dead of chthonic justice to solar light as a figure for judicial transparency. (We should recall that Argos the guard was also an all-seeing being, a panoptes.) The stretch toward the heavens concludes the play, albeit with an ambivalent Orestes who addresses Apollo partly in relief for completing the deed and partly in despair for the new murder he committed. Though they foreshadow the enlightened resolution of the final play, Orestes's words place the "imperishable fire" of Apollo not in the solar domain of Helios but in the "earth's central seat," to which the hero flees as a polluted suppliant (ln. 1036–37).

Justice and Rebirth

Up to this point, I have focused mainly on the hate-filled and warlike aspects of chthonic justice, which comprise a good majority of the *Choephoroi*'s verses. However, as I noted earlier, the appeal to Gē and retaliative justice is at times shown to serve a generative purpose, becoming a means to reach future redemption for the children of the accursed agents. Shortly before the avenging murders are committed, the chorus declares the programmatic function of the siblings' justice as aiming at the expiation of old murders that would complete and seal the family feud. Birth (*tokos*) now abandons the vendetta, preventing it from recycling itself: "γέρων φόνος μηκέτ' ἐν δόμοις τέκοι" (ln. 805; Let the old murder in / the house breed no more). After all, the goddess of the hunt is also protectress of the young, who in this case are "the orphaned children of the eagle-father" (ln. 247). I therefore turn my attention to this less visible but still-significant aspect of the play that anticipates the conclusion of the trilogy in the *Eumenides*.

It is again the women of the chorus who, in urging Agamemnon's children to summon his spirit, move between the annihilative and the generative, or even pleasurable, aspects of chthonic justice. I will thus focus on passages from Orestes's and Electra's pleas and their interchanges with the chorus and, particularly, on the distinct tropes to which each sibling resorts in their prayer—tropes that also somewhat reflect their respective gender positions.

In one of his opening invocations to Agamemnon (ln. 345–55), Orestes laments the fact that his father was deprived of a noble death in battle. He wishes that Agamemnon had died in Troy, reinforcing the masculine ideal of the "beautiful death" that seals the fate of a hero by securing his *hysterophemia*—namely, his immortality through reputation in legend. Such an imagined end would have also presumably benefitted the future of his offspring. Electra, on the other hand, presents a different dream of completion (ln. 363–71). She cares not for the heroic death in a foreign land but for the implementation of the poetic justice of retaliation: murderous kin must be slain by another kin, and such should be her father's legend even in distant lands whose people know nothing of his troubles. In her attachment to the family feud, Electra, the most vocal critic of Clytemnestra, shares much of her mother's chthonic sense of justice. Contrary to Orestes's nostalgia for *kleos*, Electra sees the *dikē* of the blood feud as the proper legacy of her hero-father. Heroic worth in her model does not stop at the *aristeia* in battle but in the dead man's meriting of revenge by his family against his family. Orestes soon joins Electra in this view, praying for Zeus's delayed Erinys to strengthen the mortal heart and hand to complete the deed for the father's sake. I direct the reader's attention to Orestes's juxtaposition of the noun τοκεῦσι, which highlights Agamemnon's role as begetter, and the verb τελεῖται, which signifies the end as both purpose and termination (ln. 385). It is as sire that Agamemnon merits the commission of the terrible deed as expression of filial duty, but the delivery[30] of this justice signals simultaneously the closure of the vendetta, which constitutes arguably the higher purpose of the trilogy. With the verb τελεῖται, Orestes condenses the formal task of the trilogy, pointing to the Aristotelian definition of tragedy as τελετή—a serious act that must be brought to its end, and potentially to its redemptive purpose, which was the purpose of any sacred ceremony as well. In the narrower context of the *Choephoroi*, this word also alludes to the summoning ritual with which he and his sister begin the preliminaries to the murder.

The chorus—similarly enthralled by the possibility of the blood feud but resigned at the sight of the murderers' impunity—dismisses Electra's wish as too good to be true, comparing it with the dreamy state of Hyperborea (ln. 373), a utopian place associated in myth with Apollonian flight.[31] The comparison of Electra's ravings to the Hyperborean dream aligns two unlikely worlds: the nether powers of revenge with a legendary and felicitous people residing beyond the North Wind, beyond human hubris and misery, a people closest to the immortals. Yet this paradoxical alignment between Hades and Hyperborea encodes something very tangible: the pleasure that accompanies the hate of dikē, which the chorus harbors and longs for, but whose absence the chorus implicitly and disappointedly registers in deeming Electra's wish for it an unattainable illusion. This is the same pleasure that Aristotle identified in the feeling of anger that motivates the justice of revenge, even though he distinguished more strictly than Aeschylus between anger and hate.

Though noble death may confer glorious reputation, it happens rather arbitrarily and impersonally on the battlefield, thus lacking this ingredient of pleasure germane to the premeditation of revenge. Death in war is nearly certain, but not individually calculated. In the scenario of dikē, pleasure is ever more intensified because of the deferred temporality of the Erinys—the "ὑστερόποινον ἄταν" (ln. 383; delayed destruction), which Orestes also mentions[32]—and the sense of personal agency of the victim, or his/her proxies, in facing the perpetrator. If, in war, the youth of the fallen warrior and the arbitrary happenstance of his death invested his loss with aesthetic meaning through epic song, in dikē, it is the ripeness of time and the overdetermined intention of the avenger that invest the victim with moral meaning, and the avenger with the equally moral glee of vindication. Revenge is a dish best served cold, says folk wisdom, encapsulating the pleasure in this delay, even though it is also this delay that misfires and even sweeps many an innocent in its passage, as I have discussed in the previous chapter.

Despite its reference to Hyperborea as illusion, the chorus concludes this strophe with a redemptive line, asserting that the day champions the children,[33] since the siblings' ritual gestures succeed in raising the chthonic powers as their allies. That the children will have the final word, so to speak, means presumably that theirs is the bloody justice that will put an end to the blood cycle. Juxtaposed to the logic of the hunt/judicial pursuit and to Walter Otto's life-demand for vindication that summons the fury, the Hyperborean interlude thematizes the other life-demand, which interrupts the hunt and lets the young be harbingers of the future. The Hyperboreans' longevity points to this futural dimension. They were famed to be a healthy and long-living people—a fantasy of a society freed from the brutishness of the hunt, the shortness of life, as well as the shade of hubris that would require the hatefulness of justice to correct it. Through the chorus's Hyperborean citation, Electra's call for justice becomes obliquely a pointer not only to the glee of destruction but also to a sense of continuity—even a cosmic resurrection—in that the children revive and guarantee the family line. The restoration of the offspring to their rightful position, which includes Orestes's return as legal heir to the throne and Electra's emancipation from enslavement in her own home, would be the beginnings of such revival. Some verses later, in what Electra herself identifies as her final invocation (ln. 500–509), obliqueness turns to decisive explicitness: almost taunting her father's spirit to come to her aid for its own sake, Electra now openly designates the offspring as the saviors of patrilineal legacy. Agamemnon's assistance is required not only for his children's future but for their rescuing of the line of Pelops,[34] and eventually, for lending a sort of immortality to Agamemnon himself (ln. 503–4).[35] Orestes's heroic ideal of the "beautiful death" in Troy that would have conferred immortality to Agamemnon is recast in Electra's demand for familial revenge, where the children-avengers act as heroic proxies in the name of the dead and defenseless father. Justice (Dikē) spells the feminine counterpoint to masculine warfare (Ares), but its Furies participate in the same activity Burkert considers to be war's distant origin: the hunt. Nonetheless, we begin to hear in this generational plea not only the vocabulary of hate but also that of salvation and immortality—the language of the life force—that will become extant in the *Eumenides*, where the spirits of blight become guardians of prosperity.

Hermes and Apollo, Gē and Helios, Hades and Hyperborea, serpent-mothers and eagle-fathers are cosmological signs of the vertical axis along which Dikē travels, sent from the high seat of Olympian Zeus but as a chthonic force that knows and desires only blood. In a stroke of genius, the playwright projects the axis mundi in Dikē's very name, which he explains through a portmanteau: Dika, writes Aeschylus, is formed by the blending of Di(os) and K(or)a (ln. 949), which means "the daughter of Zeus," who inspires wrath and destroys her enemies. Kore refers to any young maiden, and also a daughter, but it is the name primarily reserved for the underworld maiden, Persephone, daughter of the earth goddess Demeter by Zeus.[36] In addition to thematizing the axial cosmology between the high Zeus and the chthonic Kore, "Dios Kora" is an overdetermined name in the Argive cycle: both acoustically and semantically, it invokes the Dioskouroi—the mortal-immortal male twins of Zeus and Leda, who were siblings to Clytemnestra and Helen, themselves another such twin pair in myth.[37] However, whereas Castor and Pollux are known for their love, which led Pollux to share his immortality with his brother, the sisters are divided by enmity and envy, with Clytemnestra angered at her husband's campaign to retrieve the adulterous Helen. The mortal-immortal axis unites just as it divides. Chthonic in nature but Olympian in service, Dikē configures within herself this twinship that through the coupling of Leda and the swan plagues and redeems the House of Agamemnon. Moreover, Dikē's vertical itinerary reaches two different destinations as we too move from the *Choephoroi* to the *Eumenides*: entrusted to Hermes, the psychopomp and first killer among the gods, in the *Choephoroi*, Dikē's arrow[38] points decidedly toward the nether world; in the *Eumenides*, Apollo and Athena, tasked to represent the legal and rational will of Zeus, stop at the upper earth, the world of the city whose inaugural court admits to an Olympian foundation—Athena's vote—but also remembers the lower depths to which Dikē's vector initially traveled.

On the occasion of anticipating the civic space, which also moves from Argos to Athens, and having discussed at length the cosmological determinations of dikē, I would like to conclude by returning to the locale of Argos with which we started, and which, in Burkert's words, mirrors the cosmos through the figure of Argos Panoptes—the guard whose murder by Hermes founded the city. In shifting from cosmology back to the polis, however, I also wish to remind the reader that, while the polis is a cosmos, the reverse does not hold, for the cosmos contains but exceeds the polis. To rephrase it through Burkert's analysis, the city of Argos is founded on the cosmological cipher of Argos Panoptes, but Argos Panoptes is hardly an Argive citizen. From a markedly different scholarly angle, and in a commentary on another tragedy and another city, Seth Benardete offers a similar insight. Analyzing Antigone's insistence on the incommensurability of the laws of the underworld to those of the city, he writes that, for Antigone, "burial means a removal from Thebes and its concerns" because the city "is restricted to the surface of the earth," as opposed to Creon, who views the underworld as an extension below of Thebes (*Sacred Transgressions* 5). For Antigone, in other words, Thebes as a civic entity may be based on the underworld, but the underworld exceeds the city's contours.

Historically speaking, by Aeschylus's time, the city of Argos took a back seat to Athens's cultural, and Sparta's military, superiority (Burkert 162), in contrast to the unrivaled fame it enjoyed in the pre-Homeric and Homeric times, when the Greeks could all be subsumed under the name "Argives." Nonetheless, it continued to be one of few prominent Greek city-states, and one whose alliance was very much courted by both sides during the Peloponnesian War, particularly in light of its neutrality in the early phases of the war. These details are important in light of scholarly attempts to interpret the underlying ideological motives of Aeschylus and the other tragedians as *Athenian* poets. In this respect, Froma Zeitlin's work is crucial. As Geoffrey Bakewell notes, her mapping of "tragic geography is often more conceptual than real" (209), thus also pointing to unconscious ideologemes through which Attic tragedy rehearsed local problems by transposing them onto other topographies. Zeitlin, for instance, considers Thebes the tragic city par excellence, with a fixed identity that renders it the "other scene" or the negative "mirror image" of Athens, onto which Athens displaces its own unresolved anxieties.[39] Argos, on the other hand, is said to be "without firm identity," which also allows it to function as an empty screen for the projection of Athenian anxieties (Saïd 189). More recently, Angeliki Tzanetou has argued that the tragic repertoire contributed to Athens's image as a haven to outsiders, which compensated for its actually imperial and domineering attitude toward weaker city-states. Her study points to figures such as Orestes, Oedipus, and the Heracleidae as beleaguered exiles who were received generously by Athens, with the tragedians becoming somehow complicit with its civic propaganda. Accordingly, when it comes to the *Oresteia*, politically oriented scholarship views the inauguration of the court in Athens rather than Argos merely as an ideological ploy on Aeschylus's part that is meant to broadcast Athens's political superiority: excelling in philosophy and legal thought, Athens is able to produce a democratic institution such as the court of jury, of which "backward" Argos is allegedly incapable.

Such analyses can be theoretically stimulating and politically instructive, and this is certainly apropos at a time when theory theorizes—namely, *sees*—only politics and power everywhere. To a degree, the scholarly conclusion about the court of jury being specifically an Athenian institution also converges with my own earlier remark about the significance of Athens as the city that could translate the Furies into the Eumenides, and let them stand underneath its acropolis. Yet the political assumptions and valuations behind this shared conclusion could not be more dissimilar. Unlike the scholars interested in ideology critique, who view the inauguration of the Areopagus as Athens's propagandistic campaign against its inferiors, I detect in Aeschylus's text the recognition that it takes a certain type of polity to turn the bloody justice of the Erinyes into advantageous work for the social order.[40] Consequently, in making this quasi-political claim, I do not use the Athenian perspicacity concerning democracy's reliance on chthonic justice as critical fodder against the city's other failings vis-à-vis *our* notion of democracy, or even against the fragility of Athenian democracy itself. In this, I agree with historian Christian Meier, who underlines Athens's keen perceptivity during a time of radical change, which is reflected in the integrative scope of the *Oresteia*—a work Meier considers as the apex of ancient Greek political theory, negotiating a host of antitheses between old and new, male and female, blood kinship and marriage, Greek and foreign, wild and civilized: "How profoundly Athens must have been shaken by the city's upheavals to make necessary such a huge, all-embracing effort as the *Oresteia* to regain spiritual equilibrium. At the same time, the *Oresteia* demonstrates the Athenians' remarkably well-developed faculty of perception, their ability to mediate experience and to work things through, both in poetry and in public life. The Athenians possessed the capacity to be amazed by the world, a capacity that Max Weber called a prerequisite of all unbiased inquiry" (*Athens* 327). Furthermore, I do not overlook the historical fact that, despite its political failings, Athens already constituted a symbolic topos throughout the

Hellenic, and even adjacent, geography so as to become a hub for all sorts of luminaries of the ancient world who wished to live there, or at the very least, visit it.[41]

Thus, while acknowledging political critiques of Aeschylus as notable contributions to the study of tragedy, I must also indicate a threefold limit they pose to a project such as mine. In aligning myth and cult directly with ideology, whereby ideology means a limited and limiting view meriting a critical assessment, these readings compromise my effort to restore the prominence of the cosmological in Aeschylus and, in tragedy more generally, as an imitation of a grave act—that is, as an imitation of nature before all else. Secondly, by thinking of tragedy as a genre that reflects so narrowly the conflicting politics among different city-states, they downplay tragedy's appeal beyond immediate locality, even in the simple fact that its persistent themes and structures were Panhellenic: the gods and heroes that appear in the plots had resonance and recognition across all city-states; Buphonia rites existed not only in Athens but in Argos, as we saw in the introduction to this chapter; so did chthonic cults of heroes, or cults and legends of maiden sacrifices, protocols of purification, and so on. Thirdly, political interpretations should give us pause, especially in light of the present zeitgeist, which subjects everything to ideological critique without acknowledging that this critique is itself ideologically embedded. More questionably, at times such critiques proudly admit that *our* ideology is morally superior to all preceding ones. Yet to pretend that our ideology is better than that of previous cultures is not only epistemically dubious, despite its own certainty, but it repeats the same ideological blindness of which it accuses earlier epochs.

How Now? Autochthony's Time

I will outline briefly the limited, and at times distortive, lens of ideological criticism, by discussing one tragic mythologeme that has become a favorite locus of such criticism: autochthony. I isolate this particular theme largely because it pertains to the *Choephoroi* and its chthonic cult of the hero-father as guard and ground of the polis and its traditions. Civic myths of autochthony have typically been interpreted as dangerous ideologemes constructed in order to exclude foreigners or women from civic claims. In her *Children of Athena*, for instance, Nicole Loraux exposes the myths of Athenian autochthony as aiding the city's patriarchal ideology and its exclusion of women from citizenry.⁴² Loraux is likely the most prominent of the classicists to tackle this issue, but others have followed suit in areas beyond the field of Classics, and with agendas arguably not as neutral as Loraux's. As a relevant aside that nonetheless demonstrates the partiality of such criticism, I should add that, currently, myths and concepts of *indigeneity*—which is what "autochthony" means—are problematized almost exclusively within the Greek context. This is justified by the ubiquitous epistemology of power, which never defines concepts categorially but only through their relative position in a power nexus, itself precariously and instrumentally arranged, and which has retroactively construed "Greece" as synonymous with "Western hegemony." Myths of similar structure—which, as expected, can be found quite *universally*—are often not critically assessed in other contexts, at least not with the same vigor as is Greek chthonicity; on the contrary, the concept of indigeneity has rapidly risen to both cultural and disciplinary prominence.

Indeed, political perspectives on the chthonic often occlude the rich semiotic of the underworld/χθών in its relation to ancestral time and to a universality that projects itself through the local—namely, the universality of the shared feeling of mortality as well as the notion that death itself is the way to the universal, to which the cult of the dead attests.⁴³ Thus, I bracket, at least for the moment, the implicit and politically damaging identification of the chthonic with civic boundaries, stressing instead that the ancient city—if not also modern forms of political identity—is chthonic in its *temporality* prior to its geographical borders with other cities, nations, or empires. The land as circumscribed space is claimed, respected, and defended because it is, before all else, the resting place of the family dead. Sophocles illustrates this well: by the time Polyneices is killed, he is considered a traitor and an enemy of the city, effectively a noncitizen, but his political status does not prevent Antigone from fulfilling her chthonic obligation of burying him *in* Thebes. He is *of* Thebes even as he is against Thebes because "Thebes" is not merely an enclosed territory but a figure of time, the history of the dead brother's accursed genealogy as well as of his own future legacy, no matter how tainted. The claim to chthonicity constitutes above all the claim to a space where one's dead—namely, one's past, ancestry, and diachrony—are being hosted and accommodated. Put differently, a polis based on the chthonic principle has "deep time" just as does the cosmos. Such a polis is always more than a synchronic aggregate of current residents; it relies on tradition and heritage. Ideologists tend to see this ancestral factor as imaginary, thus downplaying heritage and the continuity of tradition as myths and fictions that require demythologization. However, I suppose that someone like Burkert might well say that heritage and tradition are no more fictions than is the backbone of human anatomy—a material fact and vestigial trace of our embryonic but also ancestral state. The polis functions in the present only by drawing, whether consciously or unconsciously, from the cultural deposit of the past, from the contributions of the ancestors that can be expressed variously in terms of military, economic, artistic, or other achievements that are sometimes paid, as ancient tragedy shows, with their lives, which in turn appeals to the Fury/Dikē.

It is no surprise, then, that even current social movements about racial justice perform this backward-looking glance overdeterminedly, in two opposing directions at once. Calling for the revision and even erasure of historical and literary documents, or the removal of monuments deemed complicit with a history of oppression—thus signaling the annihilative aspect of justice we saw in the *Choephoroi*—antiracist activists simultaneously appeal to the dead of past struggles and erect new heroic symbols, often with the tropes of martyrdom and saintly iconography that they problematize in their adversaries.[44] In this sense, the chthonic myth is not a lie, nor is it simply the imaginary construction of a people—which, in more fanciful and softer terms, could also spell a kind of lie—but an ancestral deposit consisting of very real commitments and very real events that become later rewritten or erased according to the present's own political needs or expediencies.

It is within this heritage-based mindset that cultural and personal gestures of carrying one's dead *with* the earth that covered them can make sense. Though still a hypothesis among archaeologists, evidence now suggests that the bluestones of Stonehenge were carried by Neolithic inhabitants of Britain when they migrated from Wales to the distant area of the Salisbury plain because beneath them were buried ancestral remains. This hypothesis, popularized in a February 2021 *National Geographic* article by Robin George Andrews, is presented with further scientific detail in the journal *Antiquity*, where the authors remark:

> In conclusion, it seems that Stonehenge stage one was built—partly or wholly—by Neolithic migrants from Wales, who brought their monument or monuments as a physical manifestation of their ancestral identities to be re-created in similar form on Salisbury Plain. . . . Stonehenge's first stage may also

have served to unite the people of southern Britain. Bluestones were brought to the land of sarsen stones and installed at a sacred axis mundi (world axis or world centre), where the sky and the earth were envisioned in cosmic harmony, and where people of different cultural and regional origins might gather for collective monument-building and feasting. (Pearson et al.)

The axis mundi, exceedingly present in the solstitial function of these henges, traverses the human world first and foremost through its dead. Likewise, in the *Choephoroi*, Hermes's travels from heaven to earth, and his *pompē*—his function as a conduit of the dead souls, for this god is a psychopomp—is part of this axial cosmology. The dead mark the deep time of the cosmological space that opens within human society and that Burkert had recognized in the narrative of the neatherd's sacrifice and its significance for the city of Argos.

Let me insert another example of this chthonic inheritance that moves from the collective to the private plane. In his intellectual autobiography *Report to Greco*, modern Greek writer Nikos Kazantzakis writes that he carried everywhere with him a clod of earth from his native Crete, squeezing it at times of anguish to receive strength from it (17). Yet, faced with mortality at the end of his existential struggle, he no longer needs to draw strength from this "fierce clay of Crete" (18); the earth now becomes an object of love and gratitude to which he bids farewell, all the while announcing the complete identification of his existence with it: "This soil I was everlastingly; this soil shall I be everlastingly" (18). This is the same Cretan land he often describes in terms of its dead, particularly those who died during the island's Ottoman occupation. The memory of his father, taking him as a child for a history lesson in the public square to venerate the hung bodies of Cretan rebels (89–90), looms large over Kazantzakis's later aesthetic and moral choices, most visibly in his insistence on the notion of the "ascent," the carrying to the end of one's own cross, that dominates *Report to Greco*. Indeed, this notion of *carrying* is also pivotal to the issue of autochthony itself: just as the prehistoric Britons carried their ancestry into the new settlement, so Kazantzakis's carrying of this handful of Cretan earth—whether literal or metaphorical—shows autochthony to be portable.

Kazantzakis's fidelity to this native amulet might appear parochial in our cosmopolitan age, but in fact points to a universality that was once again understood much earlier by Sophocles, this time in his *Oedipus at*

Colonus: addressing the Erinyes to whom Oedipus descends, the chorus pleads for a good reception of the stranger who died in a foreign land, calling the gates of Hades πολυξένοις—hospitable to many guests (ln. 1570). The chthonic discloses the universality of death because the earth eventually receives everyone anywhere, regardless of the deceased's status—social, national, or even moral, for that matter. Yet this universality is better illuminated through the specificity of the local, through the attachment to the earth that covers the family dead and so becomes a hallowed ground. With Oedipus dying far from his native land, a somewhat reverse operation occurs: the previously unremarkable locale of Colonus that receives him becomes itself inaugural, entering the map for the first time, so to speak, and becoming a universal topos as that locality. The ostensible provincialism behind Kazantzakis's attachment to a handful of "dirt" communicates a cosmological fact about human history: a piece of nature persisting *in*, and not despite, our sociality. Everyone has a "Crete," a place where one's dear ancestors are "hosted"—even if not properly buried and clearly marked, like the fallen Argives in foreign Troy, or the exile Theban king at Colonus—but Crete's meaning as container of the universal can be revealed only in this gesture of singular appropriation by which it becomes *his* Crete. This piece of earth whose keeping presents a modern instance of ancient autochthony testifies to autochthony's relation to diachrony, to rootedness not only in space but, more importantly, in time and continuity, in tradition. To be rooted means in fact to recognize the symbolic, but also eerily literal, transformation of the dead ancestors into an underground root system that supports the "family tree." Carrying this clod of earth with him in his travels, Kazantzakis carries his autochthony into his cosmopolitanism. I would argue even further that it is this archaic trace of actual nature that underlines the "cosmo-" in cosmopolitanism.

Interestingly, current ethical discussions on genocide as not simply a physical but a cultural extermination take place in parallel with a critique of autochthony as an exclusionary topos—though, again, such critique seems to be reserved in the West particularly for the ancient Greeks while exempting many other narratives of indigeneity, as I noted above. Yet these two critical positions cannot be held concurrently without acknowledgment of their underlying conceptual tension, for talk of cultural genocide is unthinkable outside the question of diachrony qua historical rootedness and continuity of tradition. Arguments about the erasure of a culture must presuppose the existence of identifiable elements that run continuously through that culture, forming those diachronic markers that make it distinct from other cultures; only then can the marginalization or persecution of this culture become effectively recognizable and enter the ethico-political discourse. Indeed, cultural genocide involves the erasure of a people not just at the moment but in history: it aims at their oblivion as a people *with* a history.

Diachrony is the "place" where change appears in the context of gradualness and evolution rather than acceleration and revolution, thus foregrounding continuity and seamlessness, not disruption and fragmentation. In diachrony, at work is the "monumental"—that is also to say, the "serious"—side of history as a grand outline seen through the lens of cosmic time, where even the most disruptive breaks, the sharpest crests and troughs of all kinds of shifts, are moderated as a result of being given a new measure, of being "put into perspective." In contrast, the synchronic is the conduit of change, fluidity, and transitoriness, where even the minutest of variations are recorded from a much closer range, thus appearing larger than they would in the depth of time.

That modernity has privileged synchrony over diachrony is rather clear in many discursive and practical fronts. Generally speaking, this preference for the synchronic dovetails with another modern valuation, that of the horizontal/mortal dimension of finitude over the vertical/cosmological dimension of infinitude.[45] More specifically, and in regard to my engagement with the language and study of myth, suffice it to say that the earlier historical-comparative perspectives have been virtually replaced by structural linguistics, which relies on a synchronic view of language—that is, on a "scientific" explanation of language's structure rather than a "philological" exploration of its storytelling patterns across various cultures and epochs. Coming yet closer to the question of autochthony I am presently discussing, modernity conceives of the polis exceedingly in synchronic terms—as a random aggregate of current urban residents—with little regard for either its diachronic dimensions as tradition and heritage or its natural landscape. Consequently, this exclusive emphasis on the synchronic, which also assumes that the diachronic has been superseded in its outdatedness and violence, underlies the critique of autochthony as a discourse of exclusion of the nonindigenous, and of all minoritized identities, including indigenous women. In so doing, however, such criticism also obviates a host of intricate relationships that its otherwise conflicting categories participate in continually.

Speaking of gender, for instance, it is worth noting that, while the chthonic world in ancient tragedy—and here in the *Choephoroi*—is chiefly appealed to and cared for by women (the female chorus and Electra), it is populated by heroes who guard the city (the line of Pelops all the way down to Agamemnon). Hence, we are reminded yet again of the trilogy's contested passage on the father's seed (*Eum.* ln. 659), the exclusive ideological treatment of which does not permit us to consider a further complexity in the masculine's participation in the chthonic. This participation, no more of the order of the heroic, is evoked in the very image of the seed, which introduces quite saliently an experience from nature that ties life and death together: buried in the earth during winter, the seed sprouts in spring, and its appearance gives human beings the miraculous sense of life's beginnings. There is yet a subtler inference to be read here about Agamemnon's fatherhood in relation to the chthonic: through the emphasis on the seed, which is both buried and emergent, Agamemnon's tragic fatherhood is rehabilitated *in* his being dead, for only as a dead ancestor does he become a civic talisman, a guardian spirit protecting Argos even though he has failed as a private father. These chthonic-related issues, carefully prepared for in the "ground" of the *Choephoroi*, should at the very least offer some additional cues as to why Apollo, the heroic god, and Athena, the citadel goddess and the "father's daughter," will valorize patrilineage in the *Eumenides*.

By way of conclusion, I should note that these issues can admit but also exceed ideological criticism, which, despite its own epistemic basis in history and historicity, ironically diminishes the historical immanence or social necessity of the ideas it critiques in favor of prescriptive rather than descriptive readings of them. Recognizing the limits of ideological interpretation does not mean that there is no space to question the valuations of any given culture—namely, the particular hierarchies or distinctions to which it gives rise. It does mean, however, as I have noted repeatedly, that such problematization is fruitful only insofar as it understands that hierarchy per se—regardless of where, when, and how it is applied—proves to be a constitutive requirement not only of ancient but also of modern thought and life. It proves indeed to be an element of necessity, and it is this overwhelming necessity that tragedy as a *descriptive* genre—a genre that looks to nature as its first source and final arbiter—discloses. Needless to say I am aware of the exhaustive effort at nuance with which various theoretical and philosophical approaches have labored to argue for a "suspension" of the hierarchy rather than a mere reversal of its various binary expressions, whether such expressions belong to the philosophical, political, ethical, social, economic, or even psychological domains. Nevertheless, at the heart of *things*, this suspension—no matter how conceptually tightly arranged and ethically well meant—is always revealed as a speculative ruse too light in itself to carry the weight of those things, too unreliable to regulate the cosmic process by which hierarchy reasserts itself. To put it in Aeschylean terms, and once again from the mouth of Prometheus, whom modernity so admired: "Craft is far weaker than necessity"; in this case, the rhetoric of suspension—no matter its necessity—finds itself rather quickly under the rubric of craft.

Eventually, Prometheus's conclusion is not that distant from Burkert's working assumption, according to which the first political forms of organization (the work of human craft par excellence) originated in the need for survival (the male brotherhoods of hunters around which tribal societies grew secure in food provision). For all the critique of functionalism Burkert's hypothesis may elicit, he is effectively translating this Promethean ontological statement into an anthropological scene and a political narrative: the polis, the crowning achievement of human craft, is first grafted onto an *external* necessity, which the polis then transforms but cannot supersede—a formula that underlies his cosmological interpretation of the neatherd Argos's murder by the youngest of the Olympians. While Burkert does not explicitly state this, I suggest that in his cosmological reading, Argos's killing thematizes on the divine plane the civilizational suppression of necessity: necessity is embodied in the figure of the hunter-guardian, whose demise allows the polis to reinvent itself as something created ex nihilo from the machinations of human will. Yet Hermes is not simply a bloodthirsty young god, indulging in the radical change of orders; he is also a guiding companion of dead souls, and as such, he registers not only the violence of political inception against nature but also the commemoration of this inaugural erasure through his participation in chthonic cult.

Chapter 5

Beyond Justice

Apollo's Youth and Athena's Dikē in the *Eumenides*

First Preamble: Aeschylus in the House of Lords or the House of Commons?

It is well established that the *Oresteia* mixes deliberately the royal house's familial intrigue with matters of the polis because "the story of the house of Atreus in many respects parallels the historical process leading to the emergence of the polis," as historian Christian Meier observes (*Athens* 320).[1] For Meier, as for others who read the *Oresteia* for its political subtext, the confrontation between the old gods and the newer Olympians reflects the concurrent strife between the old, aristocratic Areopagites and the democratic reformers of Ephialtes, while at the same time proposing a reconciliation between those rival orders (316–28). Such a reading is quite capacious in the explanatory parallels it draws. However, some mythological and poetological details of the *Oresteia* press us to reflect further on these mappings of old and new, and their underlying tension, which Meier himself acknowledges in several of his analyses of the *Oresteia*, though for different reasons and purposes than my own. For if in the politics of classical Athens the fearsome Erinyes are supposed to stand in for the old nobility, but the bright Olympians for democratic renewal, these alignments are themselves as symbolically fragile as the politics they are purported to emblematize.

The Erinyes, after all, were thought to derive from primitive, chthonic spirits of fertility, and it is to this initial role that they are restored by

Athena in this last play. Much that their retributive mission serves older and stricter values, Aeschylus's animalistic Furies are of themselves hardly a convincing embodiment of aristocratic distance and refinement. Their guardianship and vindication of family honor indeed presumes a bloody immediacy linked to a lower stratum that Jane Ellen Harrison and Walter Otto identified with another god—the one who shunned aristocratic, Apollonian repose: Dionysus.[2] This god also happens to complicate the division between old and new, a division that undergirds the "theological politics"[3] of the *Eumenides*, and that in fact defines the horizon of every politics qua contestation between the forces of maintenance and the forces of change. Contra the prior consensus about a belated, foreign divinity, Otto shows that Dionysus appeared early in Greek poetry and religion but was kept at bay because of his threatening immediacy and rebellious nature, and was only later permitted to resurface as a "stranger" and "latecomer" (*Dionysus* 53, 57, 64). Thus, we learn that the subversive latecomer is not necessarily young—Dionysian iconography portrays him both as a beardless ephebe and an older, bearded Silenus—and we might prudently add that the young, at least as far as mortal politics goes, will not remain so forever, nor will their values. Through its reversibility, nonlinear unpredictability, and simultaneity, Dionysian time complicates the politics of immanence (or politics as immanence), which relies exclusively on the temporality of linear progress even in its most conservative manifestations. In contrast to this unquestioned faith in linear advancement that all revolutionaries exhibit, thus overlooking the conspicuous "re-" of "revolution," Dionysian belatedness and recrudescence expose that revolutions are not new (nor must they necessarily be led by the young), though they tend to fly novelty's banner. Conversely, the old, when erupting unexpectedly in the present, may well produce transformative effects.[4]

In addition to this complicated temporality, Otto's emphatic references to the persecutory mythology of the god, particularly in his nature as Zagreus (the great hunter), fit rather well the template of the Erinyes as agents of pursuit. Zagreus is the most savage manifestation of the god-hunter who was himself hunted (105, 107, 109, 192), and whose cult thus centers on practices of animal dismemberment that memorialize his suffering as well as on rituals of persecution of his female attendants that imitate the pursuit against his nurses (54, 57, 76, 103, 119). Accordingly, the Pythia's petition to the gods in the opening of the *Eumenides* calls on Dionysus Bromios as the render of Pentheus—that is, in his capacity as Zagreus, as the Orphic or "first" Dionysus who was hunted by the Titans and avenged himself by hunting men (ln. 26). The Apollonian priestess compares Pentheus's death to being killed "like a hare" (λαγὼ δίκην Πενθεῖ καταρράψας μόρον), repeating not only the theme of Artemis's slain hare from the parodos of *Agamemnon* but also the syntax of dikē in the place of "as," which predicates destiny through simile. We are subtly reminded that dikē, the word also reserved for "justice," is firmly entrenched in the scene of predation and death. Additionally, the use of *μόρον*[5] for "death" fortifies the meaning of this word in the first play, where its repetition signaled the particularly gruesome fate of the king's corpse in its posthumous mutilation: the older and authoritative hero-father has met the fate of the young and reckless Pentheus.

For Harrison, too, it was this unremitting proximity of Dionysus that made him a spiritualized and spiritualizing deity in Orphism—the religious order that translated the older rites of aversion into newer mystical practices (x–xii), and was thus embraced by the poor and downtrodden in search of a power friendlier to their plight, a power more willing to mingle in their affairs and alleviate their pain than the more distant Olympians. Nietzsche has similarly theorized the Dionysian in relation to the folk song and to the collective surge (*Birth* 52). More recently, Nicole Loraux has written of the "seditious assemblies" and bloody conspiracies harbored in the theaters of Dionysus (*Mourning* 23–25). Opposite this grassroots upheaval, all the aforementioned thinkers have posited Olympian religion as an aristocratic form, which is fleshed out in the rational and public nature that Harrison detected in Homer's gods. Specifically pertinent to Apollo's regulative function in the *Eumenides*, we should mention Nietzsche's remark that this god furnishes the principle that generates and governs all Olympian deities, including Zeus himself: "The same impulse that embodied itself in Apollo gave birth to this entire Olympian world, and in this sense Apollo is its father" (*Birth* 41). The father proceeds from the son's image, in a genealogical reversal meant to exemplify Olympian essence as one of phenomenal ideality, clarity of distinctions, and rational hierarchization.

To say that the Apollonian principle represents the rational, individuated, and measured facets of existence amounts to describing a form of political enlightenment and, indeed, Apollo is both a solar and civic divinity. In turn, this also implies that Apollonian religion qua civic religion, and not mystical bacchanale, starts as an *aristocratic* form. The "first" polis, or the very possibility of a polis, hinges on an aristocratic construct, one in which distances and boundaries are observed in a steadfast manner, as opposed to the Dionysian "democracy" of leveling, whose fusional impulse, clandestine revolts, and imminent transvaluations threaten both the separateness of the various individuals that comprise the political aggregate, as well as the continuity of the fabric—the tradition—wherein these individual relations are interwoven.[6] Consequently, if we take into account the parallels between the chthonic/hunting Dionysian and the Erinyes' bloodthirsty morality that avenges *at all costs*, it becomes evident that the Erinyes cannot easily square with the old, aristocratic order any more than Apollo can be equated with revolutionary novelty.

There is yet another, anthropological line of argument concerning Indo-European social and religious hierarchy that could challenge this scholarly alignment of Aeschylus's old gods with traditionalism and the new gods with reform. In the Indo-European hierarchical order of religious and social tripartition elaborated in the works of Émile Benveniste and Georges Dumézil, fertility gods belonged to the third and lowest order, while cosmic/legal and martial gods occupied the first two positions, respectively. (Incidentally, that the first class of sovereign gods includes pairs of cosmic and contractual legislators [Varuna/Mitra, Ahura Mazda/Mithra, Odin/Tyr, Zeus/Apollo] reinforces my central point in this study about the inextricable link between dikē as jurisprudential principle and cosmology.) According to this tripartite scheme, many Indo-European mythologies share narratives of a war between the two nobler orders against the lower third, which initially fell outside the hierarchy. This war concluded with the victory of the noble alliance and the assimilation of the vanquished into a later official triad.[7] Mapping old and new along these lines, Athena and Apollo fall again under the aristocratic grouping, with the Erinyes representing the lower agricultural spirits, somewhat analogous to the early Roman household gods, the Lares and Penates.[8] The most interesting point, however, involves not the chronological sequencing itself but its symbolic efficacy: regardless of which divine grouping was more ancient, at issue is the *political* significance of the old/new divide, particularly in light of the modern consensus about what constitutes sound political development. In other words, at issue is the how and why the aristocratic—which enabled civic existence to emerge from the substratum of magic and chthonicity—has come to signify the outdated, while the democratic as a form of horizontal leveling signifies the new in perpetuity, while also being considered at every present moment as the highest and unsurpassable form of governance.

This question of old and new, or perhaps more sharply stated, of old and *young*, will be returning in many guises in this chapter. For now, it serves as an initial guidepost from which to contemplate the *Oresteia* not as a political allegory—at least not exclusively, nor even primarily—but as an encounter between two opposing, cosmic forces whose effects are most visible in the shifts and conflicts of the city, but whose necessity arrives from beyond the city-world: the battle of young and old attests to a cosmic exigency and to the sphere of Ananke, which regulates not only the genealogies of humans and their civic affairs but the economy of the universe as well. The unexpected awe of the humble guard looking up at the night sky in the opening of *Agamemnon* holds the hermeneutic key for the whole trilogy, and gives us the scale by which to measure and judge our existence in the world: What would human affairs amount to—the deaths, revolutions, wars, illnesses, births, quotidian changes, and grand movements—from the point of view of the constellations, from the timeframe required for the death of stars and the birth of planets?[9] On the one hand, the old, justice-obsessed Furies capture something of the world's death-drive—the attachment to the past only in its morbidity, which in the human polis translates into the paradox of tradition not as continuity but as expiry. On the other, the nonchalant, young Olympians, who imperiously override the last crime (the crime of the *young* son) illustrate the life force by translating through the juridical scene the immemorial demand of life to continue itself sometimes with no regard to whatever might appear morally offensive to humans. In exonerating Orestes, the Olympians announce first and foremost the justice of continuing on with life, even if past debt remains unpaid, even if hurt parties think the chase was not enough. Both these drives exist in an intimacy of opposition best captured by the image of the inexhaustible sea of death and renewal in Clytemnestra's luring speech.

Before shifting gears into the cosmology of the *Eumenides*, however, further context about the play's politics through a review of the relevant scholarship would be instructive. As the commentary is wide-ranging and impossible to address fully, I focus specifically at arguments that attend to Aeschylus's sobriety rather than blind partisanship. Daniel Blickman, for instance, discusses the politics of the *Oresteia* through the theme of pollution, whose ritual-anthropological trappings bespeak, according to him, political concerns by the time of Aeschylus. Blickman responds to Robert Parker's claims in *Miasma* that dispute the scholarly overemphasis on pollution as primarily an archaic/classical theme. The discourse of pollution was already established as early as the Homeric times, Parker argues, but it was later tragedy's obsession with homicide—particularly with kin murder (*emphylios*)—that was responsible for rendering pollution more visible in the archaic and classical age.¹⁰ While praising the evidence Parker provides in dating pollution back to Homer, Blickman believes there are reasons other than tragedy's obsession with murder that account for pollution's centrality in the life and thought of the classical age, and those reasons are of political, social, and legal nature.

Like other scholars who interpret the *Eumenides* as a response to the changed sociopolitical landscape of Athens, Blickman isolates "the theme of *dikē*, [which] through the overlap of morals, law, and political justice in that term, may be deemed the lynch-pin connecting family and city" (204). Dikē here is defined thoroughly within the semantic horizon of "justice"—namely, as a formal, political code guaranteeing fairness—without its cosmological resonance. Dikē's function as a mediating link between family and city is thanks to its political and moral nature, which Blickman considers as being shared by both the family and the city, rather than dividing them.¹¹ This is understandable given his focus on the shift from pollution as a religious, and potentially insufficient, means of regulating violence to a legal tool of implementing more efficiently the consequences of homicide in order to preserve social order in the city-state. One cannot underestimate the necessity of such a legal and sociopolitical approach to the *Oresteia* without losing sight of the complexity of the trilogy in its historical context, as well as of the very fact that the cosmology of dikē is itself not thoroughly divorceable from the polis. At the same time, however, as I am insisting throughout this study, Aeschylean dikē is not exhausted at the political threshold: though it is implicated in the changes of the nascent city-state, dikē is a *destinal* category that also reveals the nonimmanent purview of what we now term "justice."

To buttress his thesis about Aeschylus's historically specific intention of merging the fate of the royal house with that of the city, Blickman cites Friedrich Solmsen on Aeschylus's debt to Hesiod, and on the two poets' shared view of historical continuity and change. Solmsen aligns Aeschylus with Hesiod in that they both wished to move from archaic violence toward a more just age, but they were also committed to preserving the continuity of past virtues into the future: "It is safe to assume that the sequence of family catastrophes which for obvious reasons recommended themselves to Aeschylus as suitable subjects for trilogies had in their original pre-Aeschylean versions little relation to the ideas of a state like fifth-century Athens" (Solmsen qtd. in Blickman 204n42). Thus, the choice of kin murder as a theme is not dictated simply by the tragic aesthetic, which it nonetheless conveniently suits, but also by the fact that this type of violence allegorizes contemporary sociopolitical dangers behind various institutional innovations and usurpations through which new rights are granted, old jurisdictions are repealed, mistrust grows, and alliances become fragile. Amid the instability of the transitional moment, Solmsen's Aeschylus, not unlike Meier's, rises as a sober figure, gazing forward as he turns, Janus-like, both critically and respectfully toward the past. This "centrism" offers perhaps the most insightful glimpse into the playwright's politics because it captures best the larger sense of remove that inheres in Aeschylus's cosmology of dikē—his vision of the order of things (*taxis pragmatōn*)—thus also being suitable for the purposes of this study. Though the precise hermeneutical location of the center is articulated differently from commentator to commentator, the shared point of reference remains Aeschylus's treatment of the Areopagus, it being the focus of these ancient sociopolitical debates and innovations. Whether it was the target of criticism of the radical-democratic reforms, or the sole institution that could carry through and legitimize those reforms precisely because of its procedural continuity and trustworthiness, as Lindsay Hall argues (327), the Areopagus came to represent the very stakes of this fight of time against time, of innovation against tradition, and of the future against the past. The seriousness of this temporal struggle could only be played on its turf: the Areopagus was, after all, the most serious of courts, the one deciding on capital crimes and religious offenses, and the one that also had under its jurisdiction the guardianship of the laws themselves (*nomophylakia*).

Hall's commentary on the Areopagitic functions through the reforms of Ephialtes (462–61 BC) and up to the immediate aftermath of the Thirty Tyrants (404–3 BC) offers, along with a challenge of the conventional historiography of this turbulent period, an indicative sample of scholarly positions regarding Aeschylus's political leanings.[12] The *Eumenides*' positive depiction of the Areopagus as guarantor of due process leads Hall to question the historians' faith in Aristotle's rendering of the events in *Athenaiōn Politeia*, according to which Ephialtes repealed the powers of the Areopagus, and redistributed them to other institutions, thus delegitimizing it as the last aristocratic bastion.[13] The play, which was performed within three years of the reforms, could not show such confidence in the Areopagus had the recent history of its disenfranchisement been so clear-cut (Hall 319). In evaluating various responses to this problem, Hall presents a brief survey of the political commentary.

For some, Aeschylus was a reactionary fighting against the reforms—E. R. Dodds starts with this assumption but then qualifies it ("Notes"). For Ulrich von Wilamowitz-Moellendorff, Aeschylus's fictional Areopagus resembles the democratic Heliaia more than its actual counterpart, and thus the playwright must have been a democrat (Hall 320). Yet others locate Aeschylus in the political center, approving of the reforms but cautiously so. As indicated above, Dodds reaches obliquely this centrist conclusion, a move that merits elaboration because—to repeat my earlier point—such centrism (in the various forms it takes from the nearly self-contradictory articulations of Dodds or Meier[14] to Hall's own interpretation of the Areopagus as a mediating institution) affords us a subtler hermeneutic. Dodds bases his argument on the *Eumenides'* contested passage (ln. 690–95), where Athena establishes the court by warning against the laws' corruption from bad influences (κακαῖς ἐπιρροαῖσι). Whereas other scholars interpreted the bad influences to be the Ephialtic and Periclean reforms in general, Dodds identifies them narrowly with the eligibility of the lower-class *zeugitai* to the archonship of the Areopagus, which up until the discovery of the *Athenaiōn Politeia* was thought to have been introduced earlier by Aristides, and thus normalized by the time Aeschylus composes the *Eumenides*. As such, what allegedly bothers Aeschylus is not any reform, but the specific tampering with the membership criteria, and thus with the very constitution and credibility of this body. Dodds writes: "This proposal to pollute with commoners the one really aristocratic body which was left in Athens appeared fully as shocking to conservative minds as proposals to flood the House of Lords with Labour peers did some years ago to English conservatives" (20). Incidentally, this staunch conservatism fits seductively well with Aeschylean high aesthetics—the use of solemn language and the advocacy of grand old ritual in tragic form. Nonetheless, despite such initial depiction, Dodds moderates his claim by adding that Aeschylus is "not protesting against anything the democrats have already done," but "warning them against going too far in the *future*," a position he finds congruent with the play's "repeated emphasis on τὸ μέσον" (20; original emphasis): literary theme and politics converge at "the middle," which is why I detect a "centrist" reading behind this reactionary portrait. His concluding remark is quite disclosive even if one does not share his exegetical, historical, and speculative assumptions: "Aeschylus was not by temperament a reactionary, but in his old age he had begun to feel that reform was in danger of moving *too fast and too far*; that is the common experience of elderly reformers" (20; my emphasis).[15]

"Too far" and "too fast" are summary terms for tragic hubris in the coordinates of space and time. Regarding the issue of temperament, moral hesitation about the evils of excess is thoroughly commensurate with, and in fact constitutive to, tragic temperament. Dodds's assertion about the elderly man's appeal to the middle is not a mere psychologism that can be disproven once contrary empirical examples of radical elders become available. Beyond the attestable psychology of maturity, which tends to exchange unbridled experimentation for quiet cautiousness, the notion of the middle refers to what I call a "cosmological reserve," a reserve communicated in tragedy both through the heroic Apollonian remove and the chorus's reflective distance from the events.

Other scholars suspend or contain the notion of politics from overtaking the interpretive task. Hall cites Colin Macleod's opinion that Aeschylus is "aloof" from politics, noting, however, that it is not congruent with Athena's praise of the Areopagus as a bulwark of the city. Then comes Meier's reading in *The Political Art of Greek Tragedy*, which Hall finds self-contradictory because it recognizes in the *Oresteia* "a considered response" to the recent events, but maintains that Aeschylus's politics is "irrelevant" to interpretation (Hall 320). Diverging from Hall, I see in Meier's reserve the acknowledgment that authorial, and even textual, interests in political events do not reduce the drama to political messaging. Thus, without fully reviewing all these positions, I single out their broadly shared refraining from overt partisanship, whether through the concepts of centrism, aloofness, or interpretive reserve. Whereas the events of 462–61 cannot be "clinically severed" from the play's composition (Hall 320), I submit that a relative distance from empirical politics is necessary in order to appreciate what makes politics a tragic theater in the first place—that is, to cognize how much the forces acting on politics qua domain of rational deliberation are deeply unstable and often beyond rational control.[16]

Eventually, Hall's own argument, which he might view as prodemocratic (though others might charge it as "reactionary" in praising the transformative ability of an erstwhile aristocratic gerontocracy), relies on a centrist premise. His history of the Areopagus shows it to be the "constitutional anchor"[17] that managed to support the democratic process in fragile times, and to emerge after the tyranny of the Thirty as the guarantor of the vetting process (*dokimasiai*) for appointments in the newly restored democratic offices—all because of the generational continuity, and the gradual building of trust among its members who became over time more representative of the populace (326–27).

More critical toward Aeschylus's insufficiently democratic politics, Mark Griffith's essay on the *Oresteia* observes that the aristocratic elite is preserved and performs a vital role within the new civic order, as evidenced by the vertical and horizontal hierarchies between the rulers and the ruled, and among the elite families, respectively: "By focusing closely on these relationships, we shall come to recognize the processes whereby, even as 'democratic' and 'civic' pride are being reinforced, the unique and irreplaceable value of an international network of elite families is simultaneously reaffirmed. So far from being regarded as an obsolete or reactionary element under the new democracy, the old elite emerge as being essential to the prosperity and very survival of even the more 'democratic' communities" (64). Griffith's conception of these relational axes remains again firmly entrenched within a politics of power, eliding the cosmological and axiological hierarchies that inflect human relations. Of interest is his remark about the gradual decrease of lower-class voices, which happens paradoxically as the trilogy progresses toward its democratic resolution: beginning with *Agamemnon*, where lower-rank characters carry a good majority of the verses, we reach a balance of voices between the regal protagonists and the chorus of slave women in the *Choephoroi*, but in the otherwise "democratic" *Eumenides*, the lower-class voices are absent, with the jurors—the closest representatives of Aeschylus's ordinary Athenian audience—remaining silent (76–78). I submit, however, that Griffith's equivalency of the jurors' silence with the erasure of the citizenry's voice is tenuous since this silence is indicative not of insignificance but of the seriousness of the capital court. This is indeed Judith Fletcher's point concerning the gravity of decisions in cases of life and death, which, by their nature, required a space of quiet sobriety distinct from the loudness of the overcrowded popular courts (70–71). The fact that seriousness, on account of its being viewed as a vestige of an older and nobler order, falls target to democratic criticism should not automatically legitimize the assumptions behind such criticism; on the contrary, it should be cause for concern when democracy undermines the very category of seriousness for having "elitist" social trappings. Logic must be put to stand on its feet: the noble class vested itself with seriousness because seriousness is noble, not the other way around. Thus, any hierarchy of the noble versus the popular, or the quiet versus the gregarious, cannot be reduced to issues of social class alone, but is a matter of the nature of things and circumstances, which sometimes calls for the lighthearted but other times for the deadly serious. To Griffith's reproach that Aeschylus reduces the volume of ordinary voices on his way to democracy, I would respond that a silent juror can arrive at the Areopagus from the lower strata, and his silence can be just as eloquent as the poetry of *Agamemnon*'s watchman or the curses of the slave women in the *Choephoroi*.

The Areopagus could withstand tremendous political transitions, and preside over social reforms in a credible and peaceful manner, because of certain qualities inherent in its institutional structure and history: traditional continuity, ancestral authority, and procedural gradualness—all of which accommodated the process of change, even when it affected the court's own ranks, without violent disruptions. In its restraint from excess, the historical Areopagus carves out a nonhubristic space, somewhat analogous to the dramatic function of the chorus. We could even entertain the thought that Aeschylus's Areopagites comprise the "real" but silent chorus opposite the overwrought Eumenides. Whereas the unique polyphony of the incompetent assembly of elders at the end of *Agamemnon* signaled also the end of the polis, the silence of the serious Areopagites restores the tragic assembly as a reflective medium. Unlike the vocal and partisan Erinyes acting as an antichorus, the sober jurors deliberate quietly; at the same time, the numerical balance of their opposing verdicts attests both to the zone of indistinction between justice claims *and* to the civic/civilized imperative of freely contemplating and expressing rival opinions precisely in such moments of impasse.

As a suppliant led to the Areopagus for trial, Orestes summons one of Athens's primal political scenes: there is the story of Cylon and his supporters, who, after an unsuccessful coup attempt in 632 BC, ended up suppliants at the temple of Athena. Deceptively accosted by their persecutors and promised a fair trial, they—suspecting foul play—tied themselves around the statue of the goddess for protection. They were still slaughtered once out of the temple by the Alcmaeonids, the noble Athenian family from whom Pericles descended via his mother. The bloody act brought about the Cylonian curse (*Kylonian agos*), and Athens had to invite the Cretan priest Epimenides to cleanse the city. Athens thus remembers its beginnings as a powerful city-state in this scene of persecution, unholy murder, and pollution. As Blickman's essay explains, the legal consolidation of the abhorrence of murder, which initially was expressed through the religious discourse of pollution and catharsis, came with Draco's homicide laws, which ordered the relatives of the slain to proclaim the murderer as polluter at the burial, thus enhancing the public feeling of aversion at a blood crime (201). Like Cylon, Ephialtes too met a violent end, though no consensus exists about the identity of his assassin. As it often happens in times of turmoil, the most improbable of rumors travel along with the likely ones. In Ephialtes's case, the easy conjecture leads to some disgruntled aristocrats. Nonetheless, Robert Wallace presents a legitimate challenge to this speculation: had it been so, and had the radical democrats themselves not been implicated in the murder, they would have most likely "raised a witch-hunt," making him "a martyr for the democratic cause," but instead they kept silent (269). Just as in tragedy, in-house fighting may once again be more likely, and Wallace surmises that the one responsible—because also the one to profit most from such death—was Pericles and his circle (269).

In the context of such jarring stories during unstable times, Aeschylus's emphasis on "the middle," which Dodds had noted, becomes indispensable. Apropos the more specific issue of the Areopagus's relation to the middle, it appears that this middle is not located *between* the Areopagites and the reformers but was already present *within* the Areopagus itself, which, in its continuity and culture of internal trust, was able to guarantee the implementation of reforms. I should stress here that the attributes of continuity, authoritativeness, and respect for tradition[18] belong to the cluster of concepts relating to seriousness as developed in chapter 2. Therefore, the seriousness of the Areopagus is constitutively linked to its vestigial aristocracy, and furthermore, it is this *vestigial* nature that allows the court to mediate effectively the advent of the new. Hall concludes: "It is an agreeable irony that . . . this former stronghold of aristocratic power and privilege would one day play a salubrious role as the real and perceived guardian of the democratic πολιτεία in Athens's darkest hour. One notes that more modifications to government legislation in the U.K. in the last ten years have issued from the House of Lords than from the House of Commons" (327–28). Or, to put it in terms of the divine axis with which we started this political prelude to the *Eumenides*: it was through Olympian (aristocratic) reserve that law itself could be established, and that chthonic dikē could finally be shown in its rational mission and civilized service as the sending of the other daughter of Zeus—Dios Kora being now Athena rather than Persephone.

Second Preamble: Ixion's Wheel

Our second preamble is more speculative, but I hope still insightful with regard to Aeschylean dikē. Two references to the myth of Ixion[19] that perhaps appear incidental and forgettable to the modern reader were likely poignant for the ancient spectators, for whom they evinced the context of suppliance, as well as of crime and punishment, thus shedding additional light on the play and the trilogy overall. The references come from the mouths of the two gods who preside over Orestes's fate—Athena and Apollo.

First, as Athena ponders Orestes's eligibility for an audience with her, having no knowledge yet of who he is and what he has done, she compares him to a suppliant Ixion (ln. 441). Orestes corrects her promptly, asserting that he is no suppliant in need of purification, for he has already been purified (ln. 443–46). He then explains his presence on purely legal grounds, and boldly so: declaring Apollo as the moral instigator (ἐπαίτιος) of his matricide, he asks for Athena's judicial intervention to decide whether a crime committed under external duress—here, a divine command—is righteous or not (ln. 465-69). Orestes distances himself from Ixion. In correcting Athena, he also implies a subtle distinction between ritual catharsis and legal clearance, which arguably does not posit the latter as more "legitimate" than the former. I propose that Orestes's request for trial does not expect the court to validate the rite, for this assumes the court to be of higher authority in the way political readings tend to do; instead, Orestes elicits divine favor to influence the court *to conform to* the ritual by acquitting him. In this hierarchical scheme, it is the goddess who legitimizes the court to translate the ritual into civic language, and such a moment is both inaugural and meaningful about the scope and efficacy of human justice.

The second reference to Ixion occurs during Apollo's mounting argument against the Furies (ln. 717–18). The god again employs the scene of suppliance, this time to reject the Furies' demand for harsh justice, by reminding them that even Zeus was moved by Ixion's supplication and purified him. Ixion's name is thus woven into the legal and ethical fabric of the trilogy's resolution. Indeed, Ixion was of particular significance to Aeschylus, as well as to the other two major tragedians and the lesser known Timasitheus, all of whom devoted a play to him, though none has survived.[20] His myth of familial murder and pollution proves, of course, exceedingly pertinent to the *Oresteia* overall. As far as the *Eumenides* is concerned, the myth also poses questions about the impossibility of nonretributive justice and the limits of clemency.

A Lapith king, Ixion belongs to the cycle of Thessalian legend. According to Cecil Smith, the most important and perhaps most archaic part of his myth was Ixion's murder of his kin as first of its kind. His designation as first kin-slayer also persisted in later versions, and Smith imagines him as something of a "Hellenic Cain" (278), though, unlike Cain, Ixion did not aggress against a blood relative (*emphylios*). Rather, the victim is identified as his father-in-law, Deioneus/Eioneus.[21] Having invited him as his guest, Ixion threw him into a fire pit to avoid paying a bride price for his daughter, thus also violating the code of hospitality. The fire involved in the murder is visible in the poetic justice of the fiery wheel to which Ixion will be later affixed as his eternal torment.[22] Ixion's deed thus relates quite obviously to the *Oresteia*'s family intrigue as it also points to the fact that both of the *Oresteia*'s murderers were in a host-guest relationship vis-à-vis their victims, and both perverted *xenia* by feigning their roles: Clytemnestra receiving her husband with treacherous flattery, and Orestes appearing as a stranger to gain entrance to his own home and repay his mother in kind. Following the murder, a maddened Ixion sought purification from pollution, but to no avail. In Smith's interpretation of a red-figure cantharus at the British Museum depicting this myth, it appears that the purifying god Apollo has sent his priest to expel the suppliant vigorously from his altar. Here, Smith notes the typological similarities in visual representations of Ixion and Orestes as suppliants to the Delphic temple. Yet he is also mindful of the difference that the Aeschylean text makes amply clear: whereas Ixion received no sympathy from Apollo, Orestes did.

When Apollo and all mortal princes turned Ixion away, Zeus—father of all and patron god of hospitality—took pity on him, called him to Olympus, and purified him. Smith notes that this is probably a later, "Olympicizing" accretion, superimposed on the older, kin-murdering plot (278), but it is certainly a version that was in circulation by Aeschylus's time. Nevertheless, Ixion's story does not end well for him. When he arrived at Olympus, he promptly took advantage of Zeus's generosity and grew lustful of the god's consort, Hera.[23] Aware of Ixion's intentions, Zeus created a cloud in the shape of Hera to trick him, and from this strange union the race of Centaurs was born. Violating hospitality, and offending a more powerful father yet again, Ixion was not spared the second time around but was punished with one of the eternal ancient torments: strapped to a wheel of fire, he was condemned to spin around forever. Etiologically speaking, Ixion's fiery wheel reads as a solar myth; here, however, I focus on the moral and jurisprudential implications of Ixion's double crime, with Zeus's reversal being key, though this reversal remains extratextual to the *Eumenides*. The play overtly compares Ixion and Orestes as suppliants but omits mention of their eventual fates. Despite this elision, it is reasonable to infer that their respective tales must somehow correspond to their different character and behavior even as they both commit crimes.

The harsh punishment that follows the interlude of clemency in Ixion's myth begs the deeper question of the limits of lenience, and obliges us to consider these limits particularly in view of the growing, *secular* conceptions of jurisprudence that nonetheless *theologically* infinitize lenience, while releasing offending agents from responsibility. For instance, legal scholars and advocates of carceral reform routinely now propose nonpunitive forms of justice, or even the abandonment of prosecution in some cases. These proposals claim a more compassionate, more socially equitable management of crime, and in some cases may even rehabilitate the perpetrator, though this is by no means an uncontested statistical fact. The ethical question, however, is not exhausted by social pragmatics, nor by the idealistic appeal to the offender's improvement, but leaves us with a significant remainder: a nonpunitive justice that does not incur significant cost to the perpetrator does not fulfil the notion of justice as *the responsibility to suffer* for the suffering one has produced. In fact, as the chorus of *Agamemnon* twice declares, moral improvement is unthinkable outside suffering, for suffering is learning: "Zeus, who guided men to think, / who has laid it down that wisdom comes alone through suffering" (ln. 176–78). Even more pertinently to the nonpunitive legal advocates who claim the offender's moral reform as their ethical aim, the Aeschylean chorus specifies: "Justice [Dika] so moves that those only learn who suffer" (ln. 250–51). Orestes himself speaks of his earned knowledge through suffering: "I have been beaten and been taught" (ln. 276), he says to the Furies, who take pleasure at the thought of feasting on his blood and gore.

Yet another argument for judicial lenience goes as follows: punishing the culprit does not restore the losses experienced by the victim—particularly when the loss of life is concerned—and thus, there is no point in extracting payment and causing further harm. First, this quasi-utilitarian rationale relies on the suppression of the cosmology of dikē, which allows for a vast, often incomprehensible, ripple effect that the crime has—a ripple effect that extends beyond the living relations of victims and offenders, just as the cosmos exceeds the borders of civil society and human history. But second, it is worth also noting that the passage from an "enlightened" ethics of universal clemency to social justice ideologies is marked by an inconsistent consideration and use of this ripple effect: while universal clemency tends to overlook the ripple effect entirely (hence, with the victim dead, only the culprit's life matters), social justice appeals to it selectively. Indeed, the progressive advocacy for general prosecutorial lenience on the grounds that punishment fails to restore individual victims is reinterpreted in social justice advocacy. The latter resorts to a more expansive notion of justice as a ripple effect from past crimes but decides lenience and punishment on the criterion of the offender and victim's identities, thus sidelining the rational and universal basis of *isonomia*. Here is the slippage: on the one hand, the objection to prosecuting socially marginalized offenders denies the principle that all crime creates a hurtful ripple effect—a principle operative in both rational ethics and cosmic dikē; on the other hand, the ancient morality of "the sins of parents visited upon children" returns in the name of "systemic injustice," which makes moral demands for historical crimes. Extreme lenience meets the generational curse, but the difference from Aeschylus consists in the fact that both principles are now not to be thought neutrally, but selectively, according to social markers.

From the cosmological perspective, a crime marks an imbalance in the order of the world that needs to be rectified, sometimes in ways inscrutable and even antithetical to human logic, but nonetheless in some way. From this perspective, the payment may not necessarily accrue to the immediate victim, though the victim has the inalienable right to call up the Fury; the payment does accrue to the world by restoring the general pattern of things. Aeschylean dikē names the mechanism by which randomness manages to gather itself into order, delivering accidentally that which might otherwise be rationally expected: the universe somehow *happens* to catch up with the culprit. Another pair of choral lines from *Agamemnon* conveys how inscrutable divine justice can be, and how inexplicably it may arrive, as these lines reformulate dikē in the majestic paradox of a "violent grace" (χάρις βίαιος): "From the gods who sit in grandeur / grace comes somehow violent" (ln. 182–83).[24] Violent grace ensures the debt is paid, even if the proper receiver is absent. Of course, in the tragic context of the ancestral curse, where the dead were honored with a posthumous moral demand and the power of vigilance, they did in some way receive their due. In summary, to think that one can be still held responsible without punishment contravenes the seriousness of the tragic genre (and of actual crimes), at least in the sense in which I have already elaborated the concept of seriousness. Seriousness requires that the stakes be high for the agent. The agent's responsibility would not appear as such without him or her suffering a severe consequence for the deed. The last part of the Ixion myth reaffirms this point, with Zeus revoking his lenience after Ixion's repeated transgressions.

Obviously, we cannot know Aeschylus's reasons for eliding the detail of Ixion's torment, given his otherwise rigorous declarations about the consequences of misdeeds. I would, however, like to offer a speculation about the subtle dramatic effects this omission achieves: though in both instances of its citation the myth hints at the positive outcome of suppliance, the omission also works to turn Ixion into a tragic foil of Orestes. Ixion does not simply serve as a model worthy of lenience; instead, the temporary grace he enjoys, juxtaposed with the unspoken—but presumably widely known—condemnation that awaits him, contrast sharply with the final deliverance of the previously suffering Orestes. Next to Ixion, Orestes appears slightly similar but is mostly different.[25] If we keep the unmentioned punishment in mind, we can interpret Apollo's use of the myth in a way that corroborates retroactively the logic of the tragic foil. As defense witness, Apollo rebuts the Erinyes' demand for blood by reminding them of Zeus's initial mercy for someone who proved eventually unworthy of it; the inference would be that Orestes deserves all the more the mercy that Ixion abused.

It is this difference that in part accounts for the dikē Orestes receives from the Areopagus, a dikē that through his acquittal vindicates two seemingly antithetical prerogatives. On one side, it redoubles and affirms through a deliberative process nature's neutral and arbitrary impetus for the continuation of life—for why can *this* murderer be exonerated but not the previous ones, and is the flimsy excuse of patrilineal loyalty sufficient to account for such a decision? On the other, it does not obviate the human demand for moral justification, since Orestes's implicit comparison to Ixion proves him to be a *different* kind of perpetrator. This dikē is paradigmatic of Aeschylean cosmology: it acts as a centripetal force that aligns cosmos and polis along the axis mundi whenever the polis takes its measure from the cosmos (recall Burkert's cosmological link between the slain Argos and his city) but turns centrifugal whenever political hubris forgets this measure and provokes disorder (as in the tyranny of Aegisthus and Clytemnestra). Aeschylean dikē thus traverses the contested midpoint between the cosmic prerogative of just indifference and the human requirement for rational justice, between violent grace and civic convention.

The Young Gods Who Are Old: Eros, Thanatos, and the Hunt

If there is a single rubric under which one can interpret the many shifts and translations of the *Eumenides*—for instance, the translation of the very name of the Erinyes, their changing attributes from spirits of vengeance to patrons of prosperity, and the political shift from blood feud to formal judicial procedure—it would be the rift between old Titans and younger Olympians. Indeed, the grandeur of Aeschylean poetics owes very much to the fact that the playwright wrestled with a conflict of such magnitude, where the divine intergenerational conflict thematizes for human consciousness its own finitude as historical becoming—the confrontation between progress and tradition. This monumental rift, which will be resolved rather subtly with both its poles to a degree intact, is framed already in relative terms in the Pythia's prologue. The priestess recounts the genealogy of Delphi as a place of prophecy, linking Phoebus Apollo, its current claimant, to its previous titanic inhabitants (ln. 1–8). Earth, the first prophet, handed the office to her daughter Themis; with Themis's uncoerced consent, it was then inherited by her sister Phoebe, who, in turn, offered it as a "birth gift" to Phoebus, who bears her name. Though not made explicit in this genealogy, Phoebus's mother, Leto, is Phoebe's daughter.

Notable in this titanic inheritance is the mention of the legal category of uncoerced consent (θελούσης, οὐδὲ πρὸς βίαν τινός). The passing of the office to Apollo mentions the symbolism of his shared name that, along with Phoebe's gesture of the birth gift (γενέθλιον δόσιν), hint at the blood kinship between Olympians and Titans. The genealogy is thus based on a lopsided chiasmus in which the bloody Titans were already protolegal entities, while the symbolic Apollo has latent blood ties to the divine order he will oppose in the remainder of the play. The young are *of* the old, possessing an authority passed down to them from the old, no matter how the name of this authority changes, as happens in this narrative when Zeus, rather than Gaia, is said to inspire Apollo with prophecy (ln. 17–18). The usurpation of Gaia's authority by Zeus thus presents a gendered thematization of an extremely profound, iterative, and otherwise neutral, structure—indeed a cosmological structure: time's own recurring cycles of finite seasons, of day and night, which appear from the perspective of human history to progress linearly in the cumulation of these infinite repetitions. The crucial point for me here is that linearity appears only from the perspective of history but takes center stage in political and historicist interpretations, of which most paradigmatic is Hegel's reading of the play in the *Lectures on Fine Art* and his revisitation of it in the *Phenomenology*. Though I broadly share Hegel's narrative of reconciliation, I arrive there from a different path: I treat developmental linearity mainly as an epiphenomenon rather than the crux of the play, focusing instead on the repeatable cosmological pattern as a deep underlayer on which historical cumulations are superimposed. Strictly speaking, from my perspective, the ending does not articulate *primarily* the mediation between prepolitical and political forms of justice and their fully conscious reconciliation, but highlights a natural necessity that requires the end of hostilities as the only natural-cum-political response to the preceding cycle of violence. This natural necessity runs concurrently with and propels political action rather than being superseded by it. Eventually, Athena must coerce the Furies into accepting their new position, thus demonstrating the necessity of natural force over rational procedure; and eventually, prosperity and civic welfare are predicated on natural benevolence at least as much as human good will. That the question of nature is a priority for me, then, marks a substantive departure from Hegel, for whom nature is but a shackle to be removed by art and culture on the way to freedom. Nonetheless, Hegel and reconciliation will be revisited near the conclusion of this chapter.

Returning to the Pythian narrative, this generational elision of Gaia by Zeus provides a foil and a precedent for Apollo's later excuse of matricide based on the exclusive patrilineality of kinship: Clytemnestra's erasure turns out to be necessary for the establishment of another rift, analogous to the one between Zeus and the Titans.[26] Except that in the mortal world, this new rift is thematized as a political dichotomy, or better, rupture, between ancient despotism and progressive enlightenment; lest we forget, Clytemnestra is not only a spurned mother and betrayed wife but also a tyrannical usurper "deserving" of historical obsolescence. Even Apollo and Athena themselves can only be Olympian because of the elision of their own titanic mothers—the unmentioned Leto and the devoured Metis. When Apollo severs Clytemnestra's kinship to Orestes, he effectively disavows his own blood bond with the Titans, thus enabling *for* humans the political shift from archaism to enlightenment. Otherwise, the divine offspring would belong to both orders, unable to extricate the "politics" of the older from that of the younger. To drive this idea one step further: the Olympians' equal and simultaneous admission to their double genealogy entails an asynchronicity that, in political terms, would undermine the single political myth that has enjoyed consistent assent—namely, politics as linear progress away from the past's outdated conservatism and toward the future's ever-expanding amelioration. Aeschylus's patriarchal elision of the mother unexpectedly serves to affirm the progressive distinction that has become democracy's most exclusive, most prized, and thus unspoken, binary—that of a two-party regime acted out as intergenerational conflict: the confrontation of old and young not as cosmic expressions of time's *neutral* passage but—in the trope of "the classical versus the modern"—as the war between ideological formations representing broadly something like "conservatism" and "progressivism," respectively. The Erinyes' complaint against Zeus—"a young god, you have ridden down powers gray with age" (ln. 150)—encodes this translation from the rift in divine/cosmic time into the injustice of the politics of power, and more succinctly, of politics *as* power.

Nonetheless, this ideological effect at the end of the trilogy is only an epiphenomenon—and a rather ironic one—since Aeschylus, despite scholarly attempts to turn him chiefly into a political playwright, is expressly concerned with realities beyond the civic sphere as well: the reality, for instance, of temporalized existence, or of nature's immemorial engendering and destroying, which are captured in poetic rather than political language. Thus, I would recast the gods' juxtaposition of old and new not so much in terms of the progress from an erstwhile tyranny to a superior polity but in terms of a natural protophenomenon, of which one perception only leads to the narrative of politics as improvement. Before and beyond all politics, this protophenomenon marks the arrival of dikē as Fury and/or as Dios Kora, where dikē is a cosmic sending that does not always dovetail with human expectations of justice, but may even contravene them in the service of life's flux. Let me indicate this via an example: for feminist critics, Apollo's justification of Orestes seems unjustifiable, based as it is on the arbitrary exclusion of the mother from kinship.[27] But I maintain that this arbitrariness is more complex and quite disclosive, and by no means easily dismissible on feminist-theoretical grounds. Considered from a nonhuman, naturalist perspective, this arbitrariness refers to nature's generative spontaneity, its capacity to halt its own violence, allowing life activity to resume. This pattern is quite observable, and life does manage to flourish even after the most terrible catastrophes—a fact that actually offends human morality, not only because it is in itself amoral but also because human morality cannot *control* it: hence, my point about dikē's irreducible moment of indifference. Furthermore, in even posing as a justification, Apollo's enigmatic statement is a thinly veiled attempt at rationalization, pointing to the fact that all judicial advocacy relies on technicalities to exact the desired outcome. In other words, when this time around his arbitrariness is confronted from the viewpoint of logic, it does not so much fail the test as it discloses the failure of political logic per se, by exposing the remarkable fact that arbitrariness is the place where nature and politics meet, despite (or because of?) the exceeding efforts of the latter to avoid this meeting. After all, if Clytemnestra were not arbitrarily sacrificed for this passage from archaism to modernity that furnishes the founding myth of any progressive politics,[28] *someone else* would have to take just as arbitrarily her place—a necessary violence confirmed over and over by the history of revolutions and even of radical reforms.

Meier astutely observes that, whereas the Furies appeal to the authority of the old order, the new gods never explicitly use their youth as source for their authority. Their youth is mentioned only by the Furies and exclusively as a negative trait (*Discovery* 100). Still, Meier's observation is most efficacious within the historical and political context of this court scene, where "young" and "new" take their meaning along an irreversible, linear timeline. Once we admit the cosmological coordinates of the court, however—that is, dikē's destinal rather than jurisprudential aspect—the gods of "old" barbarism and the gods of "new" rationality show themselves to have existed alongside each other from time immemorial, both of them as old as the process of the changing of seasons and of generational patterns. Apollo's mocking of the Furies' age and appearance early on in the play, calling them "repulsive maidens" and "gray and aged children" (ln. 69–70; κατάπτυστοι κόραι; γραῖαι παλαιαὶ παῖδες), demonstrates this nonlinear temporality. The use of "maiden" signifies natural youth and virginity, even though they belong epochally to an old order, and while their oldness is described doubly as παλαιά (which includes anything antique) and γραῖα (which refers to the physical traits of an old woman), they are also children of sorts. The Furies partake of old and new, albeit by combining only the atavistic traits of both ages: deathly rancor and childish immaturity at once. They are the past in its stunted infancy just as Apollo was the nascent form of a mature organizing principle in Homer. Chronology happens first as genealogy before it is translated into history. Indeed, the Furies describe the dissolution of justice brought about by the new order of gods in explicitly generational and intimately familial terms: "Parents shall await / the deathstroke at their children's hands" (ln. 496–98). Prior to encountering any form of social or political injustice, one experiences rivetingly in the domain of the family the "unfairness" of time's passage, and in a certain sense, every child rings the death knell for its parents. The Furies put finitude on trial, and it is no wonder that they lose.

Dikē appeared in *Agamemnon* and the *Choephoroi* as a sending that initiates the hunt for revenge. In the *Eumenides*, the spirits of the hunt appear themselves, but next to their grotesque descriptions of the feasts of flesh they enjoy, they also foreground another aspect of dikē, toward which I have gestured repeatedly but tangentially: dikē's relation to Ananke as the realm of limits and finitude. Nowhere is this aspect shown more starkly than in the charges of Clytemnestra's ghost against the sleeping Furies who have abandoned their task of avenging her: "Sleep and fatigue, two masterful conspirators, / have dimmed the deadly anger of the mother-snake" (ln. 126–27). Before Olympian interference, and before the trial begins, the Furies' efficacy is already compromised due to their exhaustion, which is immediately coded as a sign of natural weakness. There is only so long one can chase, stay sleepless, and remain resentful, no matter how justified one's cause might be. Clytemnestra's chosen deities, whom she honors more than any other god, have quit the pursuit through no fault of their own but through natural necessity, their snores and moans being visceral signs of this primordial exhaustion. For uttering these accusatory lines alone, Clytemnestra is due great credit: once again, she emerges in her exquisite ambivalence, a villain and yet a figure with privileged access to the workings of cosmic economy. Just as in *Agamemnon* she summed up the economy of perpetual revenge in the image of the inexhaustible sea, here she conveys the opposite principle: natural exhaustion that halts further violence. The mother-snake—namely, the cosmic mother who is mirrored in the cosmic father, the chthonic hero-serpent, himself a murderer as well—is betrayed first not by the Olympians but by the exhaustion of her proxies. Sleep and fatigue are physiological processes pointing to Ananke, and even the daimons of constant vigilance relent and fall asleep. It turns out that the abundant sea of *Agamemnon* can be drained and needs a pause to regenerate.

In the political sphere, sleep and fatigue represent the historical dynamics that militate against the infinitization of justice before the latter derails into a paralyzing dialectic of resentment and guilt. These historical dynamics, however, are for the most part spontaneous processes, resulting from the passage of time that leaves no event untouched by some form of oblivion, no matter how unjust it may have been by our moral standards. Orestes understands this: "χρόνος καθαιρεῖ πάντα γηράσκων ὁμοῦ" (ln. 286; Time *purges* all things, aging with them; my emphasis).[29] The verse may sound callous, but it requires little honesty to admit that it describes *the way things are*. Who today sheds a tear for the Melian massacre, or the millions murdered by Genghis Khan? These are reminders that justice's moral outrages are relatively short-lived explosions (and perhaps this too is for the good), selective in their memory, and often serving present power relations rather than some moral ideal as the rhetoric usually suggests. Yet even if power did not manage to undercut the ideality of justice, as Socrates valiantly argued in the *Republic*, time would in its indifferent passing. Time first attenuates the events, then changes their meaning to fit present concerns, and eventually covers them with the veil of forgetfulness. The justice delivered at the end of the *Oresteia*, the dikē of Athena—a justice that matriarchy finds arbitrary and unjust—must therefore be contemplated from beyond its political inferences, for it is also a dikē that reflects two deeply interconnected expressions of necessity borne by time: the inevitability of forgetting, and the spontaneous renewal that accompanies such forgetting. I will return to this important point in the conclusion of this chapter. Meanwhile, it would be worth revisiting our organizing motif—the hunt—insofar as it consistently thematizes this old conflict between death and regeneration.

Walter Burkert had noted that the symbolism of hunting rituals concentrates on two rival but intimately related forces that exert themselves most intensely on the human being—namely, aggression and sexuality: "Sexual reproduction and death are the basic facts of life," he writes (72). Before settling into a purely political debate about the legal authority of old and new gods, the *Eumenides* stages this debate in more primordial terms: as a conflict between a death-driven dikē represented by the Furies' hunt and their defense of consanguinity as the sole criterion for justice, and a life-affirming, erotic dikē articulated in Apollo's defense of marriage as a relation that supersedes the hatred of chthonic justice. Let us consider some of the language and images that the text uses to present these two sides so that we can better understand the significance of the first argument at Delphi.

Upon waking from their slumber, the Furies immediately introduce the vocabulary of hunting, speaking of Orestes as their lost prey (ln. 147), and of their chase as that of "hounds after a bleeding fawn" (ln. 246–47); later, seeing him suppliant to Athena, they wallow in the thought of feasting on his blood (ln. 264–66). Outraged by the impropriety of their presence at his temple, Apollo lists the barbarous events of their kingdom—beheadings, stonings, impalings, and mutilations—and he pointedly describes their castrating function in terms of the destruction of young sperm, which implies the destruction of the future (ln. 185–92).[30] Their bestial violence exemplifies the dikē of revenge as the force of Thanatos, something made explicit in their celebration of Hades: "Hades is great,

Hades calls men to reckoning / there under the ground, / sees all, and cuts it deep in his recording mind" (ln. 273-75). It is reiterated in the "Song of the Furies," where they extol their office through a hymn to the destructive principle, the principle of the Night whose daughters they are (ln. 321-22). Quite clearly here the office is defined in cosmological terms: as their assigned destiny (ln. 334-35), and as ancestral prerogative and primeval privilege (γέρας παλαιόν) that they must carry out beneath the earth, away from sunlight (ln. 394-96). In yet another destinal formulation of their appointment, they speak of it as *προστεταγμένον* (ln. 208), an assignment in the form of an imperative: the duty of revenge.

Although the Furies assume phenomenal form in the play, Athena's first impression of them underlines their spectacular grotesqueness as something that defeats phenomenality itself. She describes them as nature's rejects, creatures that no natural genealogy would issue forth: in their disfigurement, they figure nature as antinature (ln. 406-14). Notably, both the Erinyes and Athena partake in antinature, she also being the result of an unnatural birth. But whereas the Erinyes are antinatural because they lack resemblance to anything beautiful and patterned, because they are *inhuman* in form (ln. 412), Athena is antinatural because her ideality nearly erases the trace of generation: in reality, she is simply an idea, and as Dios Kore (daughter of Zeus),[31] she manifests the idea of rule not so much in a new but in an inaugural form, as a subtle combination of its cosmological underpinnings and its civic ends—a "golden rule." Given that she represents Logos and Idea, Athena's description of the Furies as antinature contains an implicit argument about the misology of one-sided justice. Antinature becomes synonymous with misology, for Logos governs the pattern of the Greek cosmos, but the Erinyes, daughters of Night, remain blind to their own one-sidedness even after Apollo points it out to them.

Opposite their domain of hatred and gloom, the play presents Apollo's erotic argument (ln. 213-24). Typically associated with the cold rationality of the law, Apollo stands outside his usual civic boundaries when he launches into this early speech.[32] He summons Eros by the name of Cypris Aphrodite as herself a primordial force, as the *other* destiny, which the Furies dishonor by diminishing the moral obligations of marriage. Marriage too is appointed to men and women by fate (μόρσιμος), and Apollo as lawgiver declares that this fate is higher than oaths, and guarded by justice itself (ln. 217; ὅρκου 'στὶ μείζων τῇ δίκῃ φρουρουμένη), or in Lattimore's suggestive translation of dikē, "by right of nature." The appeal to Aphrodite as Cypris is chronologically crucial, since in the Hesiodic theogony, Aphrodite Cyprogenes is born of the seafoam and the castrated genitals of Uranus, thus making her older than Zeus, a splendid vestige of the archaic order within the newly set Olympian world. As Cypris represents love's primal force, coeval with titanic violence, so Hera Teleia (ln. 214)—the Fulfiller—functions as protector and legislator of marriage within the new order. Hera codifies what Aphrodite has already sent. Under the rubric of Eros, Apollo offers a defense of the life-principle: there is dikē that orders Thanatos, but there is also dikē that assists Eros. Insofar as both forms of dikē are articulated in terms of destiny, they express first and foremost a nonhuman, cosmological moment before they ever become judicial matters. Far from being a cold rationalist, Apollo's first advocacy in the play is on behalf of primordial pleasure and fertility to which the Erinyes will also eventually return as Eumenides. Additionally, his defense of marriage—itself a natural destiny, in his own words—is a first step away from the extremely limited scope of consanguineous justice that the Erinyes claim, and that I discuss shortly below. Even though the same god will later deny love in its filial dimension between mother and son, the life-affirming aspect of his first erotic speech is preserved elsewhere: in the final verdict that spares the offspring. Apollo does succumb to arbitrariness because the structure of justice obliges him to do so, but by favoring the young son, the young god serves the ends of life rather than those of sunless gloom, implicitly letting Eros have the final word in Athens though he lost the argument in Delphi.

This first Apollonian argument serves to refute the Furies' use of consanguinity as defense for hounding the matricide Orestes while leaving Clytemnestra at peace after she murdered her husband. In the logic of the Erinyes, because mothers and sons share blood but husbands and wives do not, murders committed against the mother are punishable, but murders committed against the husband are acceptable—a view of kinship that would also excuse Ixion's murder of his father-in-law. In appealing to shared blood to incriminate matricide while excusing spousal homicide because of the lack of shared blood, the Furies seem to compel Apollo to sever precisely the maternal blood bond *as* an incriminating agent. Though they are considered universal agents of *talio*, themselves promoting their justice as impartial and "straightforward" (ln. 312; εὐθυδίκαιοι), and though Orestes had appealed to them to aid him in revenge of his father, the Furies appear onstage only to pursue the matricide, confirming in this last play their matriarchal partisanship. To Apollo's critique of their double standards, the spirits openly admit that it is the justice of the mother's blood that makes them hunters (ln. 230–31).

Two remarks about this partisan pursuit are in order, given earlier discussions on the anthropology of the hunt, and on the more general concept of nature's arbitrariness. It seems paradoxical that in a society that assigned hunting and war to men, female daimons would hunt for the justice of women. Here it is helpful to return to Burkert's anthropological observation that this gendered division of labor among human beings is rather unusual when compared with other animals, and marks an event that recapitulated the passage of humans from animal nature to humanity proper. For most nonhuman animals, it is the females who hunt and provide for the litter, and the Furies are depicted quite literally as female bloodhounds. If homo sapiens derives from *homo necans*—that is, if predation sharpened the traits of discipline and attention necessary for building the complex forms of organization humans achieved—the other crucial factor in this evolutionary narrative was the differentiation of human sexuality from the rest of animal sexuality along a different division of labor. In this light, the end of the Furies' reign of terror does not herald simply a patriarchal event but inaugurates symbolically the quantum leap from animality to humanity proper for *both* sexes.

Regarding the concept of arbitrariness, the Furies' prejudicial stance toward matricide thematizes this arbitrariness of nature, which human justice aspires to revise by organizing and "correcting" it, having first "read" it for signs of humanity's moral concerns. For instance, the Furies' partiality to the mother can be retroactively interpreted and commended for its solidarity with the victimized woman, even though the Furies' argument of consanguinity is as obtuse as the later Apollonian exclusion of Clytemnestra from kinship; however, the latter strikes us as unduly patriarchal. At its basis, the disproportionate justice administered by the Furies is just as arbitrary as that of the newer gods whom the Furies repeatedly accuse of ruling arbitrarily, a fact that is confirmed by this deeply ironic equivalence between the Furies' rejection of marital kinship and Apollo's rejection of the son's filial bond with his mother. Indeed, how could the offspring maintain equal commitment to both parents if, according to the Erinyes, the parents abrogate their mutual obligation because they are not consanguineous? In denying the intimacy of the couple, Clytemnestra and her advocates implicitly deny Agamemnon's necessary role in the birth of her son. They deny, in other words, Eros as the singular precondition for the creation of a third being who can then share equally in both bloodlines. Thus, Apollo's eventual expulsion of Clytemnestra from the familial bond—which, significantly, comes *after* the failure of his erotic argument to stop the pursuit—could be read as an ironic and exasperated reversal of the Furies' absurdity, a taste of their own medicine, so to speak: if Clytemnestra's murder of Agamemnon is excused because she is no family to him, then she "deserves" to have her familial link with her *and his* son severed.

Special mention should be given here to Richard Kuhns's careful refutation of scholars who see in this argument only absurdity or dramatic lightheartedness on Aeschylus's part (45–46). By pointing out this potentially absurd and ironic subtext in my own remarks above, I do not disagree with Kuhns's general sense that the Apollonian thesis is fully conscious and intentional, and has to be taken seriously as a syllogism. If anything, I am saying that its absurdity or irony very much results from its conscious understanding of justice, which the Furies lack but which, in its now more extended civic scope, meets a new set of limits as the narrower natural justice once did. My difference from Kuhns, then, concerns the optimism of the developmental moral narrative that sees in civic justice either a salubrious abandonment of nature or, more moderately put, an irreversible progress from nature to polis, a historicism advanced earlier by Hegel. Instead, I am intrigued by the deep continuity of natural categories in civic jurisprudence and their enduring necessity for its functioning—whether this be the natural demand for revenge (sometimes translated as "redress") or the natural arbitrariness of all justice that law first restrains rationally via the *blind* justice of *isonomia*, but which "blindness" is then culturally reinterpreted as another arbitrariness to be shunned,[33] resulting in more kinds of arbitrariness such as those endemic to social justice practices. Putting it differently, there is no cosmology of the polis—as Kuhns seems to suggest there is, with Orestes as its "first citizen"—from which nature per se can be, or should be, thoroughly removed or superseded. Nature preserved as a *historical* remnant per Hegel is also not sufficient, and this is the reason why Aeschylus—as Kuhns recognizes astutely—locates myth and history, old gods and new gods, family and jury of peers, in a simultaneous plane that does not exactly fit conventional historical timelines. This simultaneity of nature and the court is not a mere poetic license or fanciful ploy but a profound conceptual proposal that the human polis is continually grafted onto natural exigencies.[34] Kuhns articulates this dialectic quite well in his discussion of the function of myth as a language that combines the cosmic with the political: "Myth is endowed with the cares of communal life, and the human city reaffirms its dependence on a cosmic order reflected in myth. In this way Aeschylus achieves a double perspective: he leads us to regard what ordinarily is taken to be immutable, existing out of time, as suffering the development of the temporal; and to recognize in the history of cities a reflection of the permanent order of the cosmos. The celestial and the terrestrial participate each in the order of the other" (29). The present study is particularly concerned with the way in which this "permanence" of the cosmos, its temporal and spatial monumentality, persistently underlies whatever changes occur in the process of human history.

Closing this parenthesis on Kuhns's cosmological reading, I return to Apollo's rebuttal of the Furies. The god's tremendous shift from placing marital love above consanguinity to recasting marriage as the service of one stranger to another's seed (ln. 660; ξένῳ ξένη) cannot be sufficiently explained by feminism's patriarchal critique, coming as it does at the end of a rather exhaustive attempt at reasoning with the Furies. This shift must then be recognized more broadly as the effect of an impasse constitutive to ethics, an impasse the matriarchal Furies cannot avoid either, but an impasse that nonetheless necessitates a decision in accordance with the tragic requirement of seriousness. If the Apollonian argument wins the day, it is less because of its tighter logic, and more because of its cosmological impetus, which at the moment proves more compelling than the cry for revenge embodied by the Erinyes. Apollo's defense, which tilts Athena's decision, spells the old fact that when revenge overflows, the tide changes direction, and by some ineffable necessity behind some imperceptible event, violence recedes and the world moves on. It seems that justice—whether old or new, natural or political, matriarchal or patriarchal—cannot be thought outside the frame of arbitrariness. The more interesting question then becomes evaluative: How more problematic might arbitrariness be when it results from civic attempts at "improving" nature, precisely because this kind of arbitrariness explicitly contravenes civic justice's own stated aims as well as its self-definition as deliberative moral reasoning? In this sense too, when considered narrowly only for its politics, Apollo's patriarchal intervention emerges as a civic-minded attempt to correct nature, an attempt that is now critiqued for its choice of symbolic tropes (its patriarchy), but whose overall structure (its principle of the corrigibility of nature via human techne) forms the basis of modern, progressive judicial philosophy.

The complexity of Apollo's defense is the reason for my many excursions to his argument throughout this study, by way of attempting various approaches and entries into its logic. The reader's patience might permit me to add one last comment regarding its antimaternal advocacy, a comment that joins the chthonic explanations about the seed's regenerative function, and the structural explanations about the arbitrariness inherent in all forms of justice. Before he feels obliged to dismiss the mother, Apollo defends Agamemnon's prerogative to a "proper" death—namely, his "right" to fulfil his destiny (ln. 625–39). As I have mentioned in chapter 4, in the context of heroic cults, the proper death for a warrior was death in battle. Interestingly, Apollo does not exclude the Amazons from being appropriate killers of Agamemnon, even though they were women (ln. 629). Thus, the primary injustice to Agamemnon does not consist in his demise at the hands of a woman but in his death by treachery, which is to say a form of death that annuls not only his body but his life of honor as symbolic of his warrior function as well. Clytemnestra hunted him down not in equal and honorable terms, as an Amazon would, but as a deceptive spider. At stake is the manner of death rather than the killer's gender. Apollo, Aeschylus's young god, defends the archaic honor custom of the Iliadic narrative. In the dawn of the democratic city-state, acting as advocate before an institution that guarantees the civic code, the young Olympian paves the way for a court of lenience[35] by defending not only old Eros but also the old-fashioned ideal of the "beautiful death." Suddenly, the juxtaposition of the comparative-degree adjective in "younger gods" (ln. 162, 778; νεώτεροι θεοί)[36] as opposed to the "new institutions" (ln. 490–91; νέων θεσμίων) acquires a more specific meaning: the encoding of the principle is new, but its content—embodied here by the younger Apollo—is quite old. Apollo may be "younger" than the Furies in the same sense that Homer's Apollonian world was a "response" to the preceding titanic chaos, as Nietzsche, Harrison, and Walter Otto all maintain; effectively, however, the Apollonian principle belongs to as ancient a reality as its opposite. To revisit our first preamble and its political terms, the Areopagus can guarantee democratic reforms only because of its deep, and even invisible, continuities.

Even though political readings of the *Oresteia* pay more attention to the trial scene, for my purposes it is the opening Delphic stichomythia between the erotic Apollo and the death-driven Furies that reveals the stakes of this war between the two irreducible but coeval facets of dikē. In that first scene, we become witnesses to an inaugural *polemos*, a conflict as old as time between Eros and Thanatos. Furthermore, I would argue that the later adjudication of Orestes by Athena is based on this earlier Delphic scene where the cosmological parameters of the court are laid out. The court's later acquittal does not legitimize the earlier Apollonian purification but confirms and codifies it, just as human justice formalizes the destinal nature of Dikē whether the latter appears in its retributive or lenient aspect. As Blickman noted, Draco's law required the relatives to name the criminal and swear revenge upon burial of the slain. While this proclamation is framed as a civic performance, what it proclaims is the old custom of revenge. Legal procedure encodes the victim's natural demand for payment previously expressed through religious precepts alone. Conversely, the Areopagitic lenience relies on the Delphic argument, which aims to suspend the dikē of revenge by appeal to the dikē of love, foregrounding Cypris Aphrodite over Artemis Kynegos.

Despite the text's solution of suspending revenge in favor of preserving the future generation, however, the Erinyes are not to be taken lightly. In their fixation on the hunt, they articulate in extremis what remains a staple of Aeschylean tragedy—namely, that one learns only through suffering. "There is / advantage / in the wisdom won from pain" (ln. 520–21) is the Furies' version of what the chorus of *Agamemnon* already said, and what Orestes as well concluded. Exceedingly different agents subscribe to this truth, which forms a cardinal expression of tragic seriousness: an unpunished deed, a life with no responsibility, creates a hole in the pattern of the world, a vacuum that will be filled one way or another because this is how *things* tend to work out. Orestes himself did not escape responsibility, nor is his acquittal mere lenience: he did suffer and he did pay in enduring this hunt—an argument put forth eloquently by Taplin (383). Aeschylus reserves still-more-profound lines for these otherwise abhorrent deities: "κύριον μένει τέλος," they declare (ln. 544), which Lattimore translates freely as "The all is bigger than you," but Smyth renders more faithfully as "The appointed issue abideth." Both choices nonetheless convey the depth-structure of dikē as a destinal category, with the second formulation reanimating explicitly the Aristotelian discussion of tragedy as a grave act with a certain end/purpose: an act that is *spoudaia kai teleia*; tragic act as *teletē*.

Aeschylus starts with a virgin and ends with another virgin: Artemis Kynegos and Pallas Athena; forest and city, or animal hunt and rational war/disputation. Both Athena and Artemis are connected to birth, paradoxically through their virginity. Goddess of citadels, the motherless Athena is herself a civic mother, her virginity manifesting archetypally the feminine internalization of paternal aggression, as Karl Kerényi's study has shown (*Athene* 35, 65–68). Artemis, goddess of liminality, has her sacred space at the edge of the city, where organized society ends and wild nature begins. Still according to Kerényi, although she assists during the birth pangs, Artemis is never considered a "mother"; she expresses "the untamable wildness of a particular age of maidenhood" through a close relation to the brother (24, 35). In another, rather unusual resemblance, which Aeschylus does not make explicit, Athena too is cultically linked to maiden sacrifice just as Artemis was through Iphigenia in the first play. Suffice it to say that in her identification with Aglauros, a daughter of King Cecrops, Athena summons the tragic myth of the maiden who, according to one legend, jumped to her death from the cliff of the Acropolis to save the city and the father's kingdom.[37] The dedication to the father, the fatherland, and the voluntary sacrifice for the father's kingdom recapitulate the story of Iphigenia within the sacrificial subtext of the *Eumenides*. The protectress of the city and founder of its court is not only a luminous figure but one who also attends to the darker side of sacrifice. As I have already discussed in chapter 2, this sacrificial economy, though not explicitly attached to Athena in the last play, is displaced onto Athena's own promises to the Erinyes: if they consent to dwelling under the Acropolis, they will receive their sacrificial dues in return for services to the city. They will, in a sense, sacrifice themselves for the city, like Athena's double, Aglauros, and the city will repay them in kind.

This sacrificial, chthonic side of Athena is what Kerényi calls her "darker aspect" (*Athene* 57), or what we could also call the old, archaic aspect of her Olympian youth. In his analysis of this darker side, Kerényi reveals the most unexpected connection Athena may have to Artemis—a connection that, furthermore, speaks to the cosmology of generativity and sacrifice that I am trying to emphasize. This connection involves the night and the phases of the moon. Whereas Artemis's relation to the night and the moon, particularly in her deathly capacity as huntress, is well established, Athena's is not so obvious, unless one thinks of her strong association with the owl, a predatory nightbird. Yet in considering important dates in the goddess's cult as well as her birthday, Kerényi concludes that they correspond to lunar cycles (*Athene* 62–64). The period before the goddess's emergence as a new moon (her birthday, which is the birth of the virgin)—that is, the time of moonless night—she is herself assigned the birth of a mysterious divine child, a son, who is figured in some versions to be none other than the sun/Apollo.[38] The virgin "falls" for the father, to generate for him, just as Aglauros sacrificed herself to save the father's kingdom. We have here the alternation between a mother who delivers light out of darkness, and her strange and immediate reemergence as a virgin in the new moon: "Corresponding to her essence is the blackest darkness in which only the eyes of the owl can grasp the hidden light, wherein from the conjunction of the sun and moon both luminaries once more proceed forth: first the sun, a divine child, then the new moon, the virgin. On the cosmic stage, birth follows conjunction immediately, without pregnancy" (*Athene* 88).

For Kerényi, Athena marks a psychological translation of a cosmological event. She expresses the birth of the concept of virginity-toward-the-father—the father-daughter mythologeme—as the necessary aftermath of cosmic creation, of the first nuptials between Earth and Sky, which were really a mother-son relationship (the first autochthonous/self-created being must proliferate with what she has already created), where the son turned husband, but where the position of the father was not *yet* available. Only with the appearance of father and brother can the notion of virginity take proper meaning so as to be added to the categories of mother and wife (81). Yet these "psychological" moments are not mere symbolic contingencies, nor should they be dismissed as anthropological trappings; in their anthropological framework, and their chronological sequencing of mother-right followed by father-right, they in fact preserve a cosmogonic memory and blueprint. Here is Kerényi, again, on this father-daughter mythologeme: "The humanly impossible, rapid change out of dark motherhood into bright virginity is discernible against the cosmic background. The inner tension and opposition between motherhood and a maidenhood that is dedicated to the father and signifies a prohibition against all other men is a *human reality*. . . . The father's daughter among the Gods stands beside the sons of the father, delivering over to the young men the maidens so that they will become mothers, but the lordship of the paternal spirit perdures above everything else" (*Athene* 88–89; my emphasis). This is precisely what Athena qua virgin and civic mother does as the arbiter of the court in the *Oresteia*. She figuratively gives birth again to the young son, a father's son and protégé of Apollo (the sun), which was purportedly one of the names of her mysterious child. She "delivers" him via acquittal.

Political life indeed grapples with the power of generativity,[39] and as Sara Brill notes, the Greeks tried "to harness" this power through their mythological, literary, and philosophical production as much as through their political and legal institutions (*Aristotle* 223). Nevertheless, the moment most germane to my present study comes prior to any such ideological operations that think of power primarily in instrumental terms. Generativity, and I would also add mortality, are not like any other ordinary categories, which human beings choose to invest with symbolic meanings that serve prior ideological aims; for to have already deliberated on such ideological purposes in meaning construction is to be already enculturated, whereas the powers of death and generativity do not derive from culture but inaugurate it. In short, birth and death are not reducible to being sociocultural constructs that can be contemplated with epistemic fullness, but belong to the order of exigency. Repeating Kerényi's language, I would stress that mythologemes of this order are a "human reality" (88), vividly concrete, and for this reason, also universal. To consider them chiefly as ideological effects obscures the point that we, belated readers captivated by ideology, import the most invisible, indeed abyssal, of biases to our theoretical project: the bias of what constitutes an ideological construct in the first place, which definition itself depends on the ideological fictions espoused by the theorist, and over which he or she has no epistemic mastery. Birth and death were and continue to be at the center of every (bio)politics by reason of their own regulative function in the existence of every human being, let alone of every other creature in the cosmos, including, at least in metaphor, the formation and disappearance of stars. Birth and death are riveting events, and if they receive more intense symbolization in the human world because of the human animal's more intense "politicality," this does not undermine their ultimate priority in the process of symbolization: they offer themselves as the most spectacular *sources* for political expression, forming the pivot around which human politicality turns; at the same time as they also are the origin of visible affect and concern for nonhuman animals as well.[40] Their interplay, what I have been denoting somewhat heuristically as the confrontation of Eros and Thanatos, imposes itself in every human attempt at social organization, and thus constitutes an inexorable necessity, a fact of nature that the tragedies often call *pragma/ta* (the thing/s, reality). This "realism," which I attempted earlier to unearth in Aristotle's mimetic theory, and which is conspicuously absent in contemporary cultural discourses, reasserts itself regardless of theoretical or moral discomfiture. That it had once found one of its most succinct expressions in tragedy is not surprising, since tragedy had functioned already in the ancient world as the repository of cultural disavowals, old-fashioned rituals, Homeric continuities—in effect, anachronisms—that may well have been embarrassing vestiges in polite society, though they made for popular entertainment. Tragedy opens a dangerous space, not because it is in itself benighted, but because it possesses the fortitude to name the social unmentionables.

The pursuit of justice unto death and the necessity sometimes to abandon this pursuit—an abandonment that sounds amoral but serves the amorous—are both expressions of this cosmic confrontation that Aeschylus formalized in the figures of the Erinyes and Apollo/Athena, respectively. Always tinged by revenge, the Erinyes' justice threatens the very tradition it means to protect: in their zeal to avenge the past, the Erinyes destroy the future line of the deceased, thereby extinguishing tradition. In halting the momentum of revenge, Apollo and Athena—a kouros and kore, two ephebes—side with the future; the future not as a revolutionary restart but as the promise of a certain continuity just like the continuous alternation of the lunar phases. Orestes preserves the line of Pelops. Though generativity and death can be used by politics, they remain exigent events that cannot be reliably premeditated and controlled by any political system. The vocabulary of nature, which does not disappear either from the Erinyes or from the Olympians throughout the trilogy, suggests that Aeschylus understands that political problems cannot always be solved politically. To think that they always could, or that they certainly should, risks a moment of political hubris: it assumes human beings to be thoroughly self-constituted, although the very word "human" means *of* the earth. Myth expressed this possibility of a nonhuman origin of humanity through structures and motifs that affirm autochthony, as Claude Levi-Strauss had analyzed (434–35).[41] In other words, before the concept of autochthony became ideologically problematic, its affirmation signaled the inscription of the human being into a cosmology, lest we forget the name Erichthonius, Athena's serpentine child with the fire god.

Dikē: Before and Beyond Justice

In a brief but thought-provoking essay, Yale constitutional theorist Paul Gewirtz confirms the seminal importance of the *Oresteia* for legal thought, extolling its espousal of judicial clemency and its demonstration of the positive influence emotions can have on jurisprudence (1049). Often considered to be an institution in which cold rationality must prevail, jurisprudence, according to Gewirtz, is enriched when properly informed by the emotions.[42] The Furies' emotional fanaticism, their demand for infinite revenge, is not only a threat to the law but also reinforces respect and reverence for the law (1047); hence, in a dialectical manner, these negative passions, once properly channeled, can redirect judicial procedure from a strictly persecutory endeavor to one that allows for compassion, forgiveness, and lenience. Law's capacity for clemency relies as much on an element of passion as does vengefulness, notes Gewirtz, and since passion is the precinct of the Furies, we could not hope for a merciful law without them.

Hoping for a less violent, more enlightened conception of justice, Gewirtz extols the mercy of the law just as Kuhns had belabored "the right of action" (56)—namely, the deliberative process through which the conditions that provoked the commission of a crime are assessed by a body of peers, and if deemed mitigating, may soften the verdict. In their shared conciliatory and "civilized" view of justice, they ultimately both inherit and presume Hegel's notion of "reconciliation," which I address shortly below. Additionally, both Kuhns and Gewirtz appreciate the fact that the Erinyes are indispensable to this development, with Kuhns emphasizing that even Apollo and Athena follow to an extent the law of the Erinyes in their challenge of it (31). There is, however, a difference between them regarding what each scholar sees as the catalyst for the passage from blind retaliation to merciful verdict: Kuhns attributes it to rational thinking that drives us beyond the narrow justice of consanguinity, whereas Gewirtz appeals to the opposite—the emotional nature of the Furies that provides support for the cultivation of the more refined feelings of compassion and forgiveness. As a result, Kuhns's theory of lenience centers on "the deliberative and persuasive conditions for rational morality" (56), which he aligns psychologically with the masculine principle and socially with the institution of the court; Gewirtz's analysis tilts more toward the sentiments of compassion and forgiveness as the ethical platform from where to advocate for judicial mitigation.

While I find both arguments praiseworthy in their distinct theoretical presuppositions but shared moral purposes, I take a somewhat different route, in part because of the impasse I have encountered with the currently prevalent conception of the polis as being above, or even outside of, the cosmos qua natural order and constraint. Hence, these concluding remarks foreground the cosmological necessity behind Orestes's acquittal that nonetheless is also consolidated in the trilogy through a political process. At the outset, I should remind the reader of an earlier remark: from a certain perspective, the exoneration of Orestes is not even *all that lenient*, all things considered, but the natural—namely, expected—conclusion of Apollo and Athena's successful justification of matricide. Surely matricide is a crime and Orestes is guilty, as Kuhns declares, but as he also adds, this murder was rationally proven to be of lesser importance than the murder of Agamemnon, and thus required a lesser punishment: "It remains for the trial to demonstrate that it [matricide] is not as serious as the act committed by Clytemnestra, and that Orestes can be declared *not responsible* for it" (55; my emphasis). Furthermore, the commission of matricide was coerced by a legitimate counterdemand, which—regardless of our modern moral outlook—made moral sense in Orestes's world. The final verdict, then, does not so much pronounce lenience or forgiveness but retroactively recognizes that Orestes's intermittent suffering at the hands of the Erinyes is sufficient payment for his act, thus also conforming to his earlier purification. Strictly speaking, if he is not responsible, he has already paid in excess.

I further suggest that this Olympian hyperbole of justifying Orestes's crime should be understood as the effect—not the cause—of a cosmology of dikē whose moral arbitrariness makes sense within the larger context of Aeschylean Ananke: just as in every aspect of the cosmos violence and destruction at times come to a halt in order for the pattern of reemergence to continue, so this happens too in the human world, sometimes even against the stated will of competing agents. In this I differ from Kuhns, who reads the dismissal of Clytemnestra as the inaugural *cause* of a new order. For Kuhns, Clytemnestra embodies the feminine principle of irrationality that sustains the law of the Erinyes and belongs to an old cosmology. The new cosmology, in contrast, reflects masculine rationality. In my view, this sexualized schema—incidentally central to both traditional and feminist readings of the *Oresteia*[43]—is undoubtedly rich in contested meanings, but it remains of the order of the symptom, epiphenomenon, or result of a more primary condition that involves the structure of arbitrariness behind dikē in its cosmological *and* civic forms. Accordingly, I also resist the notion of two successive cosmologies, which in itself already subordinates the cosmos to a historico-political conceptualization even in readings that favor cosmological analyses such as that of Kuhns.

As the first section of this chapter has argued, both the old and the new have always been old and paradoxically coeval. The cosmology is one but expresses itself through two intimately antithetical principles that are set against each other over time: Eros and Thanatos, Cypris Aphrodite and Artemis Kynegos, Erinyes and Apollo/Athena.

Juridically speaking, this cosmological arbitrariness means that there will always be a remainder of injustice: the "last" victim may never be sufficiently vindicated, and the "last" offender may be said to be simply released rather than "forgiven." That this last victim *happened* in the *Oresteia* to be a woman and mother is certainly worthy of further investigation or critique for its treatment of sexuality, but structurally it also shows something beyond sex and gender. It shows that the work of justice is not immune to chance, an idea actually thematized in the conclusion of the *Eumenides*: once translated, the erstwhile justice divinities are said explicitly to preside over the city's good *fortune*. The Greek word used by the Eumenides themselves (ln. 1020) and by Athena (ln. 1030) during their farewell is συμφορά, which the Liddell-Scott-Jones lexicon explains as the conjunction of different circumstances, chance, and hap.

Consider, then, an alternative scenario where chance worked differently, and the daimon that guided Orestes the alastor never showed up.[44] In this case, Clytemnestra would be spared, but her husband's death would remain unpaid. Granted, this scenario might appear "juster" in light of feminism's critique of gendered power relations, but such critique does not ultimately resolve the ethical problem of the arbitrariness of justice and its remainders; it momentarily displaces it. I submit that Aeschylus is well aware of this, and thus illuminates the source from where this arbitrariness always comes: Ananke, the cosmic necessity for both destruction and reemergence—the former operative in the majority of the trilogy, the latter concluding it with the sparing of the young and the restoration of the throne and civic life. There is no other reason why the Eumenides, who support the foundations of the polis, remain firmly nature deities even as they assume nature's benevolent aspect. Furthermore, one should not assume that benevolent nature does away with Ananke because necessity's constraints become invisible in times of prosperity: fertility is as much a spontaneous force as is blight. Thus, the scholarly frustration with the "flimsiness" of Apollo's defense and Athena's vote, and the subsequent critique of the trilogy's conclusion as an "unfair" or "arbitrary" exoneration of the son-murderer, gloss over some crucial points by blaming all this on Aeschylus's patriarchal blind spots. Instead, it may be more instructive to consider that herein the tragedian affords us his clearest and wisest vision—namely, that every justification is also unjust, even when in our moral zeal for our preferred justice cause, we tend to turn a blind eye to this constitutive and collateral injustice. Somewhat ironically, divine Dikē, which recognizes and performs this moment of arbitrariness overtly (for instance, Apollo's calling out the Furies' double standards as he also blatantly repeats them), becomes subject to criticism for its violence, when it could be appreciated for its patent exposure of this arbitrariness. At the other end, human justice, in its deliberate aim to transcend natural violence, disavows or conceals the constitutive arbitrariness that inheres in its own project precisely because it threatens this project. One can locate right here the main difference between Dikē and (human) justice: Dikē as a mode of appropriateness and appropriation[45] shows first what is appropriate to itself—arbitrariness, which nonetheless gathers itself into an unexpected order, into "violent grace"; mortal justice works rather to conceal it.

To return once more to Gewirtz: from his perspective, the Aeschylean conclusion bespeaks some sort of forgiveness, a state of mercy similar to that shown to Ixion and the Delphic Orestes via their purification. However, the limitations of this theory of clemency are shown pragmatically whenever such an enlightened narrative itself ends up justifying the distribution of mercy not universally, but selectively, often according to a political instrumentalization of the emotions. Consequently, while mercy is expected to be offered to some agents or groups, ancestral guilt and belated expiation is assigned to others. Clemency, then, appears quite whimsical in first invoking and then disavowing the very theological basis—not only in Aeschylus but also very specifically in the unnamed Christian tradition of unconditionality—from which it claims its own legitimacy and moral high ground. This slippage between universal mercy and political partiality is why the "mercy" shown to Orestes can now be critiqued as "patriarchal privilege." Starting from a strictly cosmological, rather than "ethical" perspective, I suggest that the Aeschylean resolution thematizes *first of all* and *after all* a cosmic command of dikē, which, in its "unfair" exoneration of a crime reflects a more neutral and indifferent principle located opposite the Furies. Just as the Fury represents the death-principle (the miasmatic Ares, the ever-vigilant huntress Artemis), so Apollo and Athena represent a life-principle, a kind of natural pattern according to which justice must be suspended from its infinitization toward either extreme harshness or extreme lenience: one cannot be immoderate in punishment (Orestes's pursuit had to stop) just as one cannot be immoderate in forgiveness (Ixion's first pardon had to be revoked). Dikē acts as a caesura, moving the pendulum in the opposite direction from the one that is in excess.[46] By this "neutral" or "natural" self-correcting formula, I do not mean that it is not the purpose of society also to strive to resolve moments of injustice. This is of course the mark of civilization, provided, however, that we also keep in mind that justice is one of those long-term cultural projects that profited from the virtues of vigilance, discipline, and narrow focus that distinguish the *predator*. Nevertheless, my insistence on the cosmological aspect aims to exemplify that one of the *Oresteia*'s most interesting insights—particularly in the context of a thoroughgoing campaign against nature—is that sociopolitical zealotry, whichever way it leans in different ages and societies, is not independent of the excesses that the cosmos itself negotiates, arbitrates, and sets aright. In this vein, we can understand why the goddesses of justice belong to an order of divinities first associated with chthonic fertility, then blight, then fertility again.

The translated Eumenides affirm the roots of the ethical order in arbitrary nature, and it should be emphasized that roots—no matter how invisible—must persist and grow deeper if what they support is to stand at all. In other words, with the passage of time, these roots strengthen in their subterranean domain in order to boost the long-term cultural edifice, and it is for this reason that I have proposed the "radical," albeit perhaps disagreeable, claim that human justice continues to be grounded in chthonic enmity even as it strives for rational deliberation. Chthonic persistence, in turn, illustrates that the graduation of nature into social meaning does not happen by dispelling the former's mythic violence but by supplanting it with new myths that attend the very production of meaning itself—myths such as those of "philosophical" or "civic" justice that will deliver us from the natural Fury. In case anyone presumes that by speaking of new myths I am devaluing the philosophical or the civic, I should clarify that myth, for me, is hardly a derogatory term; rather, it continues to function as it once did—an organizing principle for both life and art, the way tragedy and even the *Poetics* affirmed it.

Along with problematizing seamless notions of mercy, the persistence of the Furies, even in their translated guise, poses also a serious moral and judicial question concerning the notion of vigilantism and its own potential translation into other, less immediately recognizable forms. The need to appease, propitiate, and sacrifice anew to the Eumenides in order for them to stay satisfied underground suggests the precariousness of any theory of justice that claims to have done away with vigilantism. Indeed, different ideologies propose different conceptual and institutional parameters for justice, and may not always designate vigilante acts for what they are, particularly if such acts are deemed to be in the service of justice when present law or cultural norms fail. Refusing to recognize, or partly justifying, vigilantism as a righteous and necessary response to unjust and inadequate law, however, does not mean that justice has been successfully divorced from vigilantism. On the contrary, this practice confirms what I am trying to argue: vigilantism forms the necessary origin and, at times, inevitable end product of *any* demand for justice, both in the latter's chthonic infrastructure of hate *and* in its Uranian claim to righteous ideality that strives to right the wrong whenever legal venues fail. After all, the Furies keep vigil, while Helios surveys all. Perhaps, then, it is time to rethink the widely and unquestioningly accepted proposition that justice is always higher than the law. In its infinitized idealism, this proposition contains more dangers than is generally assumed. Albeit unconventional, one way to read the *Oresteia* is as a tale that reveals law's domain to be more benign than the ideality of justice, whose moral zeal would have demanded perpetual vigilance and endless vigilantism for *every* last victim. Idealized as they are in their beauty, Apollo and Athena are, after all, the pragmatists; the Furies, for all their external grotesqueness, operate from the terrifying assumptions of infinite ideality.

While vigilantism is classically defined as the *individual* taking justice into his/her own hands, this individualistic trait need not be an absolute constraint on that definition. Already in the *Oresteia*, we are shown Electra with the group of enslaved women in the *Choephoroi*, wishing as well as aiding and abetting in revenge. The chorus of elders as a civic body in *Agamemnon* also hails the future coming of Orestes to take revenge, not only in the name of his slain father but also of his tyrannized fellow citizens. The Lemnian women, too, committed collective revenge as vigilantes. Similarly, justice-driven rather than law-driven constituencies in later societies may well try to legitimize vigilantism on a more collective scale. What constitutes vigilantism, then, is not as clear-cut as the scenario of an "irrational" individual who unleashes his/her anger, distorted beliefs, or paranoia by bypassing legal procedure. Vigilantism passes from the stricter boundaries of ethical thought into an open ideological minefield, where many an act that could be considered vigilante by one group and one political theory is understood as righteous protest from another. That a country's legislation does not officially condone such expressions of justice as lawful does not necessarily guarantee the law's implementation, particularly if the curtailment of such acts of justice violates the particular cultural zeitgeist of justice. In short, I contend that, despite modernity's theoretical posture of shunning vigilantism universally as a form of justice, in reality it is not so. Much like the pre-Areopagitic, lawless but justice-driven clans that justified vigilantism as a necessary practice to correct the wrongs committed against them, so it holds today underneath the official technicalities that conceal the Furies the way the Parthenon once concealed them beneath its shiny surface. Naturally, what is considered immoral or unjust today is not the same as what it was back then; however, what remains constant is the moral justification that the morally invested agents have the righteous right to demand their rights, sometimes even by taking the law in their own hands, often also achieving heroic status. That modern concepts of justice are still beholden to the structure of vigilantism is shown at the very least by most gender-based critiques of the *Oresteia* itself: the overt discontent with Orestes's acquittal for his matricide as opposed to the tacit satisfaction with Clytemnestra's success at murdering Agamemnon.

Finally, one cannot write about the *Oresteia* and reflect on reconciliation without invoking Hegel, who builds from his readings of tragedy a philosophy of history in which human beings move from an abstract, unconscious mode of response to an objectively mediated, thus universal, ethical order. For Hegel, tragedy presents a major stepping stone in this linear development, and the *Oresteia*, more specifically, provides a thematization of the "objective reconciliation" between the chaotic universalism of the Furies as representatives of blind nature and the properly mediated civic process wherein actual universality resides. In the *Lectures on Fine Art*, Hegel writes that the Furies are represented as "universal powers," but not as "the gnawing of his [Orestes's] purely subjective conscience" (278); hence, Orestes's lack of penitence about the matricide despite the experience of the pursuit; hence, also, the need for a trial—as Kuhns also asserted—to make manifest the conditions surrounding the acts of revenge, which had remained obscure to the agents, and to judge such acts by the publicly deliberated criteria of civic morality. The *Eumenides* effects this objective reconciliation via the lawful and reasoned judgment of Athena that gains public assent.

It would be generally evident from Hegel's interpretation that the universality of the moral truth of justice is established precisely via this rational deliberation and assent that is, by definition, public. By extension, this means that its objectivity remains subordinate to historical circumstances and their ever-changing public consensus, provided of course that such consensus is arrived at rationally and self-consciously each time. As this *historicized* rationality is raised to the ultimate criterion for the objectively universal, the Hegelian polis may look rather antagonistic to what Kuhns described as the "permanent order of the cosmos" (29), an order whose language is myth. Yet, Aeschylus does not set aside myth and cosmos to perfect an immanent political experiment, and Kuhns pays rightful heed to this: "Orestes exists outside the ordinary course of political events, yet is made to participate in political events" (29). This poetic attunement to what remains outside politics yet is also *very real*; the sensitivity to the paradoxical but *very real* simultaneity of an immutable, monumental world and an embattled, ever-changing human spirit escapes the philosophical pen that, as I outlined in chapter 2, prefers to systematize concepts rather than to describe things as they are.

Nevertheless, despite Hegel's historicized conception of justice, J. G. Finlayson's analysis of "objective reconciliation" suggests that Hegel is not Hegelian enough. Finlayson agrees with Hegel that there is a reconciliation at the end of the *Eumenides*, but disagrees with him as to how Aeschylus brings it about—namely, through the reasoned intervention of Athena. There is nothing "objective" about Athena's discourse or her vote, since she acquits Orestes following the absurdist defense Apollo hands to her. Her reasoning—"I am a father's daughter and I side with the father"—is, in fact, no reasoning at all. Instead of relying on the insufficient rationality of Athena as the conduit toward the concrete and actualized universal, Hegel should have focused on another part of her intervention: her combative mode of persuasion that finally convinces the Furies to accept her proposal. In other words, it is not the soundness of reason but the loudness of contestation that leads to objective reconciliation. History actualizes the concept, and thus universalizes it, via contestation alone. Hegel conflated a power struggle with rational cogency, and thus missed what—still according to Finlayson—Aeschylus is telling us: "Justice, *reason*, and lawfulness are not established facts that need merely be recognized for what they are by an act of theoretical contemplation but ongoing practical tasks within the new social order, and reconciliation between the different ethical powers, between citizens and their new institutions is not a state already attained but an ongoing process" (516; my emphasis). In its impetus to steer Hegel closer to Hegel by historicizing reason along with the concepts it is meant to guarantee, Finlayson's objection eventually leads to the same point I am making through cosmology, but this convergence is due to entirely different reasons and interpretive commitments on his and my part: what Finlayson recognizes as the contestatory character of judicial universality I have identified as the natural arbitrariness that continues to underlie institutions of civic justice, and that contrasts with the invocation of a now highly relativized—because historicized—and weakened reason.

There is without a doubt something logically askew with Athena's rationale, no matter how necessary her intervention may be. There is also something *coercive* about her mode of persuasion, something that Michael Naas has astutely observed (5), but that Finlayson omits. Contestation is thus not a simple debate or an exercise in persuasion but a power struggle that does not exclude threats, aggression, and compulsion. This proximity between contestation and coercion endangers the very project of "civilizing" advance that the concepts of universality and reconciliation are supposed to usher in. Note again how Finlayson renders the dynamic and processual definition of justice as a space where there are "no established facts" but only "practical tasks," where the ever-changing social orders imply power shifts. Here, the truth of justice is never an a priori to be discovered and recognized but always an embattled, negotiated, and invented outcome. In espousing the historical contestation not only of judicial concepts and institutions but of the concept of reason itself (hence departing from Hegel in order to hegelianize him), Finlayson's statement admits to the very limits of reason as the guaranteeing procedure through which objectivity and justice are to be decided. Reason cannot decide anything because reason itself has to be decided in the power struggle. More sharply put, such processual definition points to the abyssal risk of *all* reason falling into arbitrariness, an arbitrariness from which Finlayson himself may not escape, along with the many others who also *rationally* expose the "absurdity" of Apollo and Athena's assumptions. Indeed, the very fact that we—modern critics of consanguinity but seasoned feminists—are scandalized by the Olympian position much more than by the Furies' claim that a wife's killing of her nonconsanguineous husband is acceptable, says a lot about the kinds of arbitrariness and internal contradictions allowable when reason is reduced to serving political configurations of power.

The moral certainty that politics transcends natural violence is consistently betrayed by the fact that most, if not all, actual political regimes and political theories alike have been and continue to be saturated by the vocabulary of power. Historical reality, which apparently turns out to be Hegel's and our *only* reality, vindicates Thrasymachus, who insisted contra

Socrates that justice and power are inextricable from one another. This in fact constitutes the "realism" of the cosmological politics of arbitrariness that Plato denounced but Nietzsche admired in the tragedians. There remains, however, a substantial difference between Athena's inaugural coercion and the turf wars of everyday politics; it is the difference between the truly neutral—and thus, strangely, "juster"—administering of cosmic Dikē versus the arbitrariness that results from the conceit of history and its ineffectual reason. A pattern rather than a precept, cosmic/divine Dikē, unlike human justice, does not arrive with this conceit, though it always seems to carry within itself intact the logic of necessity. As such, it precedes and exceeds the efficacy of reason, which fails to deliver as an a priori concept (at least according to historicist views), but which devolves easily into coercion in its only *actualized* modality—the contestatory modality.

I agree that there is a reconciliation of sorts (and I appreciate Finlayson's general defense of Hegel's theory of the tragic and its accord with Aristotle, who also accepted reconciliation as a possible end to tragic conflict), but I remain partial to this extrapolitical and extrahistorical cosmic element: the "rough" universal that engenders not only the Furies, but the Olympians as well. The precedence of this moment is not only chronological, and thus cannot be explained and contained within history alone. It is originary (the *archē* in archaism[47]), serving as an enduring template for politics rather than as a historical vestige in a narrative of ever-improving corrections of justice that themselves stem from something as contingent and even unscrupulous as historical power struggles. To this effect, I call attention not only to the "archaism" of the Furies but also to that of Apollo, "the god of indifferent light," as Hegel himself called him.[48] Such kind of light contains the equally archaic possibility that moral and civic enlightenment is not divorced from the neutrality of nature—a neutrality the Stoics translated into human virtue with this very term "indifference." This term likely disturbs conceptions both of rational justice, and even more, of contestatory justice, because it prizes the strength of being beyond any preference, of expecting neither rights nor rewards for any struggles or good deeds, but of accepting and working with *whatever* comes one's way.

Insofar as the politics of contestation justifies arbitrariness, even under the guise of ethical redress, it repeats within itself, but in a *more dangerous*—because deliberate—manner, the inexorable cosmic Dikē qua Ananke. It reaffirms for better or for worse (and most likely for both at different times) the rough universal that Hegel moved to mediate theoretically. Aeschylus's language—as A. E. Haigh noted, and as many poetically attuned readers have experienced on their own—remains itself somewhat unhewn in its straightforwardness, and monumental in its tone. Haigh uses phrases such as "massive strength," "massive structure," "majestic mould," and "extraordinary vigour and incisiveness" to describe it (65, 80, 81). The poet's diction is solemn but for this reason also not contrived, and this tells us something about the medium being the message: the precedence of nature over artifice, discussed earlier in relation to Aristotle's theory of tragedy, finds in Aeschylus an exemplary poetic instantiation. In Aeschylus, the priority of cosmos over polis manifests itself not merely in the themes of the *Oresteia*, but in the condensed yet thunderously assertive style of the playwright.

Epilogue

A Lying Shepherd and the Limits of Human Dikē

Much has been written about the differences among the three major tragedians, from the way they interpreted the mythical material to their distinct linguistic and dramaturgical styles. For instance, Aeschylus and Sophocles are often contrasted in that the former emphasizes the function of the *oikos* in plot structure (the tragedy of a House), while the latter innovates the genre by focusing on character, presenting us with highly individualized models of tragic heroes and heroines.[1] As for Euripides, his image as a modernizer with all the attendant accolades—rationalist, atheist, friend of women and the oppressed, even antitragic[2]—has been quite prevalent, although recently these attributions have been reassessed, sometimes because they are not entirely supported by his works, and other times because our politics militates against ancient writers reaching the moral high ground of social solidarity that we moderns reserve for ourselves.

These important and observable differences notwithstanding, there exist persistent similarities throughout the extant tragic corpus that, after all, are responsible for designating this corpus as "tragic" in the first place. More importantly, I would argue that the binding conceptual topos for all tragedians remains the same, even when they negotiate its parameters differently, or evaluate its scope with varying ethical emphases. This regulative topos has been classically referred to as the dialectic between Fate and Will, which I have here reworked in terms of the doubling of Aeschylean Dikē as external Necessity/Destiny and the human appropriation of it.[3] In such an understanding of Dikē, one's own fate is by no means simply a matter of individual possession, nor is it a "right" to subjective self-determination, nor can its appropriation be reduced to immanent, social interrelations, though it inevitably involves both the individual and the polis. This destinal, or cosmological, conception of Dikē remains vividly present in the playwrights who come after tragedy's great statesman, regardless whether or not they use the exact vocabulary of Dikē operative in Aeschylus. In other words, it is the salience of this primordial confrontation—the confrontation for the proper appropriation of the accident of existence—that decides the tragic nature of a work.

For this reason, it might be more befitting to Aeschylus to conclude not by pondering yet another of his works but by following the traces of his thinking in his illustrious rival and legatee, Sophocles. This compels me to retell a story that has been told many times over, and that has inspired as many readings as it did misreadings because it, too, is a story about misreadings and misrecognitions on the way to its terrible disclosure: a story about primal origins that has itself become a primal story. Yet this time around, the weight falls on a nearly imperceptible detail from a minor character—a shepherd—whose dissimulation exposes something dormant and opaque, perhaps as opaque as the final realization that causes the blindness of its protagonist. Let us then give *Oedipus Tyrannus* the last word.[4]

His myth is famous: the hero who was destined to slay his father and take his mother as consort, and whose parents exposed him to die as an infant precisely to avoid their own gruesome fate at his hands. Saved by a shepherd, the infant was given to someone who would, in turn, present him to the childless royals of Corinth for adoption. Unaware of the adoption, and upon hearing at Delphi of his future crimes, the adult Oedipus flees Corinth to avoid his destiny, which of course catches up with him at the crossroads outside Thebes. There he murders unknowingly his natural father, and having freed Thebes from the Sphinx's curse, is given in gratitude the widowed queen, his natural mother, as wife. The new plague that befalls the city as a result of these transgressions serves as backstage to the opening of *Oedipus Tyrannus*. From here on, Sophocles unfolds the detective plot of a responsible leader who, committed to save his city again, must first solve the riddle of his predecessor's murder. The action has happened but the consequences lie ahead.

The dreadful unfairness of Oedipus's fate holds overwhelming command over the process of interpretation. We are astounded by a fate that is at once all-too-human, yet so improbable in its perfectly drafted plausibility as to be inhuman. Confounding and overwhelming, Oedipus's drama is also eerily balanced by the compelling certainty that seals its end:

he is whom he sought to find. Indeed, despite whatever approach one may take regarding his character, motives, desires, self-reflection, degree of guilt, and so on, the premise and the outcome of his *muthos*—namely, the oracular destiny and the hero's self-realization—coincide and cannot be cast in doubt. The structure of the myth declares unremittingly that Oedipus will be/is the culprit; there is no way out, and the overdetermination of this certainty is itself the point of the tragedy.

Because of this overdetermined certainty that Sophocles imparts, and that scholarship has echoed consistently over the years, Karl Harshbarger's article "Who Killed Laius?" drew my attention for its bold gesture of posing such a question. Though I do not concur with his conclusion, the textual detail that provokes his doubt—namely, the different versions of the murder scene—is itself an interpretive gold mine. As I understand it, this ambiguity works in fact to confirm Oedipus as the incontrovertible murderer, but Harshbarger takes a different direction, which I summarize here for the sake of contrast. He advances the unusual thesis[5] that Oedipus did not kill his father, proposing instead the chorus as a likely culprit. Under the reign of Oedipus, who functions as a double of the slain Laius, thus reminding the city of his murder, the chorus's accumulated but silent guilt reaches a stress point: the chorus does not wish to admit its guilt, but it can also no longer bear its own silence, and the festering of this moral wound is literalized in the event of the plague. Oedipus, the wise sovereign, assumes the fault and becomes the voluntary sacrifice to facilitate collective atonement (130–31). For Harshbarger, the ambiguity introduced by the murder reports sustains itself as an ambiguity through to the *end*—in terms also of "purpose"—of the play.

There are two accounts of the crime that contradict each other and that confuse Oedipus himself. (One might say that this confusion perhaps entraps Harshbarger, too, who begins then to doubt Oedipus's complicity.) The first version, the one already widely accepted in Thebes, is announced by Creon, who, upon return from Delphi, advises of the need to take vengeance on Laius's murderers (αὐτοέντας/*authentas*),[6] thus introducing us to multiple culprits (ln. 104–7). Jocasta later reiterates this account as well, but specifies the crime's location at the meeting of three roads (ln. 716), a detail that unsettles Oedipus (ln. 760), leading him to step up the investigation. The second version is offered by a recalcitrant but coerced Teiresias and, though initially rejected by Oedipus, is corroborated by the latter's eventual admission of guilt. Incidentally, one of the reasons that the suggestion of other perpetrators sounds unconvincing is the marked reticence with which Teiresias confronts Oedipus at first, as if protecting him from himself—and let us keep in mind here that Teiresias holds a sacrosanct role in Sophocles. The two versions are quite similar but differ in some important details. The first speaks of many murderers and one survivor from the small royal convoy who returned to tell the story in Thebes; the second has one murderer and no survivors. Harshbarger detects yet another version suggested by lines 292–93. Here the chorus repeats Creon's version of the many wayfarers, to which Oedipus responds that he too heard this story, but adds the detail that "no one sees the one who saw it" (τὸν δ' ἰδόντ' οὐδεὶς ὁρᾷ).[7] Harshbarger interprets the lack of witnessing the witness to signify the lack of any survivor, thus counting this as a third narrative with many perpetrators but no survivor; he then links this ambiguity to what he considers the chronological contradictions of the shepherd's tale (123n2)—the latter being eyewitness to the crime, as we will see. However, Oedipus's above remark does not necessarily mean the absence of a survivor, but that the survivor chose to lay low and retreat from Theban society for understandable reasons, while his story lives on as a "rumor"—something that Jocasta's account (ln. 760–64) later supports, and with which Creon's version is compatible.

The point remains that this prevailing rumor of many accomplices enables Oedipus to exclude himself initially as a suspect since he knows that he had acted alone. It is this self-assurance based on hearsay that enables Oedipus to disbelieve and disrespect Teiresias when the seer, under duress, reveals Oedipus as Laius's murderer (ln. 362), and hints at his incestuous marriage with Jocasta (ln. 366–67). Often a messenger of bad news, Teiresias is sent angrily away, but another messenger from Corinth will lead to the confirmation of everything Teiresias said, the shepherd saw, and Oedipus feared. The messenger arrives to inform Oedipus of his ascendancy to the Corinthian throne on his father's death, which—though sad—would also be salutary news had Polybus been his natural father. Though intrigued during his youth by a drunk man's claim that he is a "counterfeit" son (ln. 779–80), Oedipus continues to think of Polybus as his sire, welcomes the death as his release from patricide, but hesitates returning to Corinth for fear of the incest part of the prophecy (ln. 976). When the messenger by way of reassurance confirms that he was adopted as an abandoned and injured infant, Oedipus presses for details about the origin of his wound. Unaware of that history, the messenger cites the shepherd as the key witness who handed him the baby. It is this humble peasant who bookends Oedipus's fate, this fate of constant transfers from place to place and from rumor to rumor: given to the local shepherd to be exposed, passed to the Corinthian shepherd to pass on to the royals as son and heir, fugitive from rumors of illegitimate parentage, self-exile to avoid the foretold crimes, tried by the contrasting rumors about Laius's death, and finally, obliged to undergo a second banishment.

The shepherd's arrival resembles in many ways the reticent entry of Teiresias, but where the seer equivocated to avoid uttering his terrible insights, the shepherd resorts to lies to avoid testifying. Upon seeing him, the messenger recognizes him immediately (ln. 1120), but the shepherd claims no memory of having seen him before (ln. 1131). A weakened memory after so many years is certainly possible, except that the shepherd's overall demeanor strongly suggests intentional evasiveness. For instance, to the question of whether he has met the Corinthian, he stalls by responding with another question about the man's profession, while pretending that he does not even understand *which* man Oedipus is asking him to identify from the group:

> OEDIPUS. Then do you know this man from having met him there?
> SHEPHERD. Met him doing what? What man do you mean?
> (ln. 1128–29)

Only when the Corinthian reveals the shepherd's dreaded memory of handing him the infant Oedipus does the shepherd admit to their acquaintance in full despair—a mood that retroactively explains the shepherd's previous lies and evasions.

By now, the shepherd has in fact lied thrice: all times with good intentions, with the wish to intervene for the better and change the grim order of things. First, he lied by omission as he silently interfered to spare the child's life. Then, he lied overtly twice more to spare himself and the city from the turmoil that could ensue from the revelation of the true killer: in the past, soon after the crime and in front of an already-enthroned Oedipus,[8] and again now, during the interrogation, for the shepherd is indeed the source of the rumor of Laius's many killers. Cowering in the presence of the murderer-turned-king, and unable to speak the unspeakable to the queen, he authored an alternative story and asked for the favor of immediate and permanent release from his duties. We hear the distant echo of his lie out of pity and fear for the queen in another scene of modern literature: the lie Joseph Conrad's Marlow says to the Intended at the end of *Heart of Darkness*—namely, that her beloved Kurtz died uttering her name instead of his demonic "The Horror! The Horror!"—so as to spare her from the truth of her idealized fiancé having turned into a monster, betrayed her with another woman, and died in complete infamy. How can the shepherd tell the queen that her husband has died at the hands of their unwanted son whom she has now wed, all because he—the underling—had disobeyed their command and spared him as a baby? How to explain that his morality, admittedly superior to that of his superiors, ended up disastrously for all involved? The heart sinks, the fear grows, and the options shrink.

To avoid more disaster, or so he thought, it was best to construct another story and disappear. The shepherd vanished because he could not bear the burden of his witness. Perhaps nobody could. Harshbarger bolsters his alternative thesis by referencing a lapse he sees in the chronology of the shepherd's actions—namely, that if the shepherd had returned immediately after the crime, Oedipus would not yet have been king, as Jocasta said (123n3). Although this is an interesting observation, it does not pose insoluble difficulties. Quite possibly, the shocked and distressed shepherd took some detours to process the scene, and perhaps even to craft the details of his account. Seeing that his delay cost him even more because the culprit is now his sovereign, it is not surprising that he begged to flee. He must have left Thebes much more quickly than he returned from the murder scene. The gist is that, whatever other objections might be raised, they cannot explain the dread with which the shepherd responds to the messenger's immediate recognition of him. Why would the shepherd shudder at the mention of the infant's rescue, had he not felt implicated in the disaster that his good deed unwittingly set in motion? The ambiguity of the murder narratives not only confirms the prevalent assumption of Oedipus's guilt but points—along with much else in this myth—to the limits of a purely immanent conception of dikē.

The abyss of human destiny is laid bare when we see the child's savior inciting as much havoc as the unconscionable parents who condemned their son to death. Human will is split between the evil decision of the parents and the good intentions of the shepherd, but both end up in disaster because tragedy spells that which is, and not necessarily what we wish to be. The gods have the upper hand because the gods are the purveyors of *ta pragmata*[9]—those "things" that remain unforeseeable and undecidable,[10] that stand firm and fixed,[11] that loom harsh and implacable,[12] or that are unknown and unexpected,[13] such that no mortals can comprehend or judge them clearly; those "things" mentioned over and over at the conclusion of numerous surviving tragedies. As these various phrases suggest, the unpredictable and undecidable nature of these things does not necessarily mean that the things must be ever changing; on the contrary, they are also described as firm and fixed, belonging to the order of the immutable, the referential, and the eternal. Signifying much more than things qua objects, *ta pragmata* comprise what we call the cosmos, or "reality,"[14] which reveal themselves to humans through the structure of Dikē. Tragedy's concluding invocations to the gods and *pragma/ta* are one and the same call. Accordingly, the justice (Dikē) appearing on the tragic stage provokes and guides the forms of justice practiced by human beings but itself belongs to another order from whence it is sent: the originary justice of things that, in Nietzsche's untimely words, "is just and unjust and equally justified in both" (*Birth* 72). The shepherd's role in the *Tyrannus* displays this well—while a servant by means of his membership in a social class, he is recast by the play as the indispensable servant of this destinal Dikē. He is the one who, through his conduct, assists the fulfillment of Oedipus's fate and brings about the destruction of the House of Labdacus. Aeschylus's stargazing guardian and Sophocles's good-hearted shepherd: through these socially subordinate figures, the playwrights reveal what in human destiny exceeds the confines of social determinations, whether wittingly or unwittingly.

At the same time, tragedy shows that human beings resist such an understanding of Dikē because it antagonizes their project of self-determination; nonetheless, even their resistance unfolds in accordance with Necessity—namely, with the "things" such as they are. Hence, the chorus's reflections about *ta pragmata* come typically at the end of an ordeal during which human beings have actively doubted or diminished the existence of these "things." The *Tyrannus* is replete with examples where oracles are mocked and tradition is belittled—examples that, we might say, attest to a crisis of values, of authority, and of legitimation. (The plague, seen from the perspective of such moral collapse, has both a physical and a metaphysical dimension.) Even the chorus, whose original stage function aligned it with divine agency, becomes an instrument of impiety. Its members doubt the claim that Teiresias possesses higher knowledge over the common man[15] and, placing their trust in mortal princes—namely, in Oedipus's innocence—they also doubt Apollo's word unless it is corroborated by empirical evidence of the crime (ln. 500–505).

Later on, and in the name of defending traditional piety against its devaluation, the chorus again suggests that if oracles do not come to pass, if empirical reality does not "prove" prophecy, divine efficacy is extinguished. Prophecy's confirmation by history is posited by the chorus as a necessary criterion for divine justice, and if insolent people remain unpunished, it follows that belief in the gods will wane. The Theban elders imply that if Oedipus is guilty, he should have been punished, and since he is not punished (yet), it means one of the following: (a) he is not guilty, thus proving the prophecy deceptive or inefficient; or (b) he is guilty and yet rewarded for his insolence, thus proving the gods unworthy of reverence.

> No longer shall I go in reverence to the inviolate navel of the earth, nor to the temple of Abae, nor to that of Olympia, if these oracles do not accord with truth, so that all mortals may point to them. But o ruler, if you are rightly thus called, Zeus, lord of all, may this not escape you and your ever deathless power! For already the oracles of Laius are fading and are being expunged, and nowhere is Apollo manifest in honour; but the power of the gods is perishing. (ln. 897–910)

In this devastating pronouncement, the chorus climaxes from the specific to the general collapse of values: no belief in the Laius prophecies, no worship of Apollo, no respect for the gods. The story of Laius has no more hold in the city; Apollo's oracles command probably as much respect as plain rumors and gossip. As for the wish for Apollo's words to come true, perhaps it speaks less of the chorus's piety and more of its desire to be vindicated for feeling already betrayed in their traditional beliefs. In other words, the chorus's yearning for concrete evidence of Apollo's victory is simultaneously an irreverent taunting of the god to prove himself to the humans so that, in turn, they can believe him. By demanding such empirical signs, the chorus espouses the secular notion of believing only upon seeing, which, in effect, announces the destruction of belief. Though Oedipus too doubts divine efficacy (ln. 965–72), it is Jocasta who diminishes oracles and divine signs in a rather curious manner. Close to the terrible revelation of her incest, Jocasta prefers the route of denial, but a denial that lies somewhere between willful ignorance and its own kind of philosophical nihilism (ln. 977–83). Exclusively subjects of *tuchē*—of accident and arbitrariness—and with no foreknowledge, human beings, according to Jocasta, lack the resources to organize their lives rationally; they must live as randomly as the playfield of forces amid which they exist. Thus, she rationalizes to herself that incest is not outside the human possibility since men often dream of laying with their mothers, and that, in fact, only people who ignore moral prohibitions and do not regret their own criminality can survive. Jocasta here reiterates Oedipus's previous theory of the true criminal as an amoral character, someone beyond good and evil, who lives undisturbed by the pangs of conscience, and who would not feel obliged to confess in the event of an official investigation (ln. 296). Ironically, although Oedipus turns out to be the *actual* criminal, he is not the "true" criminal with the amoral qualities Jocasta seems to endorse rather cavalierly if they can spare her the consequences.

Through the chorus, Oedipus, Jocasta, and implicitly even the Corinthian messenger who thinks that Oedipus cheated his fate, Sophocles is writing the process of Athens's secularization only to expose its fault lines: to challenge the illusion of politics as a purely immanent domain, as a place where human beings, shunning all reference to an outside (gods, nature, the cosmos), reduce *pragmata* into their own intersubjective affairs. The risk of such a political vision turning quite quickly into tyranny is suggested by the fact that Oedipus the statesman is not a *rex* (a king, as the play's title is often translated), but a *tyrannos*.[16] Accordingly, his final self-awareness and self-banishment from Thebes represent a release, not only of himself but of the city as a whole, from the illusion and tyranny of pure immanence.

I have tried to argue that the figure of the shepherd, so unremarkable in many ways, plays a special hermeneutic role in revealing the movement toward pure immanentism (or secular humanism, in lay contemporary terms) to be a chimera. The shepherd's lies, which are personal *and* political—the latter being "noble lies" invented by human beings to prevent civic derailment—end up exactly in derailment no matter what. Human dikē cannot surpass divine Dikē. This does not mean that these two forms of dikē/Dikē are merely oppositional, or that we can easily exchange the one for the other; rather, it means that they exist vis-à-vis one another in a hierarchical relationship that cannot be definitively overturned, though it is, by its own structure, meant to be perpetually challenged. At this point, we should recall the importance of hierarchy in the very structure of tragedy as Aristotle systematized it in the subordination of ethos (character) to *muthos* (plot). Put in slightly different terms, the plot serves as the formal equivalent of cosmic, destinal Dikē, while the character, referring to individuals, thematizes the concrete instantiations of freedom within the horizon of Dikē and the limitations of Ananke.

In this strange story about natural origins, the darkness of the *Tyrannus* is not exhausted at the particular abominations committed against Laius and Jocasta, who were equally criminal against their own nature—their offspring. Oedipus is taboo not just because of his patricide and incest but also because of some of those disconcerting "things" that necessitate this course of action. He is taboo because his fate reveals two existential facts, the simple admission of which might currently be considered an intellectual crime perhaps far worse than his own actual crimes: on the one hand, his tragedy insists that nature is (indispensable to) destiny, and all the more vengefully so the more we try to dispel it as we now do in our unqualified endorsement of artificiality and the technic; on the other hand, the shepherd's failure to save the situation, despite his best efforts at interference, exposes the limits of any politics that insists on defining itself immanently as the infinitization of human potential. Athens's nascent secular consciousness, refracted through the Theban chorus's reports on the loss of the oracle's authority, ends up the target of Sophoclean tragic irony. Cosmic Dikē and *phusis* are vindicated both on the "historical" level that the chorus hoped for, since the prophecy proved to be true, and on the ontological level through Oedipus's abyssal self-understanding.

In Sophocles, nonimmanent Dikē reappears as *ara* (curse), or *tuchē* (accident of fortune or misfortune), while Teiresias serves as the embodied locus of its manifestation. Teiresias's warnings to Oedipus present an ontological warning to humanity's blindness vis-à-vis its own horizon, particularly when this horizon is contemplated retroactively from the point of view of human origins. His question, "ἆρ' οἶσθ' ἀφ' ὧν εἶ" (Do you know who your parents are?[17]), addresses urgently the nonhuman trace of origin within the human: that singular probability that makes of one what one is, and of which one's natural parents are an irrevocable, but still only partial, marker—a destiny sent from a boundless outside ("the divine," the "cosmos," "reality," or "nature" are several names for that), yet itself bound and finite. Forgetting this exteriority, or rejecting it unthinkingly, implies Teiresias, accounts for the present and future condition of human misery. A purely immanent and socially determined dikē—which is to say, an absolute technocracy and the erasure of nature in the human—is dangerous whenever attempted, and no less dangerous than the absolute theocracy or the mechanistic natural determinism against which secular immanentism purports to be a solution.[18] What Oedipus "sees" for the first time when he becomes physically blind are the limits of human dikē. For his pursuit of riddles, Oedipus has been theorized as the prototype of the "Western," theoretical, reflexive consciousness: it remains to be thought whether his reflection is of the technic/calculative type or the contemplative type, or whether it shifts from the one to the other precisely at the moment of his physical blindness.

I have already underlined that the most serious reason why there can be no other culprit than Oedipus is because the announcement of his guilt comes from the mouth of Teiresias, and Teiresias is never an object of irony or ridicule in Sophocles. Sophocles's Teiresias is not simply an "ethical" figure; he enunciates the order of things, and thus bursts open simultaneously the domains of cosmology and ontology. Aeschylean Dikē continues in Sophocles through Teiresias. Modern culture is accustomed to think that things have changed enormously since the time of Sophocles, and that human beings have moved beyond the silly rants of two fictional blind old men. Yet we would be lying to ourselves not to admit the stark clarity with which this passage describes all the hazards that await ahead of us in our great march for progress, along with the necessary blindness they demand of us at the time of their happening:

> And I say, since you have reproached me with my blindness, that you have sight, but cannot see what trouble you are in, nor where you are living, nor with whom you share your home. Do you know from what stock you come? First, you are unaware of being an enemy to your own beneath and above the earth, and, next, the two-pronged curse that comes from your mother and your father with deadly step shall one day drive you from this land; now you have sight, then shall you look on darkness. (ln. 412–19)

Notes

Chapter 1

1. *Alafros* plays on the meaning of lightness as weightlessness and luminosity. On the Homeric topos and implications of *alafroiskiotos*, and its inheritance by Sikelianos, see Michael Paschalis.

2. See Baudelaire's "Correspondances," in *Flowers of Evil*, 18–19; also, "στήλην ἢ δένδρεον" (pillar/statue, or tree) in *Iliad* 13.437.

3. Though mostly lowercased, when context emphasizes its divine provenance, I capitalize it.

4. No matter how increasingly slight the difference between technology and technocracy proves, it is important to sustain it. The technic and the technological have been part of our understanding of the world at least as long as humanity has tried to feed, clothe, and shelter itself; the technocratic is a singularly modern phenomenon.

5. This is the term in *Phaedo* 58b. Among the meanings of *theoros*, the Liddell-Scott-Jones lexicon cites "ambassador." Theory is couched in the vocabulary of ritual through yet another context: theory as priestly art, where the priest presents the holy things to be shown (*deiknymena*) during a mystery rite, while the spectators are seeing them (*theorein*). Theater spectators also engage in *theorein*.

6. In sections 7 and 8 of *The Birth of Tragedy*, Nietzsche cites the sacred chorus as an instance of antirealism. The chorus does not represent "ideal spectatorship," thus contravening tragedy's political and didactic interpretation qua schooling of the citizenry.

7. Strange also because this anthropocentrism devalues the individualizing qualities of human beings through sociological abstractions; it decenters the person but foregrounds the limitlessness of social identity formation.

8. Again, determinism serves as the immediate disqualifying charge against nature when its facts interfere with social experimentation. However, when the same determinism assists ideology, nature is invoked as an unsurpassable limit to legitimize what a person cannot control or change.

9. Incidentally, this term "reality," which formed a classical philosophical topos at least up to the Middle Ages, has been unduly abandoned by contemporary thought.

10. A few clarifications: I use "objective" (instead of the cumbersome "objectal") to denote the thing's thingliness rather than its confirmed epistemic status, which, in Kant's terms, would have to be grounded in Understanding and its concepts. Objectivity in the latter sense requires human consensus and corroboration, when in fact I wish to stress the thing's primacy and independence from human observers. Sean Kirkland elaborates how Nietzsche, in his *Philosophy in the Tragic Age of the Greeks*, offered an idiosyncratic reading of Kant's delimitation of the thing-in-itself as a gesture of philosophical "restraint" that protects the thing from the voracity of the human will to knowledge. My present concern for the loss of the thing follows from Kant's standard reception, which sees in this delimitation an effective disappearance of the thing from any serious discussion about its knowability. The place of faith, to which Kant relegates it, is indeed a space of silence that can be read either as salutary (Nietzsche), or marginal (the standard version). If we follow Nietzsche's notion of salutary restraint, however, as Kirkland develops it, my understanding is not that dissimilar: the mode of accessibility of the thing, which I propose, is not an apprehension via operational knowledge, but an experience via *theoria*. *Theoria* refers to a quasi-sacred register, to which Kant's faith also points. In *theoria*, the thing may not be comprehensible, but it is attestable, something of the order of a miracle: the thing is phenomenalized, though not explicable.

11. Daniel Graham's translation in *The Texts of Early Greek Philosophy*, 51. For a more "poetic" rendering, see Dirk L. Couprie's translation in *Heaven and Earth in Ancient Greek Cosmology*, 93: "Whence things have their origin, / Thence also their destruction happens, / As is the order of things; / For they execute the sentence upon one another / —The condemnation for the crime—/ In conformity with the ordinance of Time." For the doxography of the fragment and its bearings on the various translations throughout the history of philosophy, and for an exhaustive bibliography of this reception, see Babette Babich. Since the fragment is related in indirect speech via Theophrastus and Simplicius, it is not quite clear where the doxographer's paraphrase ends and the quote begins. Simplicius's comment that its language is poetic has certainly inflected later interpretations, and it is his communication of the "saying" that Heidegger cites in his *Spruch des Anaximander*. Ambiguities abound as to the meaning and context of many of its terms. It is unclear whether the *apeiron* (Boundless) is part of the quote, which, in turn, makes it difficult to decide whether the stemming from and returning to (or being destroyed into) refers back to the *apeiron*. The meaning of φθορά has been variously rendered as "perishing," "destruction," "decline," "concealment," or "return." Δίκη and ἀδικία, as Babich shows, offer a kind of pretext for Heidegger's advancing his more "ontological" translation about the

(dis)jointure of presencing (the lingering/"whiling" of presence) against the gnomic/ethical reading by Nietzsche that speaks of payment. On the question of whether Anaximander effects a revolution in Greek thought, see Joseph Margolis. Margolis argues for Anaximander's antifoundationalist approach as running counter to other pre-Socratic and classical Greek philosophers who, following Parmenides, posit an *archē*/origin and abide by a principle of permanence. For my purposes, the crucial point is less whether Anaximander believes in origin or permanence and more that he articulates dikē in a cosmological context.

12. See especially 171: "Being is fittingness that enjoins: dikē." In chapter 3, my analysis of dikē as a mode of appropriating what is fitting to oneself illustrates this idea through Aeschylus's language in *Agamemnon*.

13. Heidegger's preference for Aristotle's *Physics* over his *Metaphysics* exemplifies his overall commitment to the language of the phenomenon over that of the metaphysical concept in the articulation of his ontology, as Francisco Gonzalez points out. Nonetheless, the temporal disclosure of Being opens the question of history, and by extension of politics, leading to epochal declarations. On this implicitly political and prescriptive aspect, see David Levin.

14. Here is an example in the field of social justice of the Thesean ship, or the false equivalence between Thrasymachus and Socrates, where the "same" idea is not the same at all: through political contestation that now ranks group identity higher than the ethical content of an individual act—namely, through power struggle—justice and equality before the law reverse their meaning, but keep their old names. Of course, nature can also manifest as might, but because it is truly blind, with no pretext to virtuous ends, it is less insidious. Contemplating this kind of objectivity, while admitting that higher intentions do not come without their own ethical costs, is humbling.

15. Nuria Scapin's *The Flower of Suffering* also focuses on the cosmology of justice in the trilogy. She similarly contests linear-progressive readings of the trilogy, arguing that the Aeschylean theology of Zeus does not reflect a progression of justice. Scapin too aligns Aeschylus with pre-Socratic cosmologies, seeing in his Zeus the perpetual combination of Heraclitean antinomies, in that the god dispenses both violence and grace throughout the trilogy. These are major points of contact between her study and mine, but the different disciplinary motives account for notable divergences in approach as well as in the emphasis laid by each project on Aeschylus's relevance for current discussions of justice. Scapin traces Aeschylus in the background of Xenophanes, Heraclitus, Parmenides, and Anaximander in order to yield a systematic theology of Zeus as the unitary principle of strife. My project recognizes the pre-Socratic roots of Aeschylus but proceeds via Burkert's ritual-anthropological model, in part because the latter provides for a contemporary theory of seriousness that dovetails with Aristotle's tragic mimesis. Seriousness, in turn, informs my assessment of justice as a *cultural value today*, this not being a theme in Scapin. By stressing tragic seriousness, I

also implicitly link Aristotle's "serious act" in continuity with, rather than rupture from, a pre-Socratic sacrificial logic of dikē that requires things to disappear for other things to arrive. Overall, my thesis insists on the ever-present risk that justice entails, even in its innocuous forms of grace and clemency: justice is not the opposite of violence, but presupposes it. It is not simply a matter of violence versus grace but of violence and arbitrariness within grace.

16. Unless otherwise noted, all references to Burkert are from *Homo Necans*.

17. I discuss Peradotto's argument in detail and present my differences from it in chapter 3.

18. The temporal remoteness of the hunting scene reinforces the sense of seriousness by evoking the depth of time. In this, it dovetails with tragedy, whose seriousness was in part transmitted via its presentation of acts and heroes that were already long lost to the Athenian democratic polis.

19. It is a historical irony that the resistance to Darwin, identified in the late twentieth century with fundamentalist Christianity, has now taken a different turn, with (evolutionary) biology being attacked by progressives for its "determinism" and "reductionism" on the topic of human sexuality. But whereas the former group may have worn its religious zealotry as a badge of honor, secular activists find it understandably difficult to acknowledge their own forms of zealotry.

20. See Walter Sullivan's "Questions Raised on Lorenz's Prize" in the *New York Times*.

21. Burkert cites ethology's conclusion that collective aggression is found at the dawn of community (35); he writes of sacrificial community as a social model with specific roles and hierarchies, and of collective killing as sign of loyalty in secular Athenian *hetairiai* (37; brotherhoods).

22. See Walter Otto, *Dionysus*, 24–25.

23. The abandonment of natural law and natural rights and their gradual replacement exclusively by positive rights is an example, in the juridical sphere, of this thorough denaturalization of reason.

24. We may recall the critiques of President George W. Bush's politicized use of "warrior," which was seen by detractors as a retrogressive move. Reviewing his *Portraits of Courage: A Commander in Chief's Tribute to America's Warriors* exhibition and book, art historian Melissa Warak writes of the choice of this term as "backward-looking, calling to mind the heroes of ancient Greek mythology rather than those of the modern military complex."

25. An example here is the capture and abduction of fugitive war criminal Adolph Eichmann in Argentina, and his transfer to Israel for trial, absent extradition treaties between the two countries.

26. Athena's strong civic profile hides another, less known side of hers: a cosmological side that, as in the case of the huntress Artemis, connects her to the lunar cycle. Chapter 5 discusses this.

27. Nicole Loraux's *The Mourning Voice: An Essay on Greek Tragedy* also offers an antipolitical reading of tragedy, though she does not arrive at it via Aeschylus or the question of justice.

28. Nietzsche writes: "The chorus is a living wall against the assaults of reality because it—the satyr chorus—represents existence more truthfully, really, and completely than the man of culture does who ordinarily considers himself as the only reality" (*Birth* 61).

Chapter 2

1. Harrison was influenced by Nietzsche and James G. Frazer. Gilbert Murray (of Oxford), Arthur Bernard Cook, and Francis Macdonald Cornford are the main Cambridge Ritualists. For their intellectual exchange, see Robert Ackerman; letters v and vi give a glimpse into the debate between the Ritualists and their rival, William Ridgeway, who proposed a euhemerist origin of tragedy—namely, its rise out of funeral games at the tomb of heroes (Ackerman 117). In the introduction to his translation of the *Oresteia*, Robert Fagles notes the ritual origins of tragedy, insisting on the relevance of Dionysiac ritual despite current contestations: "The ritual origins of tragedy are totally in doubt, often hotly contested. We will merely suggest how certain rites may still exist within the *Oresteia*, not as rituals in themselves, religiously observed, but freely adapted to the point of sacred parody, re-created and recast by Aeschylus' distinctive tragic vision" (18–19).

2. In *Dionysus: Myth and Cult*, Otto critiques the abstract generalization of Frazer's "vegetation deity," and reconstitutes Dionysus as a "living god." Otto was influential for Kerényi's early work.

3. See Nietzsche, *Birth*, 56.

4. This concept is also pivotal for Burkert, who registers the impregnable hierarchies that natural existence imposed on early humans and that found later expression in ritual symbology. The concept of hierarchy has been displaced in our egalitarian age; I touch on some of the ironies and problems that accompany this displacement at the conclusion of this chapter.

5. For the complexity of the concept of mimesis in Greek thought, see Stephen Halliwell, *Aesthetics*.

6. For a detailed analysis of this linguistic convergence between likeness and likelihood, see Nikolopoulou, 285–86.

7. In a pseudo-etymology, Plato links the tragic to τραχύ, which means "harsh," via alliteration (*Cratylus* 408c8), though this supports the opposite of my present claim: for Plato, the harshness does not attest to truth but stems from the falsity associated with human life, which in turn makes this life tragic. On this, see Halliwell, *Aesthetics*, 104–5.

8. For the meaning of σπουδαῖος in relation to excellence, and particularly to moral excellence, see *Nicomachean Ethics* 1.7, 1098a10–15 and 1.8, 1099a20–25.

9. In contrast, modernity aspires to the theoretical construction (and political organization) of a world in which there is no cost for any decision taken. If tragedy is no more intelligible to us, this may be the chief reason why: along with the dismantling of all kinds of binaries, what has been primarily dismantled is the dilemmatic structure of thought, and with it, the very possibility for genuine decision in ethical thinking.

10. On the accord between intellectual judgments and emotions in the *Poetics*, see Gerald Else, 374–75.

11. This notion of a mixed feeling dominates the Enlightenment aesthetics of the sublime, which turns to tragedy as its prime example. After discussing "delight" as a feeling of relief ensuing one's deliverance from terror (33–34), Edmund Burke comments on tragedy, noting that the more realistic its imitation, the more successful it is in eliciting delight (42–44). Kant's *Critique of Judgment* develops this further as a tension between the faculties of the Imagination and the Understanding. His reflections on the successive feelings of diminishment and reassurance when confronted with infinity inaugurated German Idealism's preoccupation with tragedy. For catharsis as the mixed feeling of "tragic pensiveness," see Hans Georg Gadamer, 132–34.

12. For a historical summary of theories and debates on catharsis, see appendix 5 in Halliwell's *Poetics*.

13. Unless otherwise noted, all quotations from the Greek—as well as all translations with the exception of the tragedies—are from the Loeb Classical Library.

14. Aristotle identifies praxis as a distinctive element of theater and likewise calls the tragic agents πράττοντες. The next section discusses the notion of the (sacrificial) act in detail.

15. The link between seriousness and education survives linguistically in Modern Greek, where the term for "study" is σπουδή. While the connotation of hastiness is not typically associated with careful scholarship, the sense of critical urgency grounds education in a long history of religious practice, even if this history is no longer immediately visible.

16. Deaths are not performed onstage but are communicated by messengers. The audience may hear characters being struck inside palace walls, or see a corpse carried onstage, but the moment of death is visually elided. Scholarship is divided only with respect to Sophocles's *Ajax*, which, according to some, presents the hero's suicide onstage. For this view, see Stephen Joseph Esposito.

17. Nicole Loraux ("La Main") advances a similar point, identifying action with murder. Loraux, however, develops an ideological critique of action as masculine violence that also marks political discourse. That her reading of tragedy is distinctly anti-Aristotelian in its disavowal of the murderous nature of action suggests that Aristotle may well have understood action in terms of this extremity.

18. I show later that not only the adjective σπουδαία (grave) but also that of τελεία (complete/purposeful) further embeds tragedy in ritualist semantics. For a contrasting view, see Halliwell, *Poetics*. Halliwell interprets Aristotle's theory of tragedy as "secular and naturalistic," reflecting his moral philosophy that views human affairs also in these terms (234). While I agree on naturalism, and see the logic by which naturalism and secularism are paired—in that both can be opposed to the sacred—there is a case to be made about nature's engendering of the sacred, and about tragedy's mining of this territory. Tragedy is about human affairs, but ancient "humanism" is quite distinct from the brand of secularism that dominates after the French Revolution. Tragic humanism involves the sacred.

19. The word for "neck" or "throat" at this point in *Iphigenia among the Taurians* is δέρη (ln. 1460); through the Latin *dorsum*, it might also refer to the back of the collar, per the Liddell-Scott-Jones lexicon. The same word is used in *Iphigenia at Aulis* (ln. 875, 1429, 1516, 1560), along with the synonym λαιμός (ln. 1084, 1579). For the gendered significance of throat-cutting in maiden sacrifice, see Loraux, *Tragic Ways*, 32, 38, 41, 51.

20. The advent of agriculture did not abolish blood sacrifice, nor did it substitute blood with vegetable offerings. Plants, grains, and precious liquids were introduced but remained peripheral to the central act, which still involved an animal: "Thus, the harvest is celebrated in hunting festival and in sacrifice" (Burkert 44).

21. Of her relation to the hunt and war, Vernant writes: "In the two cases, what concerns Artemis and causes her to intervene is the uncertain boundary between savagery and civilization, the boundary whose fragility is marked by both war and the hunt" (247). Similarly, Froma Zeitlin writes of her as "the goddess who in myth and cult occupies the boundary zone between the civilized and savage—specifically, in this play [*Iphigenia among the Taurians*] between Greek and barbarian identities" (*Retrospective* 450). The Arkteia festival in Brauron, where prepubescent girls served Artemis in the form of bears, celebrated a female rite of passage from childhood to womanhood. On the Arkteia, see Christiane Sourvinou-Inwood.

22. Of the gendered division of labor brought about by hunting, Burkert notes that it "has even become part of our inherited biological constitution," linking forms of labor to embodied human sexuality: "Among human beings, hunting is man's work—in contrast to all animal predators—requiring both speed and strength; hence the male's long, slender thigh. By contrast, since women must bear children with ever larger skulls, they develop round, soft forms" (17–18).

23. On the significance of virginity, which both the goddess of the hunt (Artemis) and the goddess of war (Athena) fiercely claim, see Burkert, 66–67.

24. Iphigenia's sacrifice is given various aitia going all the way back to a curse of Thyestes upon his brother Atreus for a cannibalistic/sacrificial meal of Thyestes's children. In Sophocles's *Electra*, the reason for her sacrifice turns out

to be the punishment for a hunting accident during which Agamemnon had killed a deer sacred to Artemis. For the strong intertext between the *Oresteia* and *Iphigenia among the Taurians*, and for a feminist critique of the *Oresteia*'s verdict, see Zeitlin, "Redeeming Matricide." Chapter 5 here will treat Orestes's exoneration beyond feminist criticism.

25. On cannibalism and (human) sacrifice in the Atreidae myth, see Burkert, 103–9.

26. "The Eumenides probably originated as well-disposed deities of fertility, whose name was given to the Furies either by confusion or euphemistically," notes the Oxford Dictionary (https://en.oxforddictionaries.com/definition/Eumenides). According to the Britannica, "They were probably personified curses, but possibly they were originally conceived of as ghosts of the murdered. . . . Because the Greeks feared to utter the dreaded name Erinyes, the goddesses were often addressed by euphemistic names, such as Eumenides ('Kindly') in Sicyon or Semnai ('August') in Athens" (https://www.britannica.com/topic/Furies).

27. For the element of coercion underlying the appeal to Peithō, see Michael Naas. Persuasion is not a seamless process of voluntary consent, but presupposes the exercise of compulsion to ensure that the persuading is successful: "Athene is herself using a sort of violence in order to control the violence" (5).

28. See also Aeschylus, *Seven against Thebes*, on the mutual slaughter of Eteocles and Polyneices, which fulfills a familial curse by bringing about a civil war (ln. 892–93); and Sophocles, *Electra*, on the injustice of letting Agamemnon's death go unavenged (ln. 247–48). On familial murder and civil war, see Loraux, "La Main," 179–81, where she highlights that civil war is a *stasis emphylos*—a war within the same phyle or tribe.

29. On the symbolic antagonism of wolf, bear, and dog in myth and ritual, see Burkert, 83–93, 109–116. Through a ritual of exclusion, young boys were introduced to manhood by becoming "werewolves," and joining a secret society (*Männerbund*) where they lived ferally: "By training himself in the ways of the wolf, man became a hunter and lord of the earth" (89).

30. See note 20 above.

31. Unlike this single vertical axis whose poles are occupied by gods, Heidegger's notion of the fourfold in "Building Dwelling Thinking" presents us with two intersecting axes of orientation. Heidegger considers "the thing" as the locus of a gathering of earth and sky (nature's vertical axis), and mortals and gods (culture's horizontal axis). This modern and radical rearrangement, which first removes the gods from the rubric of nature, results in a conflation, rather than separation, of mortal and divine, which both now appear coextensively under the rubric of culture. Historically finite, the gods collapse into the domain of mortal horizontality. As Michael Wheeler notes, Heidegger's coming divinity does not involve "a religious intervention in an 'ordinary' sense of the divine, but rather a transformational event in which a secularized sense of the sacred—a

sensitivity to the fact that beings are *granted* to us in the essential unfolding of Being—is restored." In our context of the hero cult, it is relevant to point out that such transformational events refer to poetic translations of ancestral heroes into divinities. Wheeler continues: "According to *Being and Time*, the a priori transcendental conditions for intelligibility are to be interpreted in terms of the phenomenon of heritage. . . . A key aspect of this idea is that there exist historically important individuals who constitute heroic cultural templates onto which I may now creatively project myself. In the later philosophy these heroic figures are reborn poetically as the divinities of the fourfold, as 'the ones to come.'" (Incidentally, Heidegger's historicized gods are not new. Euhemerus's gods were also great ancestors, later divinized.) Still, the historical expectation that a poet will rise out of a secular age to grant us a sense of the holy sounds itself strangely suprahistorical. If the god (like the poet) is merely history and culture, then this rather Romantic exceptionalism that makes the poet capable of granting a god to a godless culture elevates him—for all intents and purposes—to a suprahistorical status, above even the finite deities he promises to invent: he is not a messenger; he is *as if* a god of premodern dimensions.

32. For the etymological derivations, I consulted https://www.etymonline.com/word/grave.

33. Though Burkert recognizes that in Seneca's *Thyestes* "effective theatrical pathos springs from the religious *mysterium tremendum*" (104). For a comparative anthropological account of the first death as sacrifice, resulting in all deaths being viewed as sacrifice in Proto-Indo-European traditions, see Bruce Lincoln, especially 257. Joseph Harris cites this as well (160).

34. For a cognitive rather than physical interpretation of these feelings, see David Konstan, *Pity*, particularly his appendix, "Aristotle on Pity and Pain." In "Zum altgriechischen Mitleidsbegriff," Burkert offers an actional rather than emotional account of pity in Homer; on pity and fear, see also Elizabeth Belfiore, especially 181–89, 248–49.

35. Burkert calls the Paleolithic man "the hunting ape" (17, 18, 20). These "hunting apes" succeeded by cooperating; in that cooperation, the earliest seeds of organized culture are to be found (18).

36. In the sacrificer's flight, and the verdict of banishment for killers, Burkert sees the symbolic expression of the physiological fight-or-flight response during situations of aggression: "The biological mechanism that makes aggression change to flight was institutionalized as law" (139). There are actually two murder weapons, an axe and a knife, but just as the slayer vanishes after the kill, the knife is also thrown in the sea and made to disappear, likely as a ruse for the impending trial scene. Burkert indeed interprets the acquittal of the axe (and symbolically the participants' atonement) in light of the absence of the knife that, as the instrument that provokes the flow of blood, would have been deemed the proper murder weapon (140).

37. On the debate as to whether Athena makes or breaks the hung jury, see Judith Fletcher, 68.

38. Later expressions of this reparative function are the tropaion of war—that is, a stake adorned with the helmet and armor of the defeated—and hunting trophies (Burkert 66).

39. I refrain here from introducing the vocabulary of the tragic hero, agreeing with Bernard Knox that Aeschylean drama involves the *oikos* more than an individual's elaborate psychology (165n1).

40. Though Burkert cites mostly the animal ethologist Lorenz, the method can be traced to Darwin. Darwin's influence on the Classics should not go unnoticed, and he belonged to the intimate and familial circle of some notable British classicists. His son, Francis Darwin, married Ellen Wordsworth Crofts, lifelong friend of Jane Ellen Harrison. Their daughter Frances married classicist Francis M. Cornford, Harrison's disciple and collaborator. The figure of Darwin père loomed large over the practice of the Classics in Victorian-era Britain, and his impact on the field is especially noteworthy in light of the overall mark he left on modern thought.

41. See chapter 1.

42. What translators often render as "class of qualities" falls in Plato's text under the rubric of *phusis*. I list the instances where *phusis* appears in Greek to show what the translations conceal; for the reader's sake, the relevant terms are in italics: "ταῖς *φύσεσι*" (306e); "καὶ τὴν σώφρονα *φύσιν* καὶ τὴν ἀνδρείαν" (307c); "διαφέρεσθον *φύσει*" (308b); "ὑπὸ κακῆς βίᾳ *φύσεως*" and "ὅσων αἱ *φύσεις* ἐπὶ τὸ γενναῖον" (309a); "στημονοφυὲς" (309b); "θηριώδη τινὰ *φύσιν*" and "τῆς κοσμίας *φύσεως*" (309e); "τὴν αὐτοῦ μεταδιῶκον *φύσιν*" (310d); Plato also employs the vocabulary of *genos* (birth and generation), emphasizing the priority of noble birth that, when provided a suitable education, is more receptive to the weaving of divergent virtues within the same person: "τοῖς δ' εὐγενέσι γενομένοις τε ἐξ ἀρχῆς ἤθεσι θρεφθεῖσί τε κατὰ *φύσιν* μόνοις διὰ νόμων ἐμφύεσθαι, καὶ ἐπὶ τούτοις δὴ τοῦτ' εἶναι τέχνῃ φάρμακον, καὶ καθάπερ εἴπομεν τοῦτον θειότερον εἶναι τὸν σύνδεσμον ἀρετῆς *μερῶν φύσεως* ἀνομοίων καὶ ἐπὶ τὰ ἐναντία φερομένων" (310a); and equally, the decline of a good quality into its opposite is understood as a result of intragenerational continuity without the alloy of the opposite quality: "ἐπὶ δὲ γενεὰς πολλὰς οὕτω *γεννηθεῖσα*, νωθεστέρα *φύεσθαι* τοῦ καιροῦ καὶ ἀποτελευτῶσα δὴ παντάπασιν ἀναπηροῦσθαι" (310e).

43. We see this apotropaism in the myth of the one-eyed Horatius Cocles who averts Lars Porsenna's invasion of Rome by force of his grimace. See Georges Dumézil, 144–48.

44. According to Konstan, animals are capable of compassion, but they cannot feel pity, which requires a higher level of cognition (*Pity* 14, 17).

45. The importation of Kant is not accidental since, as mentioned earlier, Rudolf Otto's mysterium tremendum proceeds from Kant's notion of the noumenon,

and Otto explicitly references Kant's aesthetics, though he focuses on the cognitive indeterminacy of the beautiful.

46. In *Observations*, he writes that "sublime attributes stimulate esteem" (51); in the *Critique of Judgment*, he details how the sublime in nature turns out to be the subjective feeling of "respect for our own vocation" (114), meaning the respect we show to our faculty of Reason once its superiority as a regulative power becomes intuitable to us through the experience of infinity.

47. On Kant's scientific turn in the aftermath of this natural disaster, see Svend Larsen.

48. The bibliography on digital vigilantism is growing, with scholars pointing out the dangers of social-media culture normalizing a nonstatist form of social control. Case studies include incidents aligned with *both ends* of the political spectrum. This said, my critical emphasis on the social-justice end of the spectrum is because: (a) only *its* excesses tend to be overlooked by major civic and cultural institutions; and (b) global neoliberalism declares this brand of activism to have *the* monopoly on justice claims. See the journal *Global Crime*, which dedicated two issues on the topic in October 2020. See also Mona Kasra; and Kristy Hess and Lisa Waller.

Chapter 3

1. For its more literal rendering of the "lesson" of the stars, I opt here for H. W. Smyth's translation. Otherwise, I consult Richmond Lattimore's more colloquial verse translation.

2. Seth Schein also quotes this important insight. Schein discusses the concept of the cosmic order as it is expressed in the parodos, but his focus is on the narrative techniques of the chorus and on what it means to receive this cosmology from the chorus: "No chorus is omniscient in their perspective of the 'cosmic order,' but they stand outside the action and are attuned to the divine, so their song demands to be taken at least as seriously as the action itself" (379).

3. Cassandra is connected to both birds through her sorrowful song: the chorus compares her to a nightingale, but she laments that she has been offered less divine solace than the mythical songbird (ln. 1140–49); Clytemnestra refers to the dead Cassandra as "swanlike" (ln. 1444–46; κύκνου δίκην), using again the same simile construction with dikē as in "doglike." John Philip Harris notes that this passage is the earliest reference we have for "the belief that the swan sings a mournful lament once it realizes death looms" (540).

4. Recall the myth of his slaying of Argos, the vigilant guard of Io. The gods are often invested with the attributes of the creatures they slay (for instance, Pythian Apollo is invested with the powers of the dragon he kills).

5. Scholarly consensus has located this episode in Aulis, assuming that Aeschylus reworks its Homeric citation, where the predator was a serpent and

the victims young sparrows (*Il.* II. 308–11). Alan Sommerstein has proposed Argos. John Heath ("Omen") refutes Sommerstein, arguing again for Aulis on the basis of Aeschylus's debt to Homer, despite the tragedian's change of animal species (Heath, "Serpent"). On the significance of the change of animals, see also John Peradotto (243–45), who identifies Aeschylus's Artemis as the Brauronian Artemis, patron of innocent youth and fertility for whom the hare's fecundity, timidity, and innocence serve as appropriate cult symbols.

6. Peradotto cites the hunt, but insists on Artemis as protectress of both human and wild young life, abhorring indiscriminate hunters. This brackets her destructiveness as attested to, for instance, in the myth of Niobe.

7. See Walter Otto, *Homeric Gods*, 195.

8. This is an allusion to the Aristotelian connotations of the ethical nobility of tragic heroes, and of the related aristocratic heredity that is not to be always taken to coincide literally with actual aristocratic classes. Ismene, a princess by class membership, has betrayed her noble birth (εὐγενὴς πέφυκας) because her cowardly nature (ἐσθλῶν κακή) is unfitting to her heredity (*Ant.* ln. 38).

9. Lattimore translates the birds as "eagles," perhaps to preserve the kingliness of the Achaean army, and in seamless anticipation of the eagles sent by Zeus as portent. Smyth adheres to the original, which references a type of vulture that is not only a scavenger but also preys upon live animals. Aeschylus mentions that the battle cry is directed to Ares, whose bloodlust belongs to a different type of violence than the regal wrath of Zeus, and this difference may be better served by keeping the vulture and the eagle apart. In defense of Lattimore's freer translation, the Old World vulture does belong to the same family of carnivorous birds, the Accipitridae, as eagles, hawks, and kites (https://www.encyclopedia.com/science/dictionaries-thesauruses-pictures-and-press-releases/accipitridae).

10. It would be a great omission not to mention Heidegger's extensive treatment of dikē and *poros/aporos* in relation to human beings having/lacking way in his *Introduction to Metaphysics* (162). The reason for my lack of direct engagement with his insights is twofold: first, his discussion centers on *Antigone*; secondly, it is my express wish to let Aeschylus's language—famous already in his lifetime for being as profound as it was terse—establish his meanings rather than have them filtered through Heidegger and Sophocles.

11. Prior to this, the chorus in effect described Burkert's mysterium tremendum, when the irreversible leads to the unspeakable. The chorus declares that it neither saw nor would it tell what happened once the girl offered herself (ln. 239–48). That wisdom comes only through suffering is, also according to the chorus, Zeus's fixed ordinance to mortals (ln. 174–78).

12. This is not a new idea: Aeschylus follows in the well-trodden path of Homer, whose impartial treatment of both camps indicates a grasp of human conduct beyond his presumably nativist attachments to the Greek side.

13. See also Peradotto, 241: "Where Artemis is concerned, what is heavily emphasized in the *Agamemnon*, to the exclusion of nearly all her other prerogatives and attributes, is her *protective concern for the young and innocent* (an aspect of her personality which would probably have been uppermost in the mind of a fifth-century Athenian)."

14. The other side of this would be the link of war to licentiousness, the lust between Ares and Aphrodite. Burkert opportunely cites the myth of Hippolytus, whose one-sided commitment to serving Artemis and her principle of chastity caused his fall and the triumph of Aphrodite (61).

15. See Apollodorus, *Epitome* 3.21; Callimachus, "Hymn 3 to Artemis" 260ff; and Ovid, *Metamorphoses* 12.8ff.

16. See section 8 of the *Birth of Tragedy*: "Nature, as yet unchanged by knowledge, with the bolts of culture still unbroken—that is what the Greek saw in his satyr who nevertheless was not a mere ape. On the contrary, the satyr was the archetype of man, the embodiment of his highest and most intense emotions, the ecstatic reveler enraptured by the proximity of his god, the sympathetic companion in whom the suffering of the god is repeated, one who proclaims wisdom from the very heart of nature, a symbol of the sexual omnipotence of nature which the Greeks used to contemplate with reverent wonder" (61).

17. As recently as World War II, "Artemis, named for the Greek goddess of the chase and death, was an early air-to-air missile project carried out by the Royal Aircraft Establishment (RAE) beginning in late 1943. The missile was intended for radar-equipped night fighters" (Gibson and Buttler). Her association with vigilance—in the form of surveillance—extends to current weaponry: "The Army revealed the Artemis spy plane in a social-media post on Aug. 6. Artemis is a Bombardier Challenger 650 twin-engine business jet packed with sensors. It's the Army's first jet-propelled surveillance plane" (Axe).

18. Jan Kott's cosmology also suggests that Zeus is not in full mastery of the Fates, and that he too is bound by necessity (12).

19. Apropos is the current problematic of critical theoretical models of justice that, in the name of democracy, abandon *universal* equality before the law as a hegemonic, but failed, Western value. Universality need no more be extended to include all who should rightfully claim it, but effectively ought to be withdrawn from those deemed to have enjoyed it longer as a means of ethical recompense—that is, as a belated epiphany of the historical Fury.

20. On this myth, see Burkert, 103–9.

21. On Zeus as bull, and on bull sacrifice at the Buphonia, see Burkert, 77 and 135–43.

22. Athena and Artemis provide two distinct models of virginal sexuality—the former related to citizenry, the latter to wild nature. The peplos woven by the maidens was presented to Athena Polias (Athena of the city). On Athena's

concurrent attributes as virgin protectress of domesticity and motherhood, see Karl Kerényi, *Athene*. Athena expresses the father-daughter mythologeme in that her virginity formalizes the girl's internalization of the sexual aggression of the father: "She has the contradictory task of providing progeny for the father while yet remaining the father's daughter" (*Athene* 68).

23. I use Smyth's literal translation; Lattimore translates it as "Asiatic," pointing to the Trojan king, Priam, who would have celebrated triumphantly had he won, as per Clytemnestra (ln. 935).

24. It is arguable that, here, Aeschylus offers a different model of appropriating "the native" than what Hölderlin saw in Sophocles, as he described it in his letter to Böhlendorff: for Hölderlin, the road to appropriating one's nature passes inevitably through the foreign, and he noted that, while the Greeks excelled in their appropriation of the foreign, they were lost because they forgot (to return to) themselves. Aeschylus's Agamemnon is destroyed the moment he indulges in the foreign.

25. I have changed Lattimore's "God's" to the original's plural.

26. Robert Browning translated this as "exhaust" (http://www.perseus.tufts.edu/hopper/text?doc=Perseus%3Atext%3A1999.01.0224%3Acard%3D944). George Seferis, who incorporates this line in one of his poems, uses ἐξαντλῶ, which in Modern Greek also means "to exhaust," but whose literal meaning again refers to draining water.

27. David Evans also writes that Agamemnon's death can be interpreted simultaneously as punishment for his crimes and as sacrifice. In his comparative-mythological account, the death follows the Indo-European triple-death pattern of hanging (for crimes against the supreme deity), stabbing (for crimes against the military), and drowning (for crimes against sexuality), albeit with an inversion between the first and third functions. In Greece, hanging is usually associated with women and the third function, while water and the presence of ritual vessels are associated with the first (163). Thus, in Agamemnon's case, the death in the bathtub fulfils the first function, being stabbed the second, and the luxurious robes in which he is entrapped the third. Evans, however, also allows for the entangling robe to substitute for the noose (161). Agamemnon's triple fault consists in offending the gods by killing his daughter, even though her sacrifice was divine command; in causing the death of Argive youth in a war for personal honor; and in indulging in riches and concubines (164–65). On Clytemnestra as alastor, and the scholarly history of how mortals relate to divinities in Aeschylus, see Matt Neuburg.

28. See also *Choephoroi*, lines 66–74, for a similarly inexhaustible economy of blood pollution.

29. The ethical complexity behind Clytemnestra's murder of her husband and his foreign mistress will resonate in the *Choephoroi* through the chorus's

citation of the "Lemnian crime" as a prohibitive moral topos. I will address this in the next chapter.

30. Joshua Billings's critique of Anne Carson's express sympathy with Cassandra in her free translation titled *An Oresteia* raises issues indicative of the modern partiality toward Cassandra's foreignness. Such partiality, however, compromises the expansiveness of Aeschylus's tragic vision. Billings writes: "Unsurprisingly, Carson's sympathy lies with the Trojan captive Kassandra," whose voice Carson translates so as to preserve its foreignness. He continues: "Yet Carson's de-familiarizing translation practice means that her range of tones is quite limited where Aeschylus's is astonishingly wide. . . . Carson fails to do justice to the universal force of the character's parting words, as distilled a statement of the essence of tragedy as ever was written." Focusing, then, on Cassandra's words about the futility of human affairs, Billings notes that Carson's choice of apostrophe—"You, / you, / I pity"—fails to render the universality of Cassandra's statement, which includes her and everyone else in that pity. Carson's version makes her simply "vindictive," according to Billings, or, as I contend, above such pity by presuming her to be morally superior due to her status. Such ideologization, which sidelines the cosmic "order of things," is what I consider symptomatic of the contemporary forgetting of tragic neutrality.

31. This ploy is not explicit in *Agamemnon*, but forms the core of Euripides's *Iphigenia at Aulis*. Aeschylus's Clytemnestra hints at a deceptive plan (δολίαν) by which Agamemnon obtained Iphigenia (ln. 1523). The schemes leading Iphigenia and Agamemnon to their deaths are akin to Burkert's "comedy of innocence" in animal sacrifice.

32. The pejorative identification of woke culture with virtue signaling relies on this fact: vigilance, or even the performance of vigilance, is elevated to a special political virtue.

33. Beyond such officialdom, the issue is far more complex and inconvenient, since even death threats have become routine in concluding ideological arguments, at least in cyberspace. Furthermore, what is considered vigilantism is itself an ideological question, given that some acts of vindication are excused while at the same time others are deemed unacceptable.

34. Ἀγρυπνία (sleeplessness) is one term for vigil, but the actual verse reads: "φόβος γὰρ ἀνθ᾽ ὕπνου παραστατεῖ" (ln. 14; fear in sleep's place stands forever at my head).

35. See "Alastor." *Merriam-Webster*, https://www.merriam-webster.com/dictionary/Alastor. See also λάω in the Liddell-Scott-Jones lexicon. https://lsj.gr/wiki/λάω. The Latin "vigil" means similarly not only "to be awake" and "to watch" but also "to be strong, lively."

36. See Thucydides, *History of the Peloponnesian War* 5.18.2, for the term αὐτόδικος (with one's own jurisdiction and courts), which much later has come to

mean "vigilante," but which here simply confirmed the local judicial independence of areas such as Delphi that otherwise served as a Panhellenic temple. See also Nicole Loraux, "La Main," for a gender-based analysis of the hand, the act, and the self in relation to murder.

37. I must clarify what may be perceived as contradiction: I concluded the previous chapter by suggesting that the mediating function of the law is preferable—because more life-affirming—to the militancy of justice; it may now seem that I am critical of law as convention. This is not an issue once we consider the gap between the Aeschylean and modern conceptions of the law: for Aeschylus, there is no court of law without its divine (Athenian) establishment, while our conception of the law is, as I note here, divorced from such sacred (cosmological) origin. As Thanos Zartaloudis shows, the original meaning of *nomos* (law) was "apportionment," referring to a portion allotted from a sacrificial meal, thus involving the religious and cosmological registers. My thanks to Brent Adkins for alerting me to Zartaloudis's text.

38. In keeping with the notion of the bestiary, one of those characters, Leni, is web-fingered.

39. "How now?" is the question Nietzsche poses in his preface to *The Birth of Tragedy* to disabuse his readers from the erroneous assumption that he is telling us what the Greeks were. Instead, he reveals where his interests actually lie: what the Greeks mean for the moderns.

40. Thomas Carlyle's epithet for the militant and unmarried revolutionary Robespierre—"the sea-green incorruptible"—is an oft-cited example of this justice-driven puritanism (136, 153, 213, 388, 410).

Chapter 4

1. The Latin *victima* referred exclusively to a sacrificial offering, thus a creature with no resources in front of certain and inevitable death. The gravity of this definition is compromised by present notions of victimhood, where the degree of suffering can be minimal, but the claim to it guarantees quick social validation. In so investing the victim with unquestionable moral legitimacy, present culture also disregards the complexity—as in the myth of the hunter Argos—that allows for the victim to have been a predator. Here is an amusing but illustrative example of these issues from pop culture: Peter Jones of *The Spectator* writes of Meghan Markle's public fallout with the British royal family on claims of victimhood related to her identity: "Meghan Markle seems to see herself as a 'victim.' Had she called herself a *victima* in Rome, it would have been a matter of some surprise, since the ancients used that image solely with reference to animals for sacrifice. But our 'victim' is used as if one genuinely were as helpless as a *victima*. Ancients would have none of that. In place of our 'victimhood,' they used words like 'wronged, betrayed, worsted, dishonoured, neglected, injured.'"

2. For this etymology, see Gregory Nagy, 32. The sexual tension persists even in this shared domain of temporality where Hera's time involves seasonal completion but the hero's involves untimeliness through early death. Still, with deified Heracles as the heroic model, it is Hera, the feminine antagonist, who brings him to full glory and resurrects him as an Olympian (Nagy 44).

3. See particularly lines 43, 66–67, 127–28, 164, 377, 399, 489, 585, and 722.

4. For these alternatives, see H. W. Smyth's footnote on the attribution of πατρῷ' in *Choephoroi*, 159n1.

5. In Lacanian psychoanalysis, this appears as the problematic of "foreclosure"—namely, the hole in the symbolic introduced by the lack of access to the father, which results in psychosis; see *Seminar III: The Psychoses*. In Nietzsche, this is tantamount to the peril experienced in the aftermath of "the death of God"; see the madman parable in *The Gay Science*, 181.

6. On the simultaneous castration and death blow of a he-goat to Dionysus, and on the phallic symbolism of the bleeding tail of the October Horse, see Walter Burkert, 68–69.

7. Pointing to a wide comparative context beyond the Mediterranean, Burkert writes thus of sexual aggression in hunting and war: "When killed, a warrior is immediately castrated. This has occurred regularly in wars up until recent times, and it appears to be a basic element in man's fighting instinct. It can also . . . be translated into the hunter's 'battle' with his quarry. In mammals, the significance of the male reproductive organs is obvious. They stimulate aggression and hence are accorded special treatment when the quarry is cut up and distributed. It is certain that castration rituals play an important role in sacrifice, but because they largely belong to the 'unmentionables,' the ἄρρητον, we hear of them only exceptionally or by chance" (68).

8. On the subtext of mystery cults in the *Oresteia* that immortality and the seed imagery evoke, see A. M. Bowie, whose survey also offers a review of previous scholarship on the topic.

9. For the Homeric distinction between *anēr* as hero and *anthrōpos* as ordinary mortal, see Seth Benardete's "Achilles and the *Iliad*." Likewise, civic orations are addressed to *andres*, denoting the status of these men as active citizens and potential soldiers.

10. Guardianship is not exclusively attached to the male, but itself splits into two domains under the purview of each sex, revealing something of the coparticipation of both men and women in the chthonic: while the chthonic world and its rituals are guarded by women, its famed occupants are the heroes who, in turn, guard the city. I return to this near the conclusion of this chapter.

11. Kuhns cites Hubert J. Treston, E. T. Owen, William Chase Greene, and, less strongly, Friedrich Solmsen and R. P. Winnington-Ingram.

12. Aeschylus also uses στύγος for "hate"; for its relation to anger and the demand for justice, see line 392. For the Erinyes as στυγεροί (chilly ones), see Jane Ellen Harrison, 15.

13. See Froma Zeitlin, "Dynamics," which interprets the citation of the Lemnian crime as serving such a programmatic function.

14. Apollodorus relates that the women murdered their fathers along with their husbands, except Hypsipyle, who saved her father, King Thoas (*Library* 1.9.17); Apollonius Rhodius tells of the killing of all males (*Argonautica* 1.618). Both accounts postdate Aeschylus, but they communicate already existing versions of the myth. Aeschylus himself is attributed with a play about Hypsipyle. Although it is not extant, it dealt with the myth of the Lemnian women accepting the Argonauts on their island only on the condition that the latter would mate with them to repopulate the island, a demand that implicitly confirms the previous slaughter of the local men (*Fragments* 250). My point remains that this genocidal aspect makes this story an exception. The Danaids, whose myth Aeschylus treats in the *Suppliant Maidens*, also kill their husbands, but their deed does not attain the infamy of the Lemnian crime.

15. That a crime pollutes not only its perpetrator but the entire race is a central Aeschylean topos, and constitutes the premise of the *Oresteia*. Robert Parker writes: "Pollution does its best to reassert the claims of the victim against those of convenience (or even, as in the *Oresteia*, against those of broader social order). Family members who disregard it invite divine punishment" (123). It is not only the victim's blood that contaminates all in its vicinity; it is also the responsibility thereof that becomes transferable, or *communicable*, from the criminal to the future generations.

16. Herodotus recounts a story of Athenian-Pelasgian conflict where Pelasgian Lemnians abduct Athenian women for political revenge and bring them to Lemnos as concubines. The imperious attitude of the illegitimate Athenian children vis-à-vis the locals produces enmity, and the Lemnians decide to murder them along with their mothers in a plot twist that virtually reverses the gender dynamic of the earlier myth. The heinousness of child murder is then described by Herodotus thus: "From this deed and the earlier one which was done by the women when they killed their own husbands who were Thoas' companions, a 'Lemnian crime' has been a proverb in Hellas for any deed of cruelty" (*The Persian Wars* 6.139). For more on this, and for a good compilation of scholarly sources on the Lemnian crime, see Richard P. Martin.

17. A juridical synonym here would be "prejudged," which is actually tantamount to prejudicial.

18. See Kathy L. Gaca. Gaca's other publications also center on enslavement and heterosexual rape as central acts in both ancient and modern warfare.

19. This moral expectation is a Hegelianism that replaces the private feeling's natural spontaneity with the higher morality of the state. Even if we accept this Hegelian moral assumption, however, it should objectively apply not only to one woman, but to both. I can only illustrate this with a thought experiment that is contentious but should be allowed to be thought nonetheless. What if, in accordance with gender solidarity, we expected the captive maiden, the Cassandra

figure, to risk her life, even by a willingness to kill herself, in refusing to become an instrument of sexual betrayal against the wife? This scenario would now be considered outrageous because in our worldview, Cassandra is not and *can never be* responsible for her fate. A suicide would disprove such an assumption—hence, its mere contemplation is discouraged. By the same token, however, we should not expect the *despoina* to endanger her primacy, and perhaps her life, as well as the welfare and lives of her children, by unreservedly welcoming the incomer so as to satisfy civic morality's unilateral requirement of obedience.

20. See Gerald Else, 374–75, on Aristotle's structural coherence of the emotions with reason.

21. Apropos Aristotle and the emotions, the philosopher linked anger to justice: anger is "a longing, accompanied by pain, for a real or apparent revenge for a real or apparent slight, affecting a man himself or one of his friends, when such a slight is undeserved"; and immediately after, "anger is always accompanied by a certain pleasure, due to the hope of revenge to come" (*Rhetoric* 2.2, 1378a–b). In *Politics* 5.10, 1312b, Aristotle distinguishes between anger and hatred in that "Hatred is more reasonable, but anger is accompanied by pain, which is an impediment to reason, whereas hatred is painless." For an elaboration of this, see David Konstan, *Emotions*, 42. The distinctions between these cognate feelings are useful, but I stress again that the language of Aeschylus effectively blurs anger with hatred as inciters of justice. There has been a surge in recent legal scholarship on Aristotle's link between anger and Nemesis as righteous indignation; see, for instance, Christine J. Basil, and Daniela Bonnano. This pertains to Aeschylus, who might well be considered *the* poet of Nemesis.

22. Contra Aristotle, for whom hatred is more reasonable than anger, as noted above.

23. Smyth's translation.

24. See Homer, *Iliad* 5.890.

25. My translation, which preserves the name of Ares in conjunction with justice. The chorus returns to this link when speaking of a "double lion" (Clytemnestra and Aegisthus) suffering a "double assault" by Agamemnon's avenger, who is likened again to Ares (ln. 935–38). The nouns of Ἄρης and ἀρά (curse) sound significantly close together. See also Aeschylus's *Supplient Maidens*, line 1071, for the same syntax of justice against justice: "δίκᾳ δίκας ἕπεσθαι."

26. See also Burkert, 116 and 120–21. Besides its derivation from "wolf," Lykeios has been traced to "Lycia," and to "light"—the latter befitting an initially pastoral god who came to signify the light of reason. Nonetheless, Burkert remarks that for most Greeks, it meant "wolf" (121). On the double meaning of dogs and snakes as vengeful predators and curative agents, see Kuhns, 20–21, who addresses the *Oresteia*'s references to the healer Asclepius, son of Apollo.

27. On these kings and snake iconography, see Burkert on the Arrhephoria cult, 150–54; on the snake as exemplary of the chthonic substratum of Olympian deities, see Harrison's discussion of the Diasia, 12–23. A festival to Zeus, the Diasia

was originally a ritual to an underworld snake identified as Zeus Meilichios in two ancient reliefs. Arguing for a "primitive substratum" of the later Olympians, Harrison maintains that the coiled serpents of the relief do not show an "underworld aspect" of Zeus, or a Hellenic translation of a foreign deity but attest to an "autochthonous" serpent god before the "formulation of Zeus" (19).

28. On the iconography of the Erinys as serpent, the Harrisonian identification of the avenging serpent with the dead hero, and Pausanias's remark on Aeschylus being first to add snake locks to the Furies, see Cecil Smith, 279.

29. Emphasizing the transformation in this function of guardianship, Kuhns interprets Orestes as a new type of hero who "has changed from a fearful spirit of vengeance . . . to one who is endowed with divine power for the good of the *polis*" (26).

30. Pun intended, since "delivery" qua birth refers back to τοκεῦσι.

31. Hyperborea's location has no ancient consensus. Its name situates it beyond the North Wind (Boreas). It is imagined as a land of perpetual sunlight because it lies beyond the Riphean Mountains that shade the mortal world, casting humans into a state of hubris. Yet its particular geography differs in various accounts. It is found north of Thrace for Homer, Simonides of Ceos, Aeschylus, and Sophocles; near the Danube for Pindar (who nonetheless writes in his *Tenth Pythian Ode* that "neither by ship nor on foot could you find the marvelous road to the meeting-place of the Hyperboreans"); and in Britain for Hecataeus of Abdera. Apollo's two major cult sites—Delos and Delphi—fall under the auspices of the Hyperboreans, who came to worship the god's birth at Delos, according to Herodotus; in turn, Apollo flies to the Hyperboreans for a year to give them law before returning on his swan to Delphi. Swans link the human south to the ideal north through migration. On the swan and Apollonian immortality, see Karl Kerényi, *Apollo*, particularly 54–56.

32. This describes the Erinys when she first appears in *Agamemnon*, as mentioned in chapter 3.

33. Richmond Lattimore translates παισὶ δὲ μᾶλλον γεγένηται as "Power grows on the side of the children"; I prefer Smyth's rendering here: "'Tis the children that have gained the day!"

34. See Burkert, 93–103. The location of the chthonic sanctuary to Pelops as the founding Peloponnesian hero opposite the temple of Olympia (dedicated to Zeus, with Apollo figuring prominently) is used paradigmatically by Burkert to denote this nether-to-higher axis of Greek sacred space.

35. Electra had already greeted Orestes as the "hope of the seed of our salvation" in the scene of recognition (ln. 236).

36. See also *Choephoroi*, line 490, for Electra's appeal to Persephassa/Persephone.

37. Though called Zeus's sons, they are half brothers, one born of the mortal Tyndareus, the other of Zeus. Similarly, Clytemnestra is daughter of Tyndareus, while Helen is of Zeus.

38. Says Orestes of his cry for justice to his father's spirit: "This cry has come to your ear / like a deep driven arrow" (ln. 380–81).

39. See Zeitlin, "Thebes."

40. I already hinted that the Furies *were* awakened by Athens's political hubris—namely, its democratic imperialism in the Peloponnesian War; perhaps Aeschylus sensed the potential for such hubris when he kept a cautious reserve from democratic radicalism, as shown in the next chapter.

41. Historian Victor Davis Hanson stresses that, despite whatever their fine-tuned political attitudes with respect to Athens, philosophers, dissidents, and gifted craftsmen from the wider Mediterranean flocked to the city, aware of the opportunities it gave them to flourish: "'Athenianism' was the Western world's first example of globalization" (14). See also Christian Meier, *Athens*, 306–7, on the city's attraction of skilled immigrant labor, and its open trade, exotic goods, and foreign influences, which led even ancient critics to denounce it for its "effete, decadent" luxury culture.

42. Loraux is especially interesting because she advances an antipolitical interpretation of tragedy in *The Mourning Voice* but inadvertently politicizes it by viewing it exclusively through gender.

43. On death as the vehicle to objective—thus, universal—individuality, see Hegel's *Phenomenology of Spirit*, 271. J. N. Findlay's summary remark from his annotations to §451 of the *Phenomenology* is especially pertinent: "The Family exists to promote the cult of the dead" (553). For Hegel, the localized pagan mode of universality is to be surpassed by the rational universality of modern state morality, while tragedy is a step in the realization of this dialectic by which the work of freedom supersedes nature as necessity. Since I do not read tragedy "historically," I submit that its cosmological figurations of sex, family, or death cannot be supplanted by political immanence for the simple reason that the decisive ontological constraint that tragedy *recurrently* sets up against the human being is nature, and it does so in a metaphysical, nonhistorical manner. One can historicize tragedy and its choice of constraint, but one can also legitimately argue that tragedy itself does not reveal its premises as historical contingencies.

44. Notably, in an interview with Jonathan Bastian, Black Lives Matter (BLM) cofounder Melina Abdullah states that BLM is not so much a secular movement, as it was initially thought to be, but one with deep spiritual and ritual claims. To Bastian's question of "how the movement shifted into a more spiritual direction," she responds: "I think about the first night that we gathered and the summoning of ancestors to space and the very palpable spiritual energy that circulated through the group as we stood in a circle at St. Elmo Village." She adds, "All Black Lives Matter meetings and protests begin with the pouring of libation," explaining the ritual in explicitly chthonic terms: "What it looks like is the pouring of water into Earth, the pouring of water into plants, the pouring of water into flowers into something that represents the sanctity of life and Earth." The full transcript is available online.

45. Jan Kott detects this horizontal impetus in modern revolutions from Cromwell to Marx, who famously described the Paris Commune as "the storming of the heavens." Kott writes: "Revolutionary justice often employs the spatial image of 'leveling,' and it was not by chance that the Bible-educated Puritans of Cromwell, who wanted to introduce justice swiftly and thoroughly, called themselves 'levelers'" (6). There is a noteworthy distinction here between the vertical/divine Erinys of Aeschylus that was delayed, and modern justice that aspires, despite its human immanence, to be swift, immediate, and sweepingly effective.

Chapter 5

1. In another monograph, *The Discovery of Politics in Greece*, Meier also interprets the *Oresteia* as the culminating combination of Greek political and theological thought.

2. See *Eumenides*, line 500, where the Furies describe themselves as "maenads" in their frenzied wrath.

3. Meier's term, which he juxtaposes to modernity's "political theology" (*Discovery* 222); in *Prometheus Bound*, however, the old Titan is identified with progress against the younger, tyrannical Zeus. On this "entanglement" of old and new gods, see also Meier, "Umbruch," 366–74. Meier states that, unlike in the *Oresteia*, Zeus in *Prometheus Bound* acquires himself a history, something that must have sounded "outrageous" (*unerhört*) to the Greeks, because—and here Meier concurs with Karl Reinhardt—until then, the gods appeared in various guises but were not in themselves developing (370–71). In my study, I focus precisely on the "undeveloped" gods whose ahistorical, cosmological dimension I find especially intriguing for a tragic work that treats something as explicitly political as the establishment of a court of jury.

4. The "re-" in "revolution" remains to be thought as repetition, return, and even violent nostalgia and reactionary impulse—namely, everything (except violence) that revolutionaries distance themselves from. For atavism's transformative potential, see Nietzsche, *Gay Science*, 84.

5. The word sounds close to "Moira," and per the Liddell-Scott-Jones lexicon, it also means "destiny" as doom.

6. Nietzsche's Dionysian is complex, taking on various guises throughout his work. For instance, the collective enthusiasm of the folk song is not merely mob-like; in the great lyric poets, it becomes the very medium of tradition. Yet, just as Apollonian individual discipline verges on militarism, so Dionysian collectivity risks anarchy. The distinction between the two remains not only heuristically useful but phenomenologically attestable and ethico-politically urgent.

7. For instance, the Norse fertility gods are the Vanir, who, having been defeated by the Aesir of the higher dyad, became incorporated as third-class gods

in the new order. In the Roman context, the Sabine Quirinus, god of grain and the Roman curiae, was similarly incorporated in Roman civic religion after the defeat of the Sabines by Rome.

  8. In his *Phenomenology*, Hegel translates the chthonic gods whom Antigone obeys with the Roman Penates (274, 287).

  9. This is the question that my epigraph from Mikhail Bulgakov asks and to which it also responds (xii–xiii).

  10. On kin murder allegorizing civil war (*stasis emphylos*), see Daniel Blickman, 198–99; see also Nicole Loraux, "La Main," 179–80.

  11. Political dikē differs from the dikē Aeschylus uses in lieu of "as." The latter admits to a destinal nature, which remains constitutive of the family, insofar as the family manifests the natural/cosmic dimension of living together through its reliance on arbitrary and unpredictable forms of emergence, and through its fostering of equally unpredictable relations of both extreme intimacy and violence. In contrast, politics considers such unpredictability and arbitrariness obstacles to its project of citizen formation.

  12. For more on this debate, see also Anthony Podlecki's historicist interpretation; for the limits of the historicist approach, see P. J. Konradie, 25–26, who incidentally approves of Podlecki's treatment of dikē in the *Oresteia* insofar as the concept is first illumined broadly before being subjected to political correspondences.

  13. Lindsay Hall also rejects the narrative of the Thirty's restoration of the Areopagus after Ephialtes's reforms as a byproduct of this unquestioned trust in Aristotle's history. He turns to other sources and interpretations: Plutarch dates the reforms to Aristides, at the tail end of the Persian Wars; the language of some legal documents suggests that the Areopagus was disempowered later by the Thirty, not by Ephialtes (who may have simply redefined its scope of powers positively), and was restored after the fall of tyranny; finally, a text by the democrat Teisamenos extols the Areopagus upon the restoration of democracy after the Thirty. Whether Hall's challenge proves historically correct, and the later Plutarch is more trustworthy than Aristotle, is best left to classical historians. What remains relevant is his redrawing of the itinerary of the Areopagus in a manner that assigns to Aeschylus a kind of centrism, even if this is not Hall's intention.

  14. Hall views Meier's interpretation of the *Oresteia* in *The Political Art of Greek Tragedy* as contradictory because it treats the play as a response to current events but then posits a difference between interpretation and politics. On E. R. Dodds, Podlecki writes: "In the end it may seem merely a matter of personal preference, but Dodds does not seem to me to present a convincing refutation of Dover's view that the political language of the play is 'neutral, and for that very reason reconcilable with unreserved acceptance of the democratic position'" (95). In short, if Dodds meant to produce a reactionary Aeschylus, he did not succeed. I am not convinced that the only option is between reactionary or "unreserved"

democrat; hence, the notion of reserve. Similarly, Meier's "self-contradiction" allows for an important distance between political actuality and tragic drama—namely, the difference between history and poetry Aristotle prized.

15. The middle, particularly in the sense of the middle class, is indispensable to the cohesion and stability of city-states with consensual governance in Aristotle's *Politics* as well (1296a–c).

16. On tragedy's problematization of the politics of control, Patchen Markell's *Bound by Recognition* is instructive, drawing on Sophocles rather than Aeschylus. Markell reads Hegel's asymmetry in the master-slave dialectic ontologically, disputing the political desire to transform it into mutual reciprocity. For Markell, this misses the ontological dimension of the asymmetry, which is meant to subvert the very desire for mutual recognition, showing it to be a desire for a false sovereignty, one that is blind to human finitude. He asks: "Must a world of greater justice and equality also be a world of mutual transparency, a world without alienation, a world in which we can be confident of our invulnerability to all powers that we do not control ourselves?" (3); and again, "Does the pursuit of recognition, for all its democratic good intentions, actually blind us to certain ineliminable, and perhaps also valuable, aspects of our own situation?" (4). I would go much further in rephrasing his question, since I remain even more skeptical of politics as improvement project: When does the desire for democracy/equality legitimize the hubris (mortal blindness, finitude) of prohibiting all those things—favors, intimacies, accidents, contingencies, preferences—that constitute an inherent (ineliminable) part of human reality because this reality interferes with the political fantasy of the "perfect citizen"?

17. A term Teisamenos uses about the Areopagus on the occasion of the restoration of democracy.

18. Respect for tradition does not obstruct change; instead, it accommodates changes that are necessary, and not simply for the sake of change.

19. Diodorus Siculus (4.69.3–5) offers a succinct version of the myth. Timothy Gantz summarizes the tradition (718–21), reporting that the earliest literary reference to the fiery wheel is to be found in scholia to *Phoenician Women* (ln. 1185), which specify that the wheel was thrown in Tartarus (Gantz 719). I am indebted to Roger Woodard, who suggested these and a wealth of other primary and secondary sources on this myth.

20. Besides Aeschylus's *Ixion* fragments, fragments from his *Perrhaebian Women* also indicate that he was drawing on the myth of Ixion's initial crime and his purification by Zeus. See the Loeb edition of *Aeschylus*, 409–11 and 444.

21. Aeschylus does not use *emphylon* for Ixion's murder of a kin by marriage, not least because this could undermine Apollo's claim that Clytemnestra is not a genuine blood kin to her own son.

22. Pindar had already mentioned explicitly the punishment of the rotating and flying wheel in *Pythian Odes* 2.21–24; Pherecydes in fragment 51a–b (Fowler 306); and Apollodorus, postdating Aeschylus, mentions the wheel in *Epitome* 1.20.

23. Ixion's mortal wife was Dia, meaning "divine," or "belonging to Zeus." Karl Kerényi writes that Dia is another name for Hebe, or even for Hera herself as the one belonging to Zeus, or the heavenly one (*Gods* 158–60). In this sense, Ixion's pursuit of Hera doubles his earthly marriage.

24. See also Nuria Scapin, especially chapters 3 and 4.

25. He is different because he was not an eager killer, and because he already suffered. See also Oliver Taplin, 383, who writes about "the salutary suffering of Orestes' wanderings." A. M. Bowie (26n109) cites Taplin, and Alan Sommerstein's introduction to the *Eumenides*, for agreeing on this. On Orestes's reluctance to kill, and on his bewilderment about Apollo's command, see also Richard Kuhns, 31, 34. It is the rational side of Orestes, which Kuhns ascribes to the knowledge he acquired through his exile (50), and to the male proclivity for dispassion (39), that transformed him from a primitive hero to a citizen-hero through the trial.

26. I presented another entry to this Apollonian argument in chapter 3, involving the image of the seed as the male participation in the chthonic. This new approach does not aim to introduce contradiction or deliberate confusion. Rather, I wish to show that the unwieldiness of Apollo's argument is not due to nonsense but to a condensed and overdetermined logic that can be reached from different directions at once.

27. Incidentally, and quite ironically, feminism's mourned (because erased) "mother" is once again under erasure—this time, linguistically—by the "birthing person," and just as it was in Aeschylus's time, this erasure also is required by new and enlightened justice claims.

28. In principle, I do not subscribe to the pejorative connotations of myth. Here, I am using the term tactically to show that modern democracy's claim of demythologization is itself a myth.

29. H. W. Smyth's translation (as it appears at the Perseus Digital Library), which preserves the notion of purging in καθαιρεῖ. This purging does not only mean "healing," or "sublating," as Hegel might render it to keep some transformed memory of the past in the cumulative historical process; it means primarily the more decisive gesture of "dividing" and "removing" what is to be kept from what is to be discarded.

30. The seed anticipates Apollo's patriarchal argument, and refers to the split function of chthonicity that I have addressed previously: while chthonic justice entails generational destruction, the seed attests to the life-bearing potential of the netherworld—more particularly, allowing the male qua hunter/warrior to participate in the generative process.

31. The Furies address her as such in line 415. Given Aeschylus's own wordplay of Dika as Dios Kora, it appears that the Furies already implicitly accept her as the "new" instrument of justice. Athena Kore is identified as chthonic Persephone ("our Kore and Despoina") in Plato's *Laws* (796b). Kerényi discusses this in *Athene*, 50.

32. Another contradiction of this otherwise civilized god is his command to Orestes to exact blood for blood, which confuses Orestes. On this, and on its logical justification as the necessary conduit through which the new law will be established, see Kuhns, 55–61.

33. Judicial blindness is a metaphor for preventing arbitrary decisions by removing social markers that may influence the judge to unjustly favor or disfavor the accused. However, the political argument that such blindness failed in its purpose has now been deemed sufficient enough to debunk the need for such blindness.

34. See chapter 2: the translation of the Eumenides into benign nature is still nature.

35. When the Furies argue that Zeus's shackling of Cronus contradicts the Olympian priority of patricide over matricide, Apollo responds with a fascinating defense of lenience based on human finitude: the laws that bind gods and Titans are subject to reversibility, but mortal life does not enjoy this privilege (ln. 644–51). Hence, the seriousness of this court is all the more heightened.

36. Though the comparative degree in not used in line 150.

37. See Kerényi, *Athene*, 57. In another version, she commits suicide for breaking Athena's order not to look into the contents of a basket she carried, which contained a mysterious child, possibly of Athena by Hephaestus. The Arrephoria cult performs this conveyance of unmentionables. Additionally, Aglauros is an incestuous maiden (daughter and wife to Cecrops), or the product of father-daughter incest (daughter of Erechtheus with his daughter Procris). The paradox of her virginal incest figures Athena's orientation toward the father: maiden in conjugal equality with Zeus. On Athena's near coequality with Zeus, see Kerényi, *Athene*, 13–19.

38. Erichthonius is the child of a union with Hephaestus that somehow did not violate Athena's virginity; Kerényi mentions a tradition attributed to Aristotle, where her son by Haephaestus is given the name "Apollo" (*Athene* 81).

39. Regarding the implied distinction between generativity and death as sites for the exercise of power, I would recite Burkert's point that sexuality/life and aggression/death form a tight binary. Not only did power address itself to both, but they—as events emerging first in nature—lend originary legitimacy to the very processes by which power as symbolic system later reconfigures them, reducing them to imaginary narratives, and thus denaturalizing them.

40. See Sara Brill, "Animal and World in Heidegger and Aristotle," where she argues for Aristotle's continuity between human and nonhuman animals: logos does not mark a quantum leap between animality and humanity but discloses the human being as the particular animal it is, one of intense politicality. While I am in agreement with this, I also shift the emphasis away from the specialness of politicality to highlight its intensification in humans *as a response to*, thus *derivative of*, the joys and ordeals presented by the events of life and death. To buttress the priority of these events over their ensuing political symbolization (a symbolization performed to a lesser degree by other animals too—elephants

mourn), I cite Aristotle's allowance for an antisocial type of humanity: the *therion*, or beast-like person, whom tragic heroes actually resemble, is also a response to the vicissitudes of life, and perhaps as authentic a response as the successfully political one. Granted, Aristotle's thought is deeply political in its ends and does not commend such a type. In contrast, it is tragedy that illuminates those dreadful but strangely exquisite vertices where the *therion* meets the godlike in the heroic persona.

41. Myth includes both affirmations and denials of autochthony. Levi-Strauss offers a comparative structural analysis of various myths, but his analysis of Oedipus illustrates this point quite well: monsters like the Sphinx attest to the belief in chthonic origin, while monster slaying points to the human desire for self-constitution.

42. Gewirtz cites critically the opinion of Supreme Court Justice Sandra Day O'Connor that in death penalty cases, the background, character, and culpability of the perpetrator must be assessed in a morally reasoned manner rather than be swayed by emotional responses to mitigating evidence. Gewirtz prefers the more "haunting" view of Aeschylus (1049). Other than the fact that Orestes is forced into a crime by a *moral* counterdemand (thus differing from a "common" criminal like Ixion), I would also note that tragedy is replete with heroes who pay regardless of mitigating circumstances. No example is greater than Oedipus, but Heracles and Ajax also count.

43. Gewirtz also subscribes to it (1050), but disagrees with the feminist critique of the marginalization of the Erinyes (1052–53), suggesting that we focus on their inclusion.

44. See *Agamemnon*, line 1667. The chorus rebukes Aegisthus's tyrannical statements, saying that he will hold no sway over them if the daimon of Fate/Destiny/Chance sends Orestes to Argos.

45. See chapter 2 on *dikē* as a mode of being *rightfully*, of being appropriate to oneself, and the example of the guard who fulfilled his nature as vigilant protector and faithful servant to the city.

46. I borrow this image from Hölderlin's reading of Teiresias as a formal caesura that distributes the way of action in Sophoclean tragedy, tilting the text toward a balance from the excess of either too much art or too much nature.

47. See also the discussions pertaining to *archē*, hierarchy, and priority laid out in chapter 2.

48. See *Lectures on Fine Art*, 2:495.

Epilogue

1. On *oikos* versus hero, see John Jones, 82, 90; Bernard Knox, 165n1. On the importance of the heroic persona in Sophocles, see Karl Reinhardt, *Sophocles*; Cedric Whitman, *Sophocles*; and Knox, *Heroic Temper*.

2. The tradition of the rationalist-atheist Euripides begins with A. W. Verrall, *Euripides the Rationalist*; on this "ultramodern" Euripides, see Thomas E. Jenkins. Nietzsche also accused Euripides in *The Birth of Tragedy* of being a rationalist dialectician, responsible (with Socrates) for the end of tragedy. In "Euripides the Irrationalist," E. R. Dodds does not disagree with Verrall's rationalism qua Victorian anticlericalism, but proceeds to read Euripides's poetics in relation to the seventeenth-century notion of rationalism—which coincides with Nietzsche's notion of rationalism—as the thinking that prioritizes reason and that was first established in Socratic intellectualism. In this sense, Euripides the philosophical dramatist prizes intellection, but Euripides the tragic thinker describes the limitations that obstruct humanity from adhering to reason in difficult situations. Dodds writes: "For Euripides the evil in human nature is thus indestructible and rooted in heredity (which with him, as with Ibsen, takes the place of the Aeschylean Ancestral Curse)" (99). It may appear that Dodds's irrationalist Euripides counters the Nietzschean Euripides, but it does not: Dodds's Euripides is irrationalist because the constraints of human nature require him to create irrational characters, but he himself bemoans the human inability to access reason. Nietzsche identifies this Euripidean/Socratic regret about our tragic nature with rationalism.

3. As stated earlier, I distinguish here between cosmic Dikē and human dikē by way of capitalization, in the spirit of reinforcing the overall point of this study regarding the intimate but also hierarchical relation between them.

4. Unless otherwise noted, all translations of *Oedipus Tyrannus* are by Hugh Lloyd-Jones of the Loeb edition. I opted for this prose translation because it preserves more faithfully some details that I wish to emphasize in my analysis.

5. What is not unusual, however, is its reliance on psychoanalysis, an interpretive model almost synonymous with the Oedipal drama. For instance, Harshbarger's detective work is guided by the idea that "people often commit crimes *in order to be punished*" (130; original emphasis). This psychoanalytic assumption leads him—mistakenly, I believe—to equate the psychology of the chorus with that of an average spectator, who certainly wishes to escape guilt but whose lingering guilty conscience leads to his or her own capture (130). To turn the chorus into an active murderer, however, is to contravene a formal principle adhered to by all playwrights, according to which the chorus is a medium of reflection, not action.

6. Note the use of *authentēs*, the word used for killing oneself, or murdering kin and thus harming oneself symbolically. Oedipus thinks he killed a random person for his insolence, but this person was his sire. See also chapter 2 for a discussion of seriousness and authenticity.

7. Richard Jebb's translation as quoted by Harshbarger (121n2). Note that ἰδόντας is an aorist form of εἶδον whose perfect tense οἶδα means also "to know," thus also "no one sees him who knew." If there is an alternative reading of this, it is not so much that there is no survivor; rather, according to the psychoanalytic

logic of repression, no one sees (because it is taboo to do so) the culprit (Oedipus), who somehow "knows" what he cannot avow.

8. I assume that the shepherd recognized the adult Oedipus in the crime scene. It may sound far-fetched to recognize an adult after only seeing him as an infant, but Oedipus's injury marks him.

9. At times, the singular form πρᾶγμα is used; other times, the plural πράγματα; there is also the plural demonstrative pronoun τάδε (these things here).

10. See the conclusion of the chorus in Sophocles, *Ajax*, lines 1418–20; the chorus of *Oedipus Tyrannus* declares the oracle an aporia, a saying that can be neither confirmed nor denied (ln. 485).

11. See the end of Sophocles, *Oedipus at Colonus*, lines 1777–79.

12. See Hyllus's speech at the end of Sophocles, *Women of Trachis*, lines 1264–78.

13. A repeated ending of several Euripidean tragedies, where the singular form *pragma* is the very last word of the play; see *Alcestis, Andromache, Bacchae, Helen, Medea*.

14. The word derives from the Latin *res*, which also means a "thing" that is similarly not limited to trivial objects but can signify affairs, relations, occurrences, causal patterns, and so on.

15. Jocasta also doubts the seers, distinguishing between Apollo and his servants (ln. 711–12).

16. I thank Krzyzstof Ziarek for directing me to Peter Meineck and Paul Woodruff's introductory remarks in their translation of the Theban plays; there, they underline the slippage from *tyrannos* to the Latin *rex*, which is actually a translation of the Greek *basileus* (xlvii).

17. David Grene and Richard Jebb both give this translation; Hugh Lloyd-Jones translates it as "Do you know from what stock you come?"

18. Heidegger's theorization of technology/science, and his distinction between calculative and meditative thinking, furnish the modern philosophical context and terminology for this discussion. Heidegger moves beyond the instrumental view of technology, proposing that it is a way of understanding the world, therefore also generating a certain type of thinking. While he resists a simple endorsement or critique of technology, he shows its calculative thinking to be setting us into danger. See "The Question Concerning Technology," for his noninstrumental theory of technology, and *Discourse on Thinking* for these distinct types of thinking.

Works Cited

Ackerman, Robert. "Some Letters of the Cambridge Ritualists." *Greek, Roman, and Byzantine Studies* 12, no. 1 (1971): 113–36.

Aeschylus. *Oresteia*. Translated by Richmond Lattimore. In *Aeschylus*, edited by David Grene and Richmond Lattimore, 35–171. Vol. 1 of *The Complete Greek Tragedies*. Chicago: University of Chicago Press, 1959.

———. *Oresteia*. In *Aeschylus 2: Agamemnon. Libation-Bearers. Eumenides. Fragments*, trans. Herbert Weir Smyth, 1–372. Loeb Classical Library 146. Cambridge, MA: Harvard University Press, 1926.

———. *Prometheus Bound*. Translated by David Grene. In *Aeschylus*, edited by David Grene and Richmond Lattimore, 311–51. Vol. 1 of *The Complete Greek Tragedies*. Chicago: University of Chicago Press, 1959.

———. *Prometheus Bound*. In *Aeschylus 1: Suppliant Maidens. Persians. Prometheus. Seven against Thebes*, trans. Herbert Weir Smyth, 211–318. Loeb Classical Library 145. Cambridge, MA: Harvard University Press, 1926.

———. *Seven against Thebes*. Translated by David Grene. In *Aeschylus*, edited by David Grene and Richmond Lattimore, 263–302. Vol. 1 of *The Complete Greek Tragedies*. Chicago: University of Chicago Press, 1959.

———. *Seven against Thebes*. In *Aeschylus 1: Suppliant Maidens. Persians. Prometheus. Seven against Thebes*, trans. Herbert Weir Smyth, 319–420. Loeb Classical Library 145. Cambridge, MA: Harvard University Press, 1926.

———. *The Suppliant Maidens*. Translated by Seth G. Benardete. In *Aeschylus*, edited by David Grene and Richmond Lattimore, 179–214. Vol. 1 of *The Complete Greek Tragedies*. Chicago: University of Chicago Press, 1959.

———. *Suppliant Maidens*. In *Aeschylus 1: Suppliant Maidens. Persians. Prometheus. Seven against Thebes*, trans. Herbert Weir Smyth, 2–107. Loeb Classical Library 145. Cambridge, MA: Harvard University Press, 1926.

Andrews, Robin George. "3-Ton Parts of Stonehenge May Have Been Carried from Earlier Monuments." *National Geographic*, February 12, 2021. https://www.nationalgeographic.com/history/article/3-ton-parts-stonehenge-may-carried-from-earlier-monuments.

Apollodorus. *The Library*. Vol. 1, bks. 1–3.9. Translated by James George Frazer. Loeb Classical Library 121. Cambridge, MA: Harvard University Press, 1921.

———. *The Library*. Vol. 2, bks. 3.10–end, *Epitome*. Translated by James George Frazer. Loeb Classical Library 122. Cambridge, MA: Harvard University Press, 1921.

Apollonius Rhodius. *Argonautica*. Edited and translated by William H. Race. Loeb Classical Library 1. Cambridge, MA: Harvard University Press, 2009.

Aristotle. *Art of Rhetoric*. Translated by John Henry Freese. Loeb Classical Library 193. Cambridge, MA: Harvard University Press, 1926.

———. *Nicomachean Ethics*. Translated by H. Rackham. Loeb Classical Library 73. Cambridge, MA: Harvard University Press, 1926.

———. *Poetics*. Translated by Stephen Halliwell. Loeb Classical Library 199. Cambridge, MA: Harvard University Press, 1992.

———. *Politics*. Translated by Benjamin Jowett. London: Clarendon, 1908.

Axe, David. "A New Spy Plane Could Spot Targets for the U.S. Army's Thousand-Mile Weapons." *Forbes*, August 13, 2020. https://www.forbes.com/sites/davidaxe/2020/08/13/a-new-spy-plane-could-spot-targets-for-the-us-armys-thousand-mile-weapons/?sh=bf1b3ca2b876.

Babich, Babette. "Heidegger's 'Pre-Aristotelians': Nietzsche and Heidegger on Anaximander." In *Heidegger and Classical Thought*, edited by Aaron Turner. Albany: State University of New York Press, forthcoming in September 2024.

Bacon, Helen. "Aeschylus (525–456 B.C.)." In *Ancient Writers: Greece and Rome*, vol. 1, edited by Torrey James Luce, 99–155. New York: Scribner, 1982.

Bakewell, Geoffrey W. "Μετοικία in the *Supplices* of Aeschylus." *Classical Antiquity* 16, no. 2 (1997): 209–28.

Basil, Christine J. "Justice Speaks: Nemesis, Nature, and Common Law in Aristotle's *Rhetoric*." *Review of Politics* 83, no. 2 (Spring 2021): 174–95.

Bastian, Jonathan. "The Role of Spirituality and Prayer in the Black Lives Matter Movement." Interview with Melina Abdullah and Hebah Ferrag. *Life Examined*. KCRW, July 25, 2020. https://www.kcrw.com/culture/shows/life-examined/religion-slavery-black-lives-matter/black-lives-matter-blm-melina-abdullah-hebab-ferrag-interview.

Baudelaire, Charles. *The Flowers of Evil* (English and French edition). Translated by James McGowan. Oxford: Oxford University Press, 1993.

Belfiore, Elizabeth. *Tragic Pleasures: Aristotle on Plato and Emotion*. Princeton: Princeton University Press, 1992.

Benardete, Seth. "Achilles and the *Iliad*." In *The Argument of the Action: Essays on Greek Poetry and Philosophy*, edited by Ronna Burger and Michael Davis, 15–33. Chicago: University of Chicago Press, 2000.

———. *Sacred Transgressions: A Reading of Sophocles' "Antigone"*. South Bend, IN: St. Augustine's Press, 1999.

Billings, Joshua. "A Cosmic Concern for Justice." Review of Anne Carson's *An Oresteia*. *The Oxonian Review* 9, no. 4 (May 18, 2009). http://www.oxonianreview.org/wp/a-cosmic-concern-for-justice/.

Blickman, Daniel R. "The Myth of Ixion and Pollution for Homicide in Archaic Greece." *Classical Journal* 81, no. 3 (February–March 1986): 193–208.

Bonnano, Daniela. "What Does Nemesis Have to Do with the Legal System? Discussing Aristotle's Neglected Emotion and Its Relevance for Law and Politics." In *Aristotle on Emotions in Law and Politics*, edited by Liesbeth Huppes-Cluysenaer and Nuno Coelho, 237–59. Law and Philosophy Library. Cham, Switzerland: Springer, 2018.

Bowie, A. M. "Religion and Politics in Aeschylus' *Oresteia*." *Classical Quarterly* 43, no. 1 (1993): 10–31.

Brill, Sara. "Animal and World in Heidegger and Aristotle." In *Heidegger and Classical Thought*, edited by Aaron Turner. Albany: State University of New York Press, forthcoming in September 2024.

———. *Aristotle on the Concept of Shared Life*. Oxford: Oxford University Press, 2020.

Browning, Robert, trans. *Agamemnon*. In *The Poetical Works of Robert Browning*, vol. 13. London: Smith, Elder, 1889. Available online at Perseus Digital Library. http://www.perseus.tufts.edu/hopper/text?doc=Perseus%3Atext%3A1999.01.0224%3Acard%3D0.

Bulgakov, Mikhail. *The White Guard*. Translated by Michael Glenny; introduction by Orlando Figes. Everyman's Library. London: Knopf, 2024.

Burke, Edmund. *A Philosophical Enquiry into the Origin of Our Ideas of the Sublime and Beautiful*. Edited by Adam Phillips. Oxford: Oxford University Press, 1990.

Burkert, Walter. *Homo Necans: The Anthropology of Ancient Greek Sacrificial Ritual and Myth*. Translated by Peter Bing. Berkeley, Los Angeles: University of California Press, 1983.

———. "Zum altgriechischen Mitleidsbegriff." Erlangen, Germany: Inaugural-Dissertation, Friedrich-Alexander-Universität, 1955.

Callimachus. "Hymn 3 to Artemis." In *Hecale. Hymns. Epigrams*, edited and translated by Dee L. Clayman, 234–87. Loeb Classical Library 129. Cambridge, MA: Harvard University Press, 2022.

Carlyle, Thomas. *The French Revolution: A History*. Boston: Little, Brown, 1838.

Conrad, Joseph. *Heart of Darkness*. New York: Penguin Books, 2017.

Couprie, Dirk L. *Heaven and Earth in Ancient Greek Cosmology: From Thales to Heraclides Ponticus*. Astrophysics and Space Science Library 374. New York: Springer, 2011.

Diodorus Siculus. *Library of History*. Vol. 3. Translated by C. H. Oldfather. Loeb Classical Library 279. Cambridge, MA: Harvard University Press, 1939.

Dodds, E. R. "Euripides the Irrationalist." *Classical Review* 43, no. 3 (July 1929): 97–104.

———. "Notes on *The Oresteia*." *Classical Quarterly* 3, nos. 1/2 (Jan.–Apr. 1953): 11–21.

Dumézil, Georges. *Mitra-Varuna: An Essay on Two Indo-European Representations of Sovereignty*. Translated by Derek Coltman. New York: Zone Books, 1988.

Else, Gerald F. *Aristotle's "Poetics": The Argument*. Cambridge, MA: Harvard University Press, 1957.

Elytis, Odysseus. *The Axion Esti (Τὸ Ἄξιον Ἐστί)*. In Greek with a translation by Edmund Keeley and George Savidis. Pittsburgh: University of Pittsburgh Press, 1974.

Esposito, Stephen Joseph. "The Staging of Ajax's Suicide." ResearchGate. https://www.researchgate.net/publication/228174081_The_Staging_of_Ajax's_Suicide.

Euripides. *Alcestis*. In *Cyclops. Alcestis. Medea*, edited and translated by David Kovacs, 154–274. Loeb Classical Library 12. Cambridge, MA: Harvard University Press, 1994.

———. *Andromache*. In *Children of Heracles. Hippolytus. Andromache. Hecuba*, edited and translated by David Kovacs, 274–392. Loeb Classical Library 484. Cambridge, MA: Harvard University Press, 1995.

———. *The Bacchae*. In *Bacchae. Iphigenia at Aulis. Rhesus*, edited and translated by David Kovacs, 12–156. Classical Library 495. Cambridge, MA: Harvard University Press, 2003.

———. *Helen*. In *Helen. Phoenician Women. Orestes*, edited and translated by David Kovacs, 12–202. Loeb Classical Library 11. Cambridge, MA: Harvard University Press, 2002.

———. *Iphigenia at Aulis*. In *Bacchae. Iphigenia at Aulis. Rhesus*, edited and translated by David Kovacs, 166–346. Loeb Classical Library 495. Cambridge, MA: Harvard University Press, 2003.

———. *Iphigenia among the Taurians*. In *Trojan Women. Iphigenia among the Taurians. Ion*, edited and translated by David Kovacs, 152–314. Loeb Classical Library 10. Cambridge, MA: Harvard University Press, 1999.

———. *Medea*. In *Cyclops. Alcestis. Medea*, edited and translated by David Kovacs, 284–432. Loeb Classical Library 12. Cambridge, MA: Harvard University Press, 1994.

Evans, David. "Agamemnon and the Indo-European Threefold Death Pattern." *History of Religions* 19, no. 2 (1979): 153–66.

Fagles, Robert. Introduction to *The Oresteia*, by Aeschylus, 13–98. New York: Penguin Books, 1979.

Findlay, J. N. "Analysis of the Text." In *Phenomenology of Spirit*, translated by A. V. Miller, 495–591. Oxford: Oxford University Press, 1979.

Finlayson, James Gordon. "Conflict and Reconciliation in Hegel's Theory of the Tragic." *Journal of the History of Philosophy* 37, no. 3 (1999): 493–520.

Fletcher, Judith. "Polyphony to Silence: The Jurors of the 'Oresteia.'" *College Literature* 41, no. 2 (Spring 2014): 56–75.
Fowler, Robert L., ed. *Early Greek Mythography I: Text and Introduction*. Oxford: Oxford University Press, 2000.
Gaca, Kathy L. "Minding the Mistress: The Household Power Struggle to Control Female Slave Sexuality in the Ancient Mediterranean." Paper presented at the 149th Annual Meeting of the Society for Classical Studies, Boston, Massachusetts, January 6, 2018. Abstract available at https://classicalstudies.org/minding-mistress-household-power-struggle-control-female-slave-sexuality-ancient-mediterranean.
Gadamer, Hans Georg. *Truth and Method*. Translated by Joel Weinsheimer and Donald G. Marshall. London: Bloomsbury, 2013.
Gantz, Timothy. *Early Greek Myth: A Guide to Literary and Artistic Sources*. Vol. 1. Baltimore: Johns Hopkins University Press, 1993.
Gewirtz, Paul. "Aeschylus' Law." *Harvard Law Review* 101, no. 5 (1988): 1043–55.
Gibson, Chris, and Tony Buttler. *British Secret Projects: Hypersonics, Ramjets & Missiles*. Self-published: Midland, 2007.
Global Crime 21, no. 3–4 (October 2020). Special issues on digital vigilantism. https://www.tandfonline.com/action/journalInformation?show=aimsScope&journalCode=fglc20.
Gonzalez, Francisco. "The Temporality of Life: Reading Aristotle with and against Heidegger in Two Unpublished Seminars from 1923–1925." In *Heidegger and Classical Thought*, edited by Aaron Turner. Albany: State University of New York Press, forthcoming in September 2024.
Graham, Daniel W., trans. and ed. *The Texts of Early Greek Philosophy: The Complete Fragments and Selected Testimonies of the Major Presocratics*. Vol. 1. Cambridge: Cambridge University Press, 2010.
Griffith, Mark. "Brilliant Dynasts: Power and Politics in the *Oresteia*." *Classical Antiquity* 14, no. 1 (April 1995): 62–129.
Haigh, Arthur Elam. *The Tragic Drama of the Greeks*. Oxford: Clarendon, 1896.
Hall, Lindsay G. H. "Ephialtes, the Areopagus and the Thirty." *Classical Quarterly* 40, no. 2 (1990): 319–28.
Halliwell, Stephen. *The Aesthetics of Mimesis: Ancient Texts and Modern Problems*. Princeton: Princeton University Press, 2002.
———. *Aristotle's "Poetics."* Chicago: University of Chicago Press, 1998.
Hanson, Victor Davis. *A War Like No Other: How the Athenians and Spartans Fought the Peloponnesian War*. New York: Random House, 2005.
Harris, John Philip. "Cassandra's Swan Song: Aeschylus' Use of Fable in *Agamemnon*." *Greek, Roman, and Byzantine Studies* 52 (2012): 540–58.
Harris, Joseph. "Homo Necans Borealis: Fatherhood and Sacrifice in *Sonatorrek*." *Myth in Early Northwest Europe* 3 (2007): 153–74.

Harrison, Jane Ellen. *Prolegomena to Greek Religion*. New York: Meridian Books, 1955.
Harshbarger, Karl. "Who Killed Laius?" *Tulane Drama Review* 9, no. 4 (1965): 120–31.
Heath, John. "The Omen of the Eagles and Hare (Agamemnon 104–59): From Aulis to Argos and Back Again." *Classical Quarterly* 51, no. 1 (2001): 18–22.
———. "The Serpent and the Sparrows: Homer and the Parodos of Aeschylus' Agamemnon." *Classical Quarterly* 49, no. 2 (1999): 396–407.
Hegel, G. F. *Hegel's Aesthetics: Lectures on Fine Art*. Vol. 1. Translated by T. M. Knox. Oxford: Clarendon, 1975.
———. *Phenomenology of Spirit*. Translated by. A. V. Miller. With analysis of the text and foreword by J. N. Findlay. Oxford: Oxford University Press, 1979.
Heidegger, Martin. "Building Dwelling Thinking." Translated by A. Hofstadter. In D. F. Krell, ed., *Martin Heidegger: Basic Writings*, revised and expanded edition, 217–65. London: Routledge, 1993.
———. *Discourse on Thinking: A Translation of* Gelassenheit. Translated by John M. Anderson and E. Hans Freund. New York: Harper Torchbooks, 1966.
———. *Introduction to Metaphysics*. Translated by Gregory Fried and Richard Polt. New Haven: Yale University Press, 2000.
———. "The Question Concerning Technology." In *The Question Concerning Technology and Other Essays*, trans. William Lovitt, 3–49. New York: Harper & Row, 1977.
Herodotus. *The Persian Wars*. Vol. 3, bks. 5–7. In Greek with an English translation by A. D. Godley. Loeb Classical Library 119. Cambridge, MA: Harvard University Press, 1922.
Hess, Kristy, and Lisa Waller. "The Digital Pillory: Media Shaming of 'Ordinary' People for Minor Crimes." *Continuum: Journal of Media and Cultural Studies* 28, no. 1 (2014): 101–11.
Hölderlin, Friedrich. *Friedrich Hölderlin: Essays and Letters on Theory*. Edited and translated by Thomas Pfau. Albany: State University of New York Press, 1988.
Homer. *Iliad*. Translated by A. T. Murray. Revised by William F. Wyatt. Loeb Classical Library 170. Cambridge, MA: Harvard University Press, 1924.
Jenkins, Thomas E. "The 'Ultra-Modern' Euripides of Verrall, H.D., and MacLeish." *Classical and Modern Literature* 27, no. 1 (2007): 121–45.
Jones, John. *On Aristotle and Greek Tragedy*. London: Chatto & Windus, 1962.
Jones, Peter. "The Stoics Would Have Had Little Sympathy for Meghan." *Spectator*, March 20, 2021. https://www.spectator.co.uk/article/the-stoics-would-have-had-little-sympathy-for-meghan/.
Kafka, Franz. *The Trial*. Translated by Willa and Edwin Muir. New York: Schocken Books, 1968.
Kant, Immanuel. *Critique of Judgment*. Translated by Werner S. Pluhar. Indianapolis: Hackett, 1987.

———. *Observations on the Feeling of the Beautiful and Sublime*. Translated by John T. Goldthwait. Berkeley: University of California Press, 1960.
Kasra, Mona. "Vigilantism, Public Shaming, and Social Media Hegemony." *Communication Review* 20, no. 3 (2017): 172–88.
Kazantzakis, Nikos. *Report to Greco*. Translated by Peter A. Bien. New York: Simon and Schuster, 1965.
Kerényi, Karl. *Apollo: The Wind, the Spirit, and the God: Four Studies*. Translated by Jon Solomon. Dunquin Series. Dallas: Spring Publications, 1983.
———. *Athene: Virgin and Mother in Greek Religion*. Translated by Murray Stein. Woodstock, CT: Spring Publications, 1978.
———. *The Gods of the Greeks*. Translated by Norman Cameron. London: Thames and Hudson, 1980.
Kirkland, Sean D. *Nietzsche's "Philosophy in the Tragic Age of the Greeks."* Under contract at Edinburgh: Edinburgh University Press, forthcoming.
Knox, Bernard M. W. *The Heroic Temper: Studies in Sophoclean Tragedy*. Sather Classical Lectures. Berkeley: University of California Press, 1983.
Konradie, Pieter Jacobus. "Contemporary Politics in Greek Tragedy: A Critical Discussion of Different Approaches." *Acta Classica* 24 (1981): 23–35.
Konstan, David. *The Emotions of the Ancient Greeks: Studies in Aristotle and Greek Literature*. The Robson Classical Lectures. Toronto: University of Toronto Press, 2007.
———. *Pity Transformed*. London: Bloomsbury, 2015.
Kott, Jan. *The Eating of the Gods: An Interpretation of Greek Tragedy*. Translated by Boleslaw Taborski and Edward J. Caerwinski. New York: Random House, 1970.
Kuhns, Richard. *The House, the City, and the Judge: The Growth of Moral Awareness in the "Oresteia."* Indianapolis: Bobbs-Merril, 1962.
Lacan, Jacques. *The Seminar of Jacques Lacan*. Book 3, *The Psychoses, 1955–1956*. Edited by Jacques-Alain Miller; translated by Russell Grigg. New York: W. W. Norton, 1993.
Larsen, Svend Erik. "The Lisbon Earthquake and the Scientific Turn in Kant's Philosophy." *European Review* 14, no. 3 (2006): 359–67.
Levi-Strauss, Claude. "The Structural Study of Myth." *Journal of American Folklore* 78 (1955): 428–44.
Levin, David Michael. "The Court of Justice: Heidegger's Reflections on Anaximander." *Research in Phenomenology* 37, no. 3 (2007): 385–416.
Liddell, Henry George, and Robert Scott. *A Greek-English Lexicon*. Revised and augmented throughout by Sir Henry Stuart Jones with the assistance of Roderick McKenzie. Oxford: Clarendon, 1940. https://www.perseus.tufts.edu/hopper/text?doc=Perseus%3atext%3a1999.04.0057.
Lincoln, Bruce. "Death and Resurrection in Indo-European Thought." *Journal of Indo-European Studies* 5 (1977): 247–64.

Loraux, Nicole. *The Children of Athena: Athenian Ideas about Citizenship and the Division between the Sexes*. Translated by Caroline Levine. Princeton: Princeton University Press, 1994.

———. "La Main d'Antigone." *Métis* 1, no. 2 (1986): 165–96.

———. *The Mourning Voice: An Essay on Greek Tragedy*. Translated by Elizabeth Trapnell Rawlings. Ithaca: Cornell University Press, 2002.

———. *Tragic Ways of Killing a Woman*. Translated by Anthony Forster. Cambridge, MA: Harvard University Press, 1987.

Margolis, Joseph. "The Limits of Metaphysics and the Limits of Certainty." In *Antifoundationalism: Old and New*, edited by Tom Rockmore and Beth J. Singer, 13–40. Philadelphia: Temple University Press, 1992.

Markell, Patchen. *Bound by Recognition*. Princeton: Princeton University Press, 2003.

Martin, Richard P. "The Fire on the Mountain: 'Lysistrata' and the Lemnian Women." *Classical Antiquity* 6, no. 1 (1987): 77–105.

Meier, Christian. *Athens: A Portrait of the City in Its Golden Age*. Translated by Robert and Rita Kimber. New York: Metropolitan Books, 1998.

———. *The Discovery of Politics in Greece*. Translated by David McClintock. Cambridge, MA: Harvard University Press, 1990.

———. *The Political Art of Greek Tragedy*. Translated by Andrew Webber. Cambridge, UK: Polity, 1993.

———. "Der Umbruch zur Demokratie in Athen (462/61 v. Chr.)." In *Epochenschwelle und Epochenbewußtsein*, edited by Reinhart Herzog and Reinhart Koselleck, 353–80. Poetik und Hermeneutik 12. Munich: Wilhelm Fink Verlag, 1987.

Meineck, Peter, and Paul Woodruff, trans. Introduction to *Sophocles: Theban Plays*. Indianapolis: Hackett, 2003.

Morrissey, Christopher S. "Oedipus the Cliché: Aristotle on Tragic Form and Content." *Anthropoetics: The Journal of Generative Anthropology* 9, no. 1 (Spring/Summer 2003). https://anthropoetics.ucla.edu/ap0901/oedipus/.

Naas, Michael. *Turning: From Persuasion to Philosophy: A Reading of Homer's "Iliad."* Atlantic Highlands, NJ: Humanities Press, 1995.

Nagy, Gregory. *The Ancient Greek Hero in 24 Hours*. Cambridge, MA: Belknap/Harvard University Press, 2013.

Neuburg, Matt. "Clytemnestra and the Alastor (Aeschylus, *Agamemnon* 1497ff)." *Quaderni Urbinati di Cultura Classica* 38, no. 2 (1991): 37–68.

Nietzsche, Friedrich. *The Birth of Tragedy and The Case of Wagner*. Translated by Walter Kaufmann. New York: Vintage, 1967.

———. *The Gay Science: With a Prelude in Rhymes and an Appendix of Songs*. Translated by Walter Kaufmann. New York: Vintage, 1974.

Nikolopoulou, Kalliopi. "Toward the Sublime Calculus of Aristotle's *Poetics*." In *The Bloomsbury Companion to Aristotle*, edited by Claudia Baracchi, 279–93. London: Bloomsbury, 2013.

Otto, Rudolf. *The Idea of the Holy: An Inquiry into the Non-Rational Factor in the Idea of the Divine and Its Relation to the Rational.* Translated by John W. Harvey. New York: Oxford University Press/Galaxy Book, 1958.

Otto, Walter. *Dionysus: Myth and Cult.* Translated by Robert B. Palmer. Bloomington: Indiana University Press, 1965.

———. *The Homeric Gods: The Spiritual Significance of Greek Religion.* Translated by Moses Hadas. New York: Pantheon, 1954.

Ovid. *Metamorphoses.* Vol. 2, bks. 9–15. Translated by Frank Justus Miller. Revised by G. P. Goold. Loeb Classical Library 43. Cambridge, MA: Harvard University Press, 1916.

Parker, Robert. *Miasma: Pollution and Purification in Early Greek Religion.* Oxford: Clarendon, 1983.

Paschalis, Michael. "'I Removed the Mist that Clouded Your Eyes': Supernatural Vision from Homer to Sikelianos." Σύγκριση / *Comparaison* 21 (2010): 72–85.

Pearson, Mike Parker, et al. "The Original Stonehenge? A Dismantled Stone Circle in the Preseli Hills of West Wales." *Antiquity* 95, no. 379 (February 2021): 85–103. https://www.cambridge.org/core/journals/antiquity/article/original-stonehenge-a-dismantled-stone-circle-in-the-preseli-hills-of-west-wales/B7DAA4A7792B4DAB57DDE0E3136FBC33.

Peradotto, John. "The Omen of the Eagles and the HΘΟΣ of Agamemnon." *Phoenix* 23, no. 3 (1969): 237–63.

Pindar. *Olympian Odes. Pythian Odes.* Edited and translated by William H. Race. Loeb Classical Library 56. Cambridge, MA: Harvard University Press, 1997.

Plato. *Cratylus.* In *Cratylus. Parmenides. Greater Hippias. Lesser Hippias,* trans. Harold North Fowler, 1–192. Loeb Classical Library 167. Cambridge, MA: Harvard University Press, 1926.

———. *Laws.* Vol. 2, bks. 7–12. Translated by R. G. Bury. Loeb Classical Library 192. Cambridge, MA: Harvard University Press, 1926.

———. *Phaedo.* In *Euthyphro. Apology. Crito. Phaedo,* trans. Harold North Fowler, 200–406. Loeb Classical Library 36. Cambridge, MA: Harvard University Press, 1914.

———. *Statesman.* In *Statesman. Philebus. Ion,* trans. Harold North Fowler and W. R. M. Lamb, 4–196. Loeb Classical Library 164. Cambridge, MA: Harvard University Press, 1925.

Plutarch. *Theseus.* In *Theseus and Romulus. Lycurgus and Numa. Solon and Publicola,* trans. Bernadotte Perrin, 1–88. Vol. 1 of *Lives.* Loeb Classical Library 46. Cambridge, MA: Harvard University Press, 1914.

Podlecki, Anthony J. *The Political Background of Aeschylean Tragedy.* Ann Arbor: University of Michigan Press, 1966.

Reinhardt, Karl. *Sophocles.* Translated by Hazel Harvey and David Harvey. Oxford: Basil Blackwell, 1979.

Robinson, John Mansley. *An Introduction to Early Greek Philosophy*. Boston: Houghton Mifflin, 1968.

Saïd, Suzanne. "Tragic Argos." In *Tragedy, Comedy and the Polis: Papers from the Greek Drama Conference (Nottingham, 18–20 July, 1990)*, edited by Alan H. Sommerstein, 167–89. Bari, Italy: Levante, 1993.

Scapin, Nuria. *The Flower of Suffering: Theology, Justice, and the Cosmos in Aeschylus's "Oresteia" and Presocratic Thought*. Trends in Classics 97. Berlin: De Gruyter, 2020.

Schein, Seth L. "Narrative Technique in the Parodos of Aeschylus' *Agamemnon*." In *Narratology and Interpretation: The Content of Narrative Form in Ancient Literature*, edited by Jonas Grethlein and Antonios Rengakos, 377–98. Berlin: De Gruyter, 2009.

Seferis, George. *Mythistorema*. In *George Seferis: Collected Poems*, translated and edited by Edmund Keeley and Philip Sherrard, 1–28. Princeton: Princeton University Press, 1995.

Shelley, Mary. *Frankenstein: Or the Modern Prometheus*. New York: Penguin Classics, 1992.

Smith, Cecil. "The Myth of Ixion." *Classical Review* 9, no. 5 (June 1895): 277–80.

Smyth, Herbert Weir, translator. *Aeschylus II: Agamemnon. Libation-Bearers. Eumenides*. Loeb Classical Library 146. Cambridge, MA: Harvard University Press, 1926.

Sommerstein, Alan H. "Aesch. *Ag*. 104–59 (The Omen of Aulis or the Omen of Argos?)." *Museum Criticum* 30/31 (1996) [1997]: 87–94.

Sophocles. *Ajax*. Translated by John Moore. In *Sophocles*, edited by David Grene and Richmond Lattimore, 213–268. Vol. 2 of *The Complete Greek Tragedies*. Chicago: University of Chicago Press, 1959.

———. *Ajax*. In *Ajax. Electra. Oedipus Tyrannus*, edited and translated by Hugh Lloyd-Jones, 27–163. Loeb Classical Library 20. Cambridge, MA: Harvard University Press, 1994.

———. *Electra*. Translated by David Grene. In *Sophocles*, edited by David Grene and Richmond Lattimore, 333–93. Vol. 2 of *The Complete Greek Tragedies*. Chicago: University of Chicago Press, 1959.

———. *Electra*. In *Ajax. Electra. Oedipus Tyrannus*, edited and translated by Hugh Lloyd-Jones, 165–321. Loeb Classical Library 20. Cambridge, MA: Harvard University Press, 1994.

———. *Oedipus at Colonus*. Translated by Robert Fitzgerald. In *Sophocles*, edited by David Grene and Richmond Lattimore, 79–155. Vol. 2 of *The Complete Greek Tragedies*. Chicago: University of Chicago Press, 1959.

———. *Oedipus at Colonus*. In *Antigone. The Women of Trachis. Philoctetes. Oedipus at Colonus*, edited and translated by Hugh Lloyd-Jones, 409–599. Loeb Classical Library 21. Cambridge, MA: Harvard University Press, 1994.

———. *Oedipus the King*. Translated by David Grene. In *Sophocles*, edited by David Grene and Richmond Lattimore, 11–76. Vol. 2 of *The Complete Greek Tragedies*. Chicago: University of Chicago Press, 1959.

———. *Oedipus Tyrannus*. In *Ajax. Electra. Oedipus Tyrannus*, edited and translated by Hugh Lloyd-Jones, 323–483. Loeb Classical Library 20. Cambridge, MA: Harvard University Press, 1994.

———. *The Women of Trachis*. In *Antigone. The Women of Trachis. Philoctetes. Oedipus at Colonus*, edited and translated by Hugh Lloyd-Jones, 129–252. Loeb Classical Library 21. Cambridge, MA: Harvard University Press, 1994.

Sourvinou-Inwood, Christiane. *Studies in Girls' Transitions: Aspects of the Arkteia and Age Representation in Attic Iconography*. Athens, Greece: Kardamitsa, 1988.

Sullivan, Walter. "Questions Raised on Lorenz's Prize." *New York Times*. December 15, 1973, 9.

Taplin, Oliver. *The Stagecraft of Aeschylus: The Dramatic Use of Exits and Entrances in Greek Tragedy*. Oxford: Clarendon, 1989.

Thucydides. *History of the Peloponnesian War*. Vol. 3, bks. 5–6. Translated by C. F. Smith. Loeb Classical Library 110. Cambridge, MA: Harvard University Press, 1921.

Tzanetou, Angeliki. *City of Suppliants: Tragedy and the Athenian Empire*. Ashley and Peter Larkin Series in Greek and Roman Culture. Austin: University of Texas Press, 2012.

Vernant, Jean-Pierre. *Mortals and Immortals: Collected Essays*. Edited by Froma Zeitlin. Princeton: Princeton University Press, 1991.

Verrall, A. W. *Euripides the Rationalist: A Study in the History of Art and Religion*. Cambridge: Cambridge University Press, 1895.

Wallace, Robert W. "Ephialtes and the Areopagos." *Greek, Roman, and Byzantine Studies* 15, no. 3 (Fall 1974): 259–69.

Warak, Melissa. "Warriors and Volunteers: A Review of George W. Bush, *Portraits of Courage*." *Art Journal* (July 2, 2018). http://artjournal.collegeart.org/?p=9949.

Wheeler, Michael. "Martin Heidegger." In *Stanford Encyclopedia of Philosophy*. Stanford University, 1997–. Article published Oct. 12, 2011. https://plato.stanford.edu/entries/heidegger/.

Whitman, Cedric. *Sophocles: A Study of Heroic Humanism*. Cambridge, MA: Harvard University Press, 1951.

Zartaloudis, Thanos. *The Birth of Nomos*. Edinburgh: University of Edinburgh Press, 2020.

Zeitlin, Froma I. "The Dynamics of Misogyny: Myth and Mythmaking in the *Oresteia*." In *Women in the Ancient World*: *The "Arethusa" Papers*, edited by John Peradotto and John Patrick Sullivan, 159–93. Albany: State University of New York Press, 1984.

———. "Redeeming Matricide? Euripides Rereads the *Oresteia*." In *The Soul of Tragedy: Essays on Athenian Drama*, edited by Victoria Pedrick and Steven M. Oberhelman, 199–225. Chicago: University of Chicago Press, 2005.

———. *The Retrospective Muse: Pathways through Ancient Greek Literature and Culture*. Ithaca, NY: Cornell University Press, 2023.

———. "Thebes: Theater of Self and Society in Athenian Drama." In *Greek Tragedy and Political Theory*, edited by J. Peter Euben, 101–41. Berkeley: University of California Press, 1986.

Index

Abdullah, Melina, 217n44
absence, of fathers, 111–12, 213n5
action, 17, 40, 43, 63–64, 68, 180–81
  consequences and, 186
  gravity of, 30, 38, 51–52, 130
  modernity and, 54–55
  murder and, 44, 202n17
  tragedy and, 44–45
  vigilance and, 115
activism, 24–25
  justice and, 17
  violence and, 73–75
Aeschylus, 7, 10–11, 26, 199n15. See also *Agamemnon; Choephoroi; Eumenides*
  aristocracy and the Areopagus and, 145–46, 148–50, 167, 219n13
  democracy and, 146–50
  feminist critiques of, 51, 115, 118, 158, 166, 174–76, 221n27
  Homer and, 84, 95, 207n5, 208n12
  Kafka and, 103–5
  politics of, 146–50
  Prometheus Bound, 13, 59, 218n3
  reconciliation and, 139, 179–82
Agamemnon (Aeschylus), 21, 61, 143
  cosmic dikē in, 86, 92–93, 95–96, 98
  dogs in, 77–80, 86–87, 90, 97, 105

  parodos of, 45, 81–82, 84–94, 141, 207n2
Agamemnon (character), 81–83, 93
  death of, 94–95, 97, 167, 174, 210n27
  dikē and, 95–96, 98
  fatherhood and, 110–14, 124–27, 136
aggression, 19–20, 200n21
  culture and, 65–67
amor fati, 100, 104
Ananke. *See* necessity
Anaximander, 10–11, 25–26, 198n11
ancestors, 111, 113, 132, 134
  heroes as, 50–51, 109–10
anger, justice and, 119–20, 125, 215n21
animals, 18–19, 79, 206n44. *See also* dogs
  birds, 80–81, 84–85, 87–88, 207n3, 208n9
  cattle, 56, 94, 109–10
  dream interpretation and, 122–23
  humanity and, 84, 92–93, 171–72, 222n40
  hunting and, 49, 67–68, 97, 109
  predation and, 80–81, 87, 208n9
  sacred, 57, 78, 81, 89–94, 204n24, 207n5

239

animals *(continued)*
  sacrifice of, 16-17, 45, 51-59, 67, 88-89, 112-13
  snakes, 80, 122-23, 160, 215n27
  tragic heroes and, 222n40
anthropocentrism, 2, 197n7
  nature and, 9, 63
  technocracy and, 5, 194
anthropology, 164
  cosmological, 14-21, 110-11, 137
  ritual and, 38, 51, 60-62, 65-66, 142-43, 199n15
  tragedy and, 20-21, 30-31
Antigone (character), 8, 63, 128, 131
Aphrodite, 116-17, 162-63, 168, 175, 209n14
Apollo, 121, 123, 151-52, 222n32
  Athena and, 127, 136
  Dionysus and, 141-42, 218n6
  Eros and, 161-65
  on fathers, 114-15
  Furies and, 158-59, 166-68, 182
  Zeus and, 156-57
arbitrariness, 176, 199n15
  cosmos and, 2, 37-38, 120-21, 175, 182
  dikē and, 23, 25-26, 98-99, 166, 181
  nature and, 92-95, 155, 158-59, 163-65
  necessity and, 174-75, 182-83
  social justice and, 23, 99-100, 165
the Areopagus, 90, 147
  aristocracy and, 145-46, 148-50, 167, 219n13
Ares, 120, 209n14, 215n25
  Dikē and, 126-27
Argos (character), 56-57, 72-73, 77-78, 108-11, 207n4
Argos (city), 75
  Athens and, 127-30
  as cosmos, 107-16

aristocracy, 82, 208n8
  the Areopagus and, 145-46, 148-50, 167, 219n13
  democracy and, 139-42, 146, 148, 150
  hierarchy and, 148-49
Aristotle, 199n13, 202n14, 219n13
  Burkert and, 29-30, 38-46, 51-52
  nature and, 31-32, 65-66, 119
  Poetics, 30-38, 44-45, 53-55
  Politics, 215n21, 220n15
  ritual interpretation of tragedy and, 29-31, 43-45, 54-55, 61, 97, 201n1, 203n18
  seriousness and, 34-35, 67, 69
  tragic mimesis of, 8, 16-17, 30-33, 36-40, 51, 69, 130, 199n15
Artemis, 209n22
  Athena and, 169-70
  hunting and, 21, 45-46, 78-81, 168, 175, 203n21, 208n6
  nature and, 82, 88, 91-94
  sacred animals of, 81, 89-90, 204n24, 207n5
  virginity and, 89-90, 103, 168-70, 203n21, 203n23
  war and, 90, 209n14, 209n17
Athena, 151, 180-81
  Apollo and, 127, 136
  Artemis and, 169-70
  cosmology and, 25-26, 200n26
  as Dios Kora, 127, 150, 158, 221n31
  Furies and, 157, 162
  motherhood and, 168-70, 209n22
  ritual and, 45-48
  Zeus and, 169-70, 222n37
Athens, 26-27, 45-47, 75, 217n41
  Argos and, 127-30
  Eumenides and, 102, 108, 163
autochthony, 130-31, 136-37, 172, 223n41
  earth and, 133-34

Index | 241

modernity and, 132, 134–35
nativism and, 72–76, 79, 208n12, 210n24
axis mundi, 13–14, 50, 155, 204n31
   Hermes and, 21–22, 108, 123, 127, 132–33
   ritual and, 132–33
   seriousness and, 51–52

Babich, Babette, 198n11
Bacon, Helen, 78
Bakewell, Geoffrey, 128
balance, 10–11, 88, 154, 223n46
   injustice and, 90–91
   order and, 129–30
Benardete, Seth, 128
biology, hunting and, 17–18, 20, 38–39, 62–63, 65–66, 114–15
birds, 80–81, 84–85, 87–88, 207n3, 208n9
Black Lives Matter (BLM), 217n44
Blickman, Daniel, 143–45, 149, 168
BLM. *See* Black Lives Matter
Brill, Sara, 171
Burke, Edmund, 202n11
Burkert, Walter, 24–25, 73, 209n14. See also *Homo Necans*; hunting
   Aristotle and, 29–30, 38–46, 51–52
   cosmological anthropology of, 14–21, 110–11, 137
   Darwin and, 17–19, 62, 200n19, 206n40
   mysterium tremendum of, 16, 18, 21, 52–53, 208n11
   ritual and, 41, 50–52, 55–60, 109, 201n4, 205n36
   ritual anthropology and, 38, 51, 60–62, 65–66, 142–43, 199n15
   seriousness and, 15–17, 19–20, 61–62, 65–70
   three stages of ritual sacrifice and, 55, 57–60

Bush, George W., 200n24

cannibalism, 46, 66–67, 92–93, 97–98, 203n24
Carlyle, Thomas, 212n40
Cassandra (character), 93, 97–100, 207n3, 211n30, 214n19
   prophecy of, 78, 80, 94, 109
catharsis, tragedy and, 37, 60–61
cattle, 56, 94, 109–10
centrism, political, 146–47, 150, 220n15
change, 146
   cosmology and, 174–75
   deities and, 140–42
   modernity and, 195
   tradition and, 140, 149, 220n18
Choephoroi (Aeschylus), 85, 107, 111, 114, 210n29
   autochthony and, 130–37
   axis mundi and, 21–22, 108, 123, 127, 132–33
   chthonic dikē in, 61, 80–81, 116–24
   Dikē in, 113, 120–21, 126–27
   vengeance and, 124–30
chorus, 84–91, 116–18, 124–26, 149, 197n6, 208n11. *See also* parodos
   of *Oedipus Tyrannus*, 187, 191–94, 224n5, 225n10
chthonic dikē, 3–4, 73–74, 107, 221n30
   in *Choephoroi*, 61, 80–81, 116–24
   hate and, 116–20, 125–27, 178, 213n12
   social justice and, 132, 217n44
   Uranian dikē and, 13, 25–26, 50–51, 75–76, 123, 177–78
chthonic earth, polis and, 8, 108–9, 127–28
chthonic world, 213n10
   gender and, 135–36, 221n26, 221n30

chthonic world *(continued)*
  sacrifice and, 49–50
  snakes and, 122–23, 215n27
  time and, 131
civic dikē, 22–23, 165–70, 174, 177, 181. *See also* social justice
civic good, 175
  cosmos and, 63–64
  Furies and, 25, 46–51, 57–58, 102
  violence and, 154–55, 176
Clytemnestra (character), 80, 157, 164–65, 174, 207n3
  dream of, 122–23
  murder of, 57, 61, 159–60
  vengeance of, 93–98, 100–101, 118, 210n29
compensation, tragedy and, 10–11
Conrad, Joseph, 190
consequences, 56–57, 83–84
  action and, 186
  destiny and, 91–92
  lenience and, 43, 153–54, 167–68, 173–74, 176
  punishment as, 50–51, 85–86, 116–18, 153–55, 192
cosmic dikē, 2, 4–5, 78–79, 153–54, 159, 198n11
  in *Agamemnon*, 86, 92–93, 95–96, 98
  humanity and, 182, 191, 194, 224n3
cosmological anthropology, of Burkert, 14–21, 110–11, 137
cosmology, 107–9, 130
  Athena and, 25–26, 200n26
  change and, 174–75
  crime and, 154
  dikē and, 72–73, 142, 144, 172, 199n15
  Dikē and, 22, 127, 182, 194, 224n3
  earth and, 111
  morality and, 17–18, 88
  necessity and, 75–76
  politics and, 11–13, 22, 115–16, 165–66
  time and, 156–57
cosmopolitanism, 63, 74, 115–16, 133–34
cosmos, 190–91
  arbitrariness and, 2, 37–38, 120–21, 175, 182
  Argos as, 107–16
  civic good and, 63–64
  history and, 166
  humanity and, 93–94
  nature and, 7–10, 96–98
  Orestes and, 108, 111, 123
  polis and, 8, 63–65, 78, 110–11, 155, 173–74, 183
courts, 59, 75–76, 101–5, 129, 167–68, 218n3
  emotions and, 173, 223n42
  nature and, 165–66
  seriousness of, 148–49, 222n35
craft, necessity and, 9, 43, 59, 65, 98, 137
crime
  cosmology and, 154
  Lemnian, 116–17, 214n14, 214n16
  morality and, 192–93
  pollution and, 117, 215n15
cult, 59–60, 222n37
  myth and, 29–30, 44, 130
culture, 30, 38, 110
  aggression and, 65–67
  hunting and, 55–56, 205n35
  seriousness and, 14, 39–40, 62, 65–67
  woke, 74, 211n32

Darwin, Charles, 17–19, 62, 200n19, 206n40
death, 5–7, 172
  of Agamemnon, 94–95, 97, 167, 174, 210n27

family and, 131–34
heroes and, 122–23, 167
power and, 40–41, 171
sexuality and, 117
time and, 55
universality and, 131, 134, 217n43
war and, 125–26
deities, 139, 218n7, 219n8
  change and, 140–42
  genealogy of, 81, 90–91, 141, 150, 156–59, 162–63, 169–70
  humanity and, 82, 90–91, 192–93, 204n31
  Olympians and Titans and, 155–72
  youth and, 155–72
Delos, 5–6, 216n31
Delphi, 122–23, 152, 163, 167–68, 211n36, 216n31
  prophecy and, 156, 186–87
democracy, 26, 71, 129
  the Areopagus and, 90, 145–50, 167, 219n13
  aristocracy and, 139–42, 146, 148, 150
  hubris and, 220n16
  in modernity, 159, 221n28
  youth and, 142–43
destiny, 144, 190–91
  consequences and, 91–92
  dikē and, 77–81, 85–87
  Dikē and, 185–86
  family and, 219n11
  law and, 162–63
  nature and, 194
  necessity and, 121
diachrony, 131, 134–35
digital vigilantism, 100, 207n48, 211n33
dikē, 2, 19, 185, 193–95. *See also* chthonic dikē; cosmic dikē
  Agamemnon and, 95–96, 98
  arbitrariness and, 23, 25–26, 98–99, 166, 181

in *Choephoroi*, 108, 120, 124–25
civic, 22–23, 165–70, 174, 177, 181
cosmology and, 72–73, 142, 144, 172, 199n15
destiny and, 77–81, 85–87
earth and, 108, 113, 116
as Eros and Thanatos, 161–63, 167–68
generational, 23, 110–11, 113–15, 126–27, 214n15
hunting and, 121–22, 161–65
morality and, 160–61
necessity and, 91
political, 144, 219n11
as regeneration, 46–47, 55, 116, 124, 158, 161, 167
Uranian, 13, 25–26, 50–51, 75–76, 123, 177–78
as violence, 23–25, 144–45, 154–55, 157–63, 166, 176–77, 199n15
war as, 120–21
Zeus and, 78, 84–87
Dikē, 78–79, 168, 191, 224n3
  Ares and, 126–27
  in *Choephoroi*, 113, 120–21, 126–27
  cosmology and, 22, 127, 182, 194, 224n3
  destiny and, 185–86, 193
  nature and, 91, 176–77
dilemmatic thought, 35, 202n9
  tragedy and, 21, 23, 42–43, 70
Dionysus
  Apollo and, 141–42, 218n6
  Furies and, 139–40
Dios Kora, Furies and, 127, 150, 158, 221n31
Dodds, E. R., 146–47, 150, 219n14, 224n2
dogs, 121
  in *Agamemnon*, 77–80, 86–87, 90, 97, 105
  law and, 102–5

244 | Index

domesticity, 51, 94–95, 209n22
dream interpretation, 79–80, 107
  animals and, 122–23

earth, 48, 122–24, 156, 170. *See also* axis mundi
  autochthony and, 133–34
  chthonic, 8, 108–9, 127–28
  cosmology and, 111
  dikē and, 108, 113, 116
education, 39–40, 202n15
Electra (character), 113–14, 124–26, 178, 216n35
Electra (Sophocles), 57–58
Elytis, Odysseus, 72–73
emotions, 53–54, 215n21
  courts and, 173, 223n42
  ethics and, 68
  hate as, 116–23, 125–27, 178, 213n12
  politics and, 176
  seriousness and, 67, 69
Ephialtes, 139, 145–46, 149–50, 219n13
epiphany, reality and, 52–53
Erinyes. *See* Furies
Eros, 167
  Apollo and, 161–65
  Thanatos and, 161–63, 168, 171
ethics, 55–56, 68
  order of, 177
ethology, 18–19, 200n21
Eumenides, 57–58, 177–78, 204n26
  Athens and, 102, 108, 163
  Furies as, 47–51, 92, 129, 155–56, 163, 175, 217n40
Eumenides (Aeschylus), 13–14, 22, 46–51, 59, 61
  cosmology of, 25–26
  hunting and, 159–61
Euripides, 59, 185, 224n2, 225n13
  Iphigenia among the Taurians, 44–46, 203n24

Iphigenia at Aulis, 44–45, 203n19, 207n5, 211n31
Evans, David, 210n27

Fagles, Robert, 201n1
family, 25–26, 49–51, 119, 159. *See also* fathers; motherhood
  death and, 131–34
  destiny and, 219n11
  generational dikē and, 23, 110–11, 113–15, 126–27, 214n15
  murder and, 143–45, 151–52, 163–64, 220n21
  nature and, 136
Fates, 91, 209n18
  Furies and, 13–14, 50
fathers, 109, 170
  absence of, 111–12, 213n5
  Agamemnon and, 110–14, 124–27, 136
  Apollo on, 114–15
  heroes and, 113–15
  hierarchy and, 141
  seed and, 22, 115, 136, 167, 221n26, 221n30
feminist critiques, of Aeschylus, 51, 115, 118, 158, 166, 174–76, 221n27
Finlayson, J. G., 180–82
Fletcher, Judith, 59, 148
Furies, 22, 98
  Apollo and, 158–59, 166–68, 182
  Athena and, 157, 162
  civic good and, 25, 46–51, 57–58, 102
  Dionysus and, 139–40
  Dios Kora and, 127, 150, 158, 221n31
  as Eumenides, 47–51, 92, 129, 155–56, 163, 175, 217n40
  Fates and, 13–14, 50
  law and, 74–76, 101–2

nature and, 46–48, 162
sacrifice and, 49–51, 97
Thanatos and, 161–65
vigilantism and, 177–78
future, 13, 50–51, 77–78, 121, 123–24, 126
tradition and, 144–46, 172, 178–79

Gadamer, Hans-Georg, 53
Gē. *See* earth
gender, 213n10
chthonic world and, 135–36, 221n26, 221n30
hunting and, 46, 164, 203n22
politics and, 130–31, 217n42
ritual and, 55
vengeance and, 116–19
genealogy, of deities, 81, 90–91, 141, 150, 156–59, 162–63, 169–70
generational dikē, 23, 110–11, 113–15, 126–27, 214n15
generativity, 46–47, 115, 158, 221n30
justice and, 124–30
politics and, 171–72
Gewirtz, Paul, 172–73, 176, 223nn42–43
gravity, of action, 30, 38, 51–52, 130
Griffith, Mark, 148–49
guard (character), 21, 77–78, 86–87, 95, 97, 100–101
guardianship, 114–15, 213n10

Haigh, A. E., 183
Hall, Lindsay, 145–47, 150, 219nn13–14
Halliwell, Stephen, 21, 34, 203n18
Harrison, Jane Ellen, 29, 66–67, 122, 141, 201n1, 215n27
Harshbarger, Karl, 187–88, 224n5
hate, 121–23
chthonic dikē and, 116–20, 125–27, 178, 213n12

Hegel, Georg Friedrich Wilhelm, 156–57, 182, 214n19, 217n43, 219n8
reconciliation and, 173, 179–80
Heidegger, Martin, 7, 11–12, 198n11, 199n13, 204n31, 225n18
Introduction to Metaphysics, 208n10
Hera, 56, 109–10, 163, 213n2
Zeus and, 152, 221n23
Heraclitus, 8, 10–11, 83
Hermes, 109
axis mundi and, 21–22, 108, 123, 127, 132–33
Herodotus, 117–18, 214n16
heroes, 204n31, 213n2
as ancestors, 50–51, 109–10
death and, 122–23, 167
fathers and, 113–15
tragic, 35, 61, 81–83, 206n39, 222n40
vengeance and, 124–25
hierarchy, 41
aristocracy and, 148–49
fathers and, 141
ideology and, 136–37
modernity and, 70–72
nature and, 8–9, 32, 201n4
seriousness and, 69–72
tragedy and, 34–35, 119
history, 2–3, 134–35, 145
cosmos and, 166
nature and, 13–14, 50
reason and, 180–81
Homer, 3, 27, 34, 66–67, 143–44, 167
Aeschylus and, 84, 95, 207n5, 208n12
Homo Necans (Burkert), 46, 54, 79, 200n21, 203n22, 205n35
cosmological anthropology of, 14–21, 110–11, 137
seriousness and, 15–17, 19–20, 61–62, 65–70

246 | Index

hubris, 79, 87, 93–96, 125–26
　democracy and, 220n16
　political, 11–12, 155, 172
　tragedy and, 147
humanity, 88–89
　animals and, 84, 92–93, 171–72, 222n40
　chthonic dikē and, 177
　cosmic dikē and, 182, 191, 194, 224n3
　cosmos and, 93–94
　deities and, 82, 90–91, 192–93, 204n31
　necessity and, 143
　order and, 7–8
　predation and, 16, 68
　violence and, 19–20
hunting, 16, 73–74, 140–41
　animals and, 49, 67–68, 97, 109
　Artemis and, 21, 45–46, 78–81, 168, 175, 203n21, 208n6
　biology and, 17–18, 20, 38–39, 62–63, 65–66, 114–15
　culture and, 55–56, 205n35
　dikē and, 121–22, 161–65
　Eumenides and, 159–61
　gender and, 46, 164, 203n22
　morality and, 79–80
　of Orestes, 80, 121–22
　as pursuit of justice, 14, 56–57, 75, 78, 94, 102–3, 168–69
　ritual and, 14–15, 40–41, 60, 122, 161
　sacrifice and, 30–31, 59–60
　sexuality and, 55, 89–90, 213n7
　vigilance and, 100–101
　war and, 24, 87, 126–27, 213n7
Hyperborea, 125–26, 216n31
hypervigilance, 24, 73–74, 76

identity, 23, 25–26, 74, 110, 197n7
　ship of Theseus and, 5–7, 199n14

ideology, 7, 71, 128–29, 158, 171, 178, 211n33
　autochthony and, 130–32, 172
　hierarchy and, 136–37
imitation, 44
　nature and, 30–34, 36–43, 65, 130
　tragic mimesis as, 8, 16–17, 30–33, 36–40, 51, 69, 130, 199n15
incest, 188, 192–94, 222n37
injustice, 10, 23, 75–76, 118, 158–59
　arbitrariness and, 175–76
　balance and, 90–91
　morality and, 24–25
innocence, sacrifice and, 56–57, 67, 98, 100, 211n31
Introduction to Metaphysics (Heidegger), 208n10
Iphigenia (character), 44–46, 80–82, 85–86, 89, 97–99, 169, 203n24
Iphigenia among the Taurians (Euripides), 44–46, 203n24
Iphigenia at Aulis (Euripides), 44–45, 203n19, 207n5, 211n31
isonomia, 71, 120, 209n19
　nature and, 12, 92–93, 165
　objectivity and, 12, 25, 74
　social justice and, 22–23, 43, 154, 199n14
Ixion's wheel, 150–55, 220nn19–22, 221n23

Jocasta (character), 187–88, 190, 192–94, 225n15
Jones, Peter, 212n1
justice, 2, 23. *See also* dikē
　anger and, 119–20, 125, 215n21
　balance and, 10–11, 88
　generativity and, 124–30
　hunting and, 15, 17, 56–57, 74
　law and, 121–22, 178–79
　modernity and, 4, 117–19, 218n45

predation and, 103, 122
sacrifice and, 46–47

Kafka, Franz, *The Trial*, 102–5
Kant, Immanuel, 52–53, 62, 198n10, 202n11
  mysterium tremendum and, 69, 206n45, 207n46
Kazantzakis, Nikos, 133–34
Kerényi, Karl, 29, 169–71, 201n2, 221n23, 222n38
Kirkland, Sean, 198n10
Kleist, Heinrich von, 26
Konstan, David, 67, 206n44
Kott, Jan, 13–14, 50, 209n18, 218n45
Kuhns, Richard, 12–13, 36–37, 115, 165–66, 173–74, 216n29, 221n25
  Hegel and, 180

law, 12, 156, 173, 199n14, 212n37. See also *isonomia*
  the Areopagus and, 90, 145–50, 167, 219n13
  destiny and, 162–63
  dogs and, 102–5
  Furies and, 74–76, 101–2
  justice and, 121–22, 178–79
  murder and, 59, 149–50
  nature and, 23, 92, 200n23
  ritual and, 151
  vigilance and, 102–3
  violence and, 24
Laws (Plato), 39–40
Lemnian crime, 116–17, 214n14, 214n16
lenience, 43, 167, 173
  morality and, 176
  for Orestes, 48–49, 57, 168, 174–76
  social justice and, 153–54
  victimhood and, 153–54
liminality, 46, 89–90, 92, 107, 169

Loraux, Nicole, 68, 130–31, 141, 202n17, 217n42
Lorenz, Konrad, 19, 65, 206n40

mantic art, 79, 88, 91, 105. See also prophecy
Markell, Patchen, 220n16
matricide, 121–23, 151, 157, 163–64, 174, 179, 222n35
Meier, Christian, 129, 139, 147, 159, 219n14
  theological politics and, 140, 218n3
Meuli, Karl, 56
mimesis. See imitation
modernity, 7, 24, 26–27
  action and, 54–55
  autochthony and, 132, 134–35
  change and, 195
  democracy in, 159, 221n28
  dilemmatic thought and, 202n9
  hate and, 119–20
  hierarchy and, 70–72
  justice and, 4, 117–19, 218n45
  morality and, 98–99, 211n30
  technology and, 9
  tragedy and, 99–100
  universality and, 22–23, 209n19
  vigilantism and, 179
  violence and, 25
Moirai. See Fates
morality, 117–18, 190
  cosmology and, 17–18, 88
  crime and, 192–93
  dikē and, 160–61
  hunting and, 79–80
  injustice and, 24–25
  lenience and, 176
  modernity and, 98–99, 211n30
  nature and, 12–13, 92–93, 158
  polis and, 214n19
  sacrifice and, 212n1
  tragedy and, 83–84, 208n8

248 | Index

Morrissey, Christopher, 45
motherhood, 80, 121–25, 157–58, 163–65, 221n27
   Athena and, 168–70, 209n22
   snakes and, 160
murder, 188
   action and, 44, 202n17
   chorus and, 187, 224n5
   of Clytemnestra, 57, 61, 159–60
   family and, 143–45, 151–52, 163–64, 220n21
   hate and, 116–17
   law and, 59, 149–50
   lenience and, 174
   theater and, 42–43, 202n16
mysterium tremendum, 58
   of Burkert, 16, 18, 21, 52–53, 208n11
   Kant and, 69, 206n45, 207n46
   seriousness and, 53–54
myth, 89–90, 108, 110–11, 122–23, 177
   of autochthony, 130–35, 172, 223n41
   cult and, 29–30, 44, 130
   history and, 13–14, 50
   Ixion's wheel, 150–55, 220nn19–22, 221n23
   Lemnian crime, 116–17, 214n14, 214n16
   nature and, 103–5
   politics and, 157–59, 165–66, 221n28
   sacrifice in, 51, 56, 109

Nagy, Gregory, 5–6
nativism, 72–76, 79, 208n12, 210n24
nature, 54, 197n8, 204n31, 223n46
   anthropocentrism and, 9, 63
   arbitrariness and, 92–95, 155, 158–59, 163–65
   Aristotle and, 31–32, 65–66, 119

   Artemis and, 82, 88, 91–94
   cosmos and, 7–10, 96–98
   courts and, 165–66
   destiny and, 194
   Dikē and, 91, 176–77
   family and, 136
   Furies and, 46–48, 162
   hierarchy and, 8–9, 32, 201n4
   history and, 13–14, 50
   imitation and, 30–34, 36–43, 65, 130
   isonomia and, 12, 92–93, 165
   law and, 23, 92, 200n23
   mantic art and, 79, 88, 91, 105
   morality and, 12–13, 92–93, 158
   myth and, 103–5
   necessity and, 62–63, 65, 78–79
   objectivity and, 4, 52–53, 199n14
   order and, 47, 86–87
   phusis, 12, 63, 95, 194, 206n42
   politics and, 94–95, 157
   seriousness and, 8, 59, 62–64, 100
   tragedy and, 62–63, 92
   violence and, 3–4, 33, 47
necessity, 24–25, 90, 160–61
   arbitrariness and, 174–75, 182–83
   cosmology and, 75–76
   craft and, 9, 43, 59, 65, 98, 137
   destiny and, 121
   dikē and, 91
   humanity and, 143
   nature and, 62–63, 65, 78–79
   prophecy and, 191
   sacrifice and, 81–83
neutrality, 12, 27, 93, 120, 155–56, 179–82, 199
Nietzsche, Friedrich, 141, 198nn10–11, 201n28, 224n2
   amor fati of, 100, 104
   tragedy and, 8, 197n6, 212n39
novelty, tradition and, 7, 11–12, 15, 140, 142

objectivity, 27, 72, 179–81. *See also* universality
  isonomia and, 12, 25, 74
  nature and, 4, 52–53, 199n14
  thingliness and, 198n10
Oedipus at Colonus (Sophocles), 57–58, 133–34
Oedipus Tyrannus (Sophocles), 44–45, 84, 186, 190, 225n8
  chorus of, 187, 191–94, 224n5, 225n10
  prophecy in, 187–89, 194–95, 225n10, 225n15
Olympians, Titans and, 155–72
order, 167
  balance and, 129–30
  ethical, 177
  humanity and, 7–8
  nature and, 47, 86–87
  tripartite, 54–55, 61, 91, 142, 210n27
order of things, 35, 47, 58, 72, 86, 211n30
  pragma/pragmata as, 9–11, 25–26, 145, 171
Orestes (character), 124–26, 179, 216n35, 217n38
  cosmos and, 108, 111, 123
  hunting of, 80, 121–22
  lenience for, 48–49, 57, 168, 174–76
  suffering of, 15, 151–53, 155, 221n25
  trial of, 59, 149, 151, 167–68
Otto, Rudolf, 16, 52–54, 69, 206n45
Otto, Walter, 29, 72–73, 140, 201n2

Parker, Robert, 143–44, 214n15
parodos, of *Agamemnon*, 45, 81–82, 84–94, 141, 207n2
patricide, 186–88, 194, 222n35
peace, 48–49, 64, 72, 101, 121, 149
Peloponnesian War, 217n40

Peradotto, John, 14, 81–83, 208n6
Phaedo (Plato), 5–7, 197n5
philosophy, 6–7, 37–38, 72, 177, 198n11
  poetry and, 31–36, 85
  politics and, 27, 74–75, 171
  tragedy and, 33–34, 58
phusis, 12, 63, 95, 194, 206n42. *See also* nature
Plato, 31, 201n7
  Laws, 39–40
  Phaedo, 5–7, 197n5
  Statesman, 63–65, 206n42
pleasure, 32, 153
  poetry and, 31, 36–38
  tragedy and, 37, 202n11
  vengeance and, 125–26
Plutarch, 5–6, 219n13
Podlecki, Anthony, 219n14
Poetics (Aristotle), 30–38, 44–45, 53–55
poetry
  philosophy and, 31–36, 85
  pleasure and, 31, 36–38
polis, 102
  chthonic earth and, 8, 108–9, 127–28
  cosmos and, 8, 63–65, 78, 110–11, 155, 173–74, 183
  morality and, 214n19
  politics and, 139–50
political *dikē*, 144, 219n11
political hubris, 11–12, 155, 172
politics, 8, 86
  of Aeschylus, 146–50
  centrism in, 146–47, 150, 220n15
  cosmology and, 11–13, 22, 115–16, 165–66
  emotions and, 176
  gender and, 130–31, 217n42
  generativity and, 171–72
  myth and, 157–59, 165–66, 221n28

politics *(continued)*
  nature and, 94–95, 157
  philosophy and, 27, 74–75, 171
  polis and, 139–50
  power and, 158, 171, 181–82, 219n13
  religion and, 30, 193
  theological, 140, 218n3
  time and, 140, 157–58, 160–61
  tragedy and, 26–27, 128–30, 147, 220n16
Politics (Aristotle), 215n21, 220n15
pollution, 56, 143–44, 146, 149–52
  crime and, 117, 214n15
power, 71, 90–91, 111, 118–19, 222n39
  death and, 40–41, 171
  politics and, 158, 171, 181–82, 219n13
pragma/pragmata, 18, 190, 225n13
  as order of things, 9–11, 25–26, 145, 171
  as reality, 27, 171–72, 191–92
praxis, 44, 202n14
prayer, 1–2, 48–49, 107–8, 113, 124–25
  reality and, 3–4
predation, 24
  animals and, 80–81, 87, 208n9
  humanity and, 16, 68
  justice and, 103, 122
Prometheus, 9, 137
Prometheus Bound (Aeschylus), 13, 59, 218n3
prophecy
  of Cassandra, 78, 80, 94, 109
  Delphi and, 156, 186–87
  necessity and, 191
  in *Oedipus Tyrannus*, 187–89, 194–95, 225n10, 225n15
  reality and, 58–59, 191–92
  war and, 81, 87, 90

punishment, 50–51, 85–86, 116–18, 153–55, 192
purification, 103, 151–52, 212n40
pursuit of justice, 24–25, 47, 74, 140, 172
  hunting as, 14, 56–57, 75, 78, 94, 102–3, 168–69

reality, 6, 9, 35, 198n9, 225n14
  epiphany and, 52–53
  imitation and, 31–34
  pragma/pragmata as, 27, 171–72, 191–92
  prayer and, 3–4
  prophecy and, 58–59, 191–92
  ritual and, 42
  theoria and, 27
  tragedy and, 16–17, 99–100, 190–91
reconciliation
  Aeschylus and, 139, 179–82
  Hegel and, 173, 179–80
redemption, tragedy and, 57–58, 113–14, 124–26
regeneration, dikē as, 46–47, 55, 116, 124, 158, 161, 167
religion, 17, 104, 110–11
  politics and, 30, 193
reparation, 60, 206n38
revolutions, 24, 74–75, 135, 218n4, 218n45
  Dionysus and, 141
  transformation and, 140, 147
ritual
  anthropology and, 38, 51, 60–62, 65–66, 142–43, 199n15
  Athena and, 45–48
  axis mundi and, 132–33
  Burkert and, 41, 50–52, 55–60, 109, 201n4, 205n36
  gender and, 55
  hunting and, 14–15, 40–41, 60, 122, 161

law and, 151
reality and, 42
seriousness and, 41–43, 58
theater and, 37–39, 52, 54
theory and, 5–6, 197n5
vengeance and, 47–49
violence and, 18
ritual interpretation of tragedy, 29–31, 43–45, 54–61, 201n1, 203n18
ritual sacrifice, three stages of, 55, 57–60
Robinson, John Mansley, 10

sacred animals, 57, 78, 91–94
of Artemis, 81, 89–90, 204n24, 207n5
sacrifice, 14–15, 44, 203n20, 203n24, 205n36
of animals, 16–17, 45, 51–59, 67, 88–89, 112–13
chthonic world and, 49–50
culture and, 30
dilemmatic thought and, 42–43
ethics and, 55–56
Furies and, 49–51, 97
Hermes and, 108–9
hunting and, 30–31, 59–60
innocence and, 56–57, 67, 98, 100, 211n31
justice and, 46–47
morality and, 212n1
in myth, 51, 56, 109
necessity and, 81–83
sexuality and, 112–13
violence and, 45
Scapin, Nuria, 199n15
Schein, Seth, 207n2
seed, fatherhood and, 22, 115, 136, 167, 221n26, 221n30
Seferis, George, 1–4, 27, 210n26
seriousness, 21, 104, 145, 148, 150
Aristotle and, 34–35
axis mundi and, 51–52

Burkert and, 15–17, 19–20, 61–62, 65–70
of courts, 148–49, 222n35
culture and, 14, 39–40, 62, 65–67
education and, 40, 202n15
emotions and, 67, 69
hierarchy and, 69–72
mysterium tremendum and, 53–54
nature and, 8, 59, 62–64, 100
ritual and, 41–43, 58
of tradition, 39–41
tragedy and, 15–17, 42–43, 154, 199n15, 200n18
vengeance and, 85, 187, 224n6
sexuality, 213n2
culture and, 110
death and, 117
hunting and, 55, 89–90, 213n7
sacrifice and, 112–13
war and, 89–90, 209n14, 213n7
shepherd (character), 186, 188–91, 193–94
ship of Theseus, 5–7, 199n14
SJW. See social justice warrior
Smith, Cecil, 151–52
snakes, 80
chthonic world and, 122–23, 215n27
motherhood and, 160
social justice, 103–5
arbitrariness and, 23, 99–100, 165
chthonic dikē and, 132, 217n44
identity and, 26, 74
isonomia and, 22–23, 43, 154, 199n14
lenience and, 153–54
ship of Theseus and, 199n14
social justice warrior (SJW), 24–25, 73
Socrates, death of, 5–7
Solmsen, Friedrich, 144

252 | Index

Sophocles, 8, 11
   Electra, 57–58
   Oedipus at Colonus, 57–58, 133–34
   Oedipus Tyrannus, 44–45, 84, 186–95, 224n5, 225n8, 225n10, 225n15
Statesman (Plato), 63–65, 206n42
suffering, 168
   lenience and, 153–54
   of Orestes, 15, 151–53, 155, 221n25
synchrony, 131–32, 135

taboo, 93, 194, 224n7
Taplin, Oliver, 77, 221n25
technocracy, 63
   anthropocentrism and, 5, 194
   technology and, 197n4
technology, 194–95, 225n18
   modernity and, 9
   technocracy and, 197n4
Thanatos, 167–68, 171
   Furies and, 161–65
theater, 27, 30–31, 41, 75, 141, 147
   murder and, 42–43, 202n16
   ritual and, 37–39, 52, 54
Thebes, 8, 122, 128, 131, 186–88, 193
theological politics, 140, 218n3
theoria, 5–6, 198n10
   reality and, 27
   theory compared to, 9–10, 27
theory, 7
   ritual and, 5–6, 197n5
   theoria compared to, 9–10, 27
Theseus, ship of, 5–7, 199n14
thingliness, 9–10, 27, 190–91. See also *pragma/pragmata*
   objectivity and, 198n10
three stages of ritual sacrifice, 55, 57–60
time, 2–4, 39, 200n18
   chthonic world and, 131
   cosmology and, 156–57
   death and, 55
   diachrony and, 131, 134–35
   politics and, 140, 157–58, 160–61
Titans, Olympians and, 155–72
tradition, 131–32
   change and, 140, 149, 220n18
   culture and, 38–39
   future and, 144–46, 172, 178–79
   novelty and, 7, 11–12, 15, 140, 142
   seriousness of, 39–41
   violence and, 144–45
tragedy, 4, 6–7, 172, 185
   action and, 44–45
   anthropology and, 20–21, 30–31
   axis mundi of, 13–14, 50, 204n31
   catharsis and, 37, 60–61
   compensation and, 10–11
   dilemmatic thought and, 21, 23, 42–43, 70
   hierarchy and, 34–35, 119
   hubris and, 147
   modernity and, 99–100
   morality and, 83–84, 208n8
   nature and, 62–63, 92
   Nietzsche and, 8, 197n6, 212n39
   philosophy and, 33–34, 58
   Plato and, 201n7
   pleasure and, 37, 202n11
   politics and, 26–27, 128–30, 147, 220n16
   reality and, 16–17, 99–100, 190–91
   redemption and, 57–58, 113–14, 124–26
   ritual interpretation of, 29–31, 43–45, 54–61, 201n1, 203n18
   seriousness and, 15–17, 42–43, 154, 199n15, 200n18
   theoria and, 9–10
   three stages of ritual sacrifice and, 55, 57–60
   tripartite order of, 54–55, 61, 91, 142, 210n27

tragic heroes, 35, 61, 81–83, 206n39
  animals and, 222n40
tragic mimesis, of Aristotle, 8, 16–17,
    30–33, 36–40, 51, 69, 130,
    199n15
transformation, 36–37, 46–47, 123,
    134, 204n31, 216n29. *See also*
    change
  revolutions and, 140, 147
trial, of Orestes, 59, 149, 151, 167–68
The Trial (Kafka), 102–5
tripartite order, of tragedy, 54–55, 61,
    91, 142, 210n27
Trojan War, 2, 77, 84
Troy, 2, 78, 82, 87, 93–94, 124, 126
Tzanetou, Angeliki, 128–29

universality, 43, 74, 92–93, 179–80
  death and, 131, 134, 217n43
  modernity and, 22–23, 209n19
Uranian dikē, chthonic dikē and, 13,
    25–26, 50–51, 75–76, 123, 177–78

vengeance, 50, 84
  Choephoroi and, 124–30
  of Clytemnestra, 93–98, 100–101,
      118, 210n29
  gender and, 116–19
  heroes and, 124–25
  pleasure and, 125–26
  ritual and, 47–49
  seriousness and, 85, 187, 224n6
  vigilance, 101
  war and, 49
Vernant, Jean-Pierre, 45–46
victimhood, 45, 67–68, 88, 99–100,
    109, 212n1
  lenience and, 153–54
vigil, 74, 77–78, 103, 123, 211nn34–35
vigilance, 90, 209n17
  action and, 115
  hunting and, 100–101

hypervigilance, 24, 73–74, 76
law and, 102–3
vengeance, 101
  as vigilantism, 22–24, 56–57, 94,
      100–102, 178–79
  woke culture as, 74, 211n32
vigilantism, 73–74, 211n36
  digital, 100, 207n48, 211n33
  Furies and, 177–78
  modernity and, 179
  vigilance as, 22–24, 56–57, 94,
      100–102, 178–79
violence, 15–16
  activism and, 73–75
  arbitrariness and, 199n15
  civic good and, 154–55, 176
  dikē as, 23–25, 144–45, 154–55,
      157–63, 166, 176–77, 199n15
  humanity and, 19–20
  law and, 24
  modernity and, 25
  nature and, 3–4, 33, 47
  ritual and, 18
  sacrifice and, 45
  tradition and, 144–45
virginity, 209n22, 222n37
  Artemis and, 89–90, 103, 168–70,
      203n21, 203n23

war, 3, 200nn24–25, 206n38
  arbitrariness and, 120
  Artemis and, 90, 209n14, 209n17
  death and, 125–26
  as dikē, 120–21
  hunting and, 24, 87, 126–27, 213n7
  Peloponnesian War, 217n40
  prophecy and, 81, 87, 90
  sexuality and, 89–90, 209n14,
      213n7
  Trojan War, 2, 77, 84
  vengeance and, 49
Warak, Melissa, 200n24

Wheeler, Michael, 204n31
woke culture, 74, 211n32

youth
   deities and, 155–72
   democracy and, 142–43

Zartaloudis, Thanos, 212n37

Zeitlin, Froma, 128, 203n21
Zeus, 56
   Apollo and, 156–57
   Artemis and, 93–94
   Athena and, 169–70, 222n37
   dikē and, 78, 84–87
   Fates and, 91, 209n18
   Hera and, 152, 221n23

www.ingramcontent.com/pod-product-compliance
Lightning Source LLC
Chambersburg PA
CBHW021837220426
43663CB00005B/288